Arsenic Under the Elms

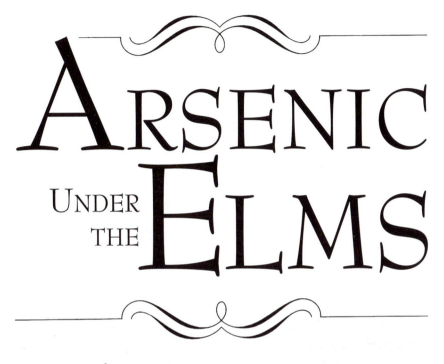

ARSENIC UNDER THE ELMS

Murder in Victorian New Haven

VIRGINIA A. McCONNELL

Westport, Connecticut
London

Library of Congress Cataloging-in-Publication Data

McConnell, Virginia A., 1942–
     Arsenic under the elms : murder in Victorian New Haven / Virginia
A. McConnell.
       p.   cm.
     Includes bibliographical references and index.
     ISBN 0–275–96297–0 (alk. paper)
     1. Poisoning—Connecticut—New Haven—Case studies.   I. Title.
HV6555.U52M33   1999
364.15′23′097468—dc21   99–19261

British Library Cataloguing in Publication Data is available.

Library of Congress Catalog Card Number: 99–19261
ISBN: 0–275–96297–0

First published in 1999

Praeger Publishers, 88 Post Road West, Westport, CT 06881
An imprint of Greenwood Publishing Group, Inc.
www.praeger.com

Printed in the United States of America

∞™

The paper used in this book complies with the
Permanent Paper Standard issued by the National
Information Standards Organization (Z39.48–1984).

10 9 8 7 6 5 4 3 2 1

Copyright Acknowledgment

The author and publisher gratefully acknowledge permission for the use of the following material:

"Herbert Marshall," "Lyman King," "Fiddler Jones," "Jeremy Carlisle," "Barry Holden," "Percival Sharp," "Mrs. Williams," "Thomas Rhodes," "Eugenia Todd," and "Amelia Garrick" from *Spoon River Anthology* by Edgar Lee Masters. Originally published by the Macmillan Co. Permission by Hilary Masters.

To my supporter, my encourager, and my biggest fan,
whose belief in me has been a sustaining life force:
My Mother,
Mary Alice Kendall McConnell

CONTENTS

Illustrations follow page 123.

ACKNOWLEDGMENTS

A research project like this one doesn't get finished without a lot of help. Primarily, I am indebted to Jackson Vance, the librarian at Walla Walla Community College's Clarkston Center, who was so patient and so timely with all my interlibrary loan requests, and always willing to listen to my ramblings about the two cases.

I am also indebted to the librarians at the Connecticut State Library in Hartford who honored all those loan requests, and who were so gracious and helpful during my visit there.

Researchers of past events would have to spend inordinate amounts of time and money were it not for the Family History Centers run by the Church of Jesus Christ of Latter Day Saints, and to them and their archives in Salt Lake City, I owe a huge debt.

Large thank-yous go to Lisa Greenville and her desktop publishing class, and especially Barbara Petty, for helping to clean up some of the pictures and drawings from the newspaper microfilm.

Thanks to Walla Walla Community College for the grant allowing me to visit Connecticut to see the murder sites for myself.

I owe a special debt to Joel Helander, author of the first book on the Mary Stannard murder, *Noose and Collar*, for generously sharing his sources and giving me a tour of Rockland. Thanks also to Tom Hopkins, current owner of the Stannard property, for the photo of Charlie Stannard and for allowing me to wander around and take pictures.

Mila Rindge of the Madison Historical Society sent me a copy of *Poor Mary Stannard*, photocopied at her own expense. Jim Campbell and Robert Egleston of the New Haven Colony Historical Society provided gracious access to their files and pictures on the Jennie Cramer case. Professor Robin Winks of Yale promoted the book in his talk there in October 1997.

Barbara Hays, R.N., M.S.N., of the Clarkston Center's School of Nursing, answered numerous questions while I was working on this and found an invaluable 1927 medical text. My student, Ginny Vassar, rescued a 1909 dictionary from the trash and loaned me the 1885 Kellogg book on Victorian ideals of masculine and feminine behavior.

I'd also like to thank Hilary Masters for his kind permission to use the poems from Edgar Lee Masters' *Spoon River Anthology*.

I would be amiss if I did not mention all those newspaper reporters, long gone now, who covered these events. They did not merely report the facts, but fleshed out the people and surroundings so well that I was able to see and hear them as if I had been there myself.

And, finally, to my editor at Praeger, Heather Ruland Staines, who took a chance on the project and on me, and was an encouraging voice throughout.

PREFACE

Anyone who has ever longed for a time machine only needs to spend a few hours reading through old newspapers to realize that the past is still alive. It's alive in two senses: in the "you-are-there" eavesdropping feeling you get as you scroll through the issues, and in the awareness you have that, as different as some things might have been back there, not all that much has changed over the centuries.

Murder provides us with a mirror of an era. Today, our impersonal, technological society has spawned random, stranger versus stranger violence: drive-by shootings, serial killings, cold-remedy tamperings. In the Victorian era, where abortion was illegal and bastardy strongly condemned, there was a great temptation for a young man to rid himself of "an inconvenient woman." Yet, in both eras, the old motives still prevail, motives that have been around since Cain and Abel: power, revenge, money, sex, jealousy, fear of discovery.

The murders of Mary Stannard in 1878 and of Jennie Cramer just three years later are unique in their similarities and in what they reveal about life in the microcosm of New Haven County in the late nineteenth century. Two young women in their early twenties, both of a lower class than the suitors accused of murdering them, were found with lethal doses of arsenic in their systems. The world, through its reporters, flocked to New Haven's door to cover these stories and, with the second death especially, since it followed so closely on the heels of the first, New Havenites worried about what that world would think of them.

These murders are unique from a forensic point of view as well. The proximity of this relatively small New England city to a major research institution (Yale) and a major international city (New York) gave New Haven access to advanced forensic techniques that would not have been available to any other city of its size.

For example, while the Jennie Cramer case hinged largely on supposed eyewitness testimony, the Mary Stannard trial was the beneficiary of the most sophisticated arsenic testimony ever presented in a courtroom at that time. Its import back then was similar in significance to modern breakthroughs in DNA and fiber analysis.

But in other respects, crime detection in the Victorian era was almost primitive. Police officers, especially in relatively quiet areas such as New Haven County, were primarily watchmen and peacekeepers. They were not trained in detection or in crime scene preservation. Moreover, any curious citizen or newspaper reporter was allowed to (and did) perform the functions now reserved for police detectives: searching the crime scene for clues, interrogating suspects and witnesses, doing background investigations, and performing time and distance tests to verify or disprove alibis.

Detective work was also done by the inquest jury, which was hastily formed by the coroner immediately after a homicide was discovered. Jurors were taken from the local citizenry and were more often than not part of the crowd of onlookers at the scene or merely passing by. No one seemed to have been concerned about conflict of interest, as many inquest jurors were also witnesses to key events of the crime.

Another curious aspect was that, although inquest jurors had the duty to investigate, they also had to bear their own costs of investigation. The result of this was that many leads were not followed because of the expense involved. Inquest jurors were not sworn to secrecy, and often achieved their fifteen minutes of fame by making statements to the press. Still others jealously guarded their information, not even sharing it with fellow jurors. Competition among jurors was rampant, and they seldom acted in unison in their investigative efforts.

Members of the press were probably the most professional and efficient in methods of interrogation. Lamenting the fact that they were denied access to one of the participants in the Jennie Cramer case, *New York Times* reporters boasted that they could have succeeded in getting information where the police and the inquest jurors had failed.

However, reporters were primarily concerned with scooping their rivals and selling newspapers, and not at all with the rights of defendants. They printed rumors as facts, gave editorial comments about the principals, the witnesses, and the jurors, and made definitive statements about their belief in a defendant's guilt or innocence. Although jurors were told not to read the newspapers, they were never sequestered except for deliberations.

The two high-profile trials that are the subject of this book lasted three months each. By our standards today, this is not a long time, but for the nineteenth century it was probably at least twice as long as it should have been. Trials were prolonged by excessive wrangling between attorneys (not allowed today) and by the backward refusal of many states, notably Connecticut, to provide independent court reporters at trials. The lack of a court reporter forced attorneys to take their own transcripts, and they frequently had to stop proceedings so they could catch up with the testimony. If an attorney had no transcript of testimony from the current or a preceding trial, he would spend inordinate amounts of time trying to get a witness to admit a prior contradiction.

But probably the biggest difference between that era and our own is the way witnesses and attorneys viewed perjury and tampering with evidence. Both of those exist today, of course, but it is (one hopes) rare, and the legal consequences are serious. In the nineteenth century, however, tampering with evidence was so widespread that attorneys would not allow opposing counsel to handle crucial items unless a deputy were present. Lay witnesses changed their testimony from trial to trial, and bribery was also prevalent.

The prevailing opinion seemed to be that if an attorney or witness firmly believed in a defendant's guilt or innocence, evidence or statements that would help or hurt that defendant could be adjusted "in the interests of justice." Witnesses took it upon themselves to decide what testimony was or was not relevant to the case, and thought nothing of changing facts they considered not probative. And they routinely lied to protect themselves from public embarrassment.

If the Victorian era was lax in the matter of fair trials, however, it nonetheless had strict parameters for feminine behavior. In the Mary Stannard case, the defendant's wife was presented as the perfect model of womanhood, while the victim, an unwed mother of the lowest class, was contrasted unfavorably with her. In the Jennie Cramer case, the young prostitute involved with the Malley boys was constantly derided in the press, and there was a universal feeling that the conspiracy among the three to rob the victim of her virtue was a far more serious crime than murder. At both trials, women spectators were criticized for showing what was considered to be an unseemly interest in the lurid details of sex and violence that came out in the testimony.

The tragedies of Mary Stannard and Jennie Cramer, then, give structure to a study of how journalism, law, medicine, and morality worked back then and how they have since evolved. At the same time, they allow us to eavesdrop on the people of Victorian New England, to listen to their speech patterns, their opinions, and to *see* the clothes they wore and the tools they used and the food they ate—not as examples in a history text or artifacts in a museum, but as vibrant and real.

The deaths of these two young women over one hundred years ago spotlight the lives of people who would otherwise never have come to our attention. Murder takes the ordinary, unremarkable existences of the victim, the accused, and those closely connected with them, and makes them extraordinary. People like Mary Stannard, Herbert Hayden, Jennie Cramer, and even the somewhat prominent Malleys would have passed unnoticed into oblivion but for these events.

And to think for a moment about the grief of those left behind—the Stannards, the Hawleys, the Cramers—is to come to a realization about our connection with *all* humans from the past, whose sorrows and despairs are not different from our own. It makes us more aware of our own small roles in the flow of humanity.

A word about the narrative structure: All dialogue is either verbatim as reported or a reasonable facsimile of what was said. Thoughts, motives, and actions of the people involved, where not specifically stated in the sources, are based on my own analysis of what I determined to be most probable, given the evidence, testimony, and psychological profile of each individual. It was often not possible to determine from the witnesses who was telling the truth, and sometimes even the reporters at the trials had different versions of what was said there (and, of course, there were no official transcripts to check). In that case, I had to read between the lines and make a decision as to what was *most likely* to have been said.

Finally, my goal was to re-create these past events and people in such a way as to give you the impression that I was personally familiar with them. If, after you finish reading, you feel that you know them also, then I have succeeded in that goal.

PART I

THE MURDER OF MARY STANNARD

Chapter 1

MARY

This is life's sorrow:
That one can be happy only where two are;
And that our hearts are drawn to stars
Which want us not.

—Edgar Lee Masters, "Herbert Marshall,"
Spoon River Anthology

THURSDAY, AUGUST 29, 1878

For the third consecutive morning, twenty-one-year-old Mary Stannard held her head over the glory hole in the Studleys' privy and vomited. The stench rising up from the hole, combined with the airless closeness of the outhouse, increased her nausea and it was some minutes before she could stand upright again. She clutched her stomach in pain. Then she sank to the floor and wept.

There was a banging on the door alternating with an attempt to open it. "Mama! Mama!" Her two-year-old son's voice escalated in tones of frustration; he was about to work himself into one of his tantrums. "I'll be right out, Willie," she assured him. "Don't you be banging and waking people up."

The first morning Mary had thought her sickness was simply the result of the previous night's supper, although no one else had felt any ill effects. The second morning brought an uneasiness that she quickly put away because she did not want to think about it. Then there was the cramping in her stomach and the swelling tightness in her breasts. But now the fact was unavoidable: there was every indication that she was about to become a mother . . . again.

Again. That was the source of Mary's despair this humid August morning, and she didn't know if she had the strength to face it. She had no husband and no prospect of one. Two years ago, when Willie was born, an unusually understanding community put aside its prejudice against women who bore bastards because Mary was such an honest, repentant, hardworking young woman—virtuous, really, despite her lapse.[1]

And she had no trouble finding work in their homes, for which she was ever grateful. The truth was that the Rockland community loved Mary. She was always ready to lend a hand with the sick, she was almost always cheerful, and she never shied away from hard work.[2]

But it was not likely that the community would forgive a second time. Mary thought ahead to the looks she would have to endure, to the stiff but polite rejections of her offers of work. And how would she support herself and Willie and another child? How would she help out her father, who depended on her income? What decent man would ever marry her now?

No, she would *not* go through this again. She would get rid of this impending problem. Or she would kill herself.

Mary stood up and unlatched the privy door. In spite of her assurances, Willie had not stopped banging on it. She took her son's hand and walked toward the house where she had been hired two weeks ago to help out with housework. Edgar Studley's wife and daughters were taking a trip to Europe and Mary had come to Guilford from her home in nearby Rockland to be with his elderly mother, Jane, and take over the bulk of the chores for the household.[3]

The communities of Middletown, Durham, Rockland, Madison, and Guilford, Connecticut, form a backwards "L," leading into the city of New Haven at its tip. Rockland, which has never had its own post office and today has no zip code, is fifteen miles from Middletown, Guilford, and New Haven.

The towns at the base of the "L" are closer to Long Island Sound and here is where the richest land lies. North of this area, notably Rockland (aptly named), is what was formerly a wild, untillable settlement, populated in 1878 with poor farmers and laborers. The major industry then was the making of charcoal, which employed even very young children.[4]

Mary Stannard began her working life at a young age, as did most of the Rockland area residents, and had very little education. But even by Rockland standards, the Stannard family was poor, and Mary was "put out to work," as they phrased it, probably when she was about fourteen or fifteen. She was patient, docile, and robust, so her chores ranged from taking care of children to feeding pigs.[5]

No task was too menial for Mary to undertake. She was strong and capable despite her small size and was glad to get any work at all.

Sometimes Mary commuted from her home and sometimes she boarded at the home where she was working. When she arrived at the Studleys' in Guilford on August 18, she was looking forward to a long period of employment. The only thing that could spoil it would be bad behavior on Willie's part, but Mary wanted Willie with her; she so often had to leave him at home, and she was afraid she was missing his growing up.[6]

Willie's conception came about as the result of giving in to the constant flir-
tations on the part of a young married man in a family Mary had been employed with in the town of Northford during the summer of 1875. Willie was
born the following April, when Mary was just nineteen.[7]

Mary was far below the young man in class and she knew that nothing could
come of it, especially since he was married. But she had spent many long hours
dreaming of a family life for herself, and in the end she allowed herself to be seduced by him. She had never betrayed him by revealing his name and had not
yet decided what she would tell Willie when he got old enough to ask about his
father.

Mary was not what could be considered a loose or easy woman. Indeed, she
had even quit a position once when a fellow employee pressed his attentions
upon her.[8] But she was vulnerable, ingenuous, simple, and uneducated. She
was eager to please and easily influenced.[9]

Mary so longed for a family of her own that she sometimes grew wistful just
talking about it. It wasn't sex that she wanted so much as stability and emotional intimacy, and it was easy to confuse one for the other.

Of all Mary's traits, however, there was one that everyone agreed on: she
never lied. Her honesty could be counted on implicitly, and it was a quality that
was highly valued by the community she lived and worked in, a quality that
earned her a second chance after her disgrace.[10]

Now Mary led her son back to the Studleys' kitchen to resume her chores
and think about her predicament. She had missed the signs of pregnancy because of her typically irregular menstrual periods. According to her calculations, she was about five months along. This might make a termination of the
pregnancy difficult, but she intended to do just that.

Mary's menstrual periods had always been irregular; in fact, she had started
another one just that day. She would have thought this to be impossible, except
that her former employer, Rosa Hayden, had menstruated while expecting her
second child, so it was not unheard of.[11]

Mary sat Willie at the big worktable with a piece of charcoal and some
butcher paper to draw on while she finished up the dishes. She was so preoccupied that she didn't hear old Mrs. Studley come in, and she started violently
when her name was called. Mrs. Studley chided her for daydreaming and Mary
burst into tears.

"Oh, Mrs. Studley," Mary sobbed as her employer tried to comfort her, "I'm
in such trouble and I don't know what to do about it. I'd like to kill myself."

"Why, what's wrong, Mary?" Mrs. Studley asked, alarmed.

"I think I'm about to become a mother," Mary wailed. "How could I have
let this happen to me again? I'm sure you'll think me just awful."

Jane Studley was a very large, very unflappable woman in her late sixties with children of her own. She took a no-nonsense approach to Mary's dilemma and asked her why she thought she was pregnant.

Mary related her symptoms, after which the older woman took Mary into her bedroom and examined her physically. She felt Mary's breasts and palpated her stomach. The breasts were hard and swollen, and she thought she could feel a lump in the abdomen. But when she checked the girl's underpants, she found evidence of menstruation.[12]

"I believe you're right, Mary," she said; "there does seem to be something there. You've got your monthly, though, so maybe you're really not pregnant."

Mary was so relieved at Mrs. Studley's nonjudgmental approach that she blurted out the whole story to her: She had been employed in the Rockland home of the Reverend Mr. Herbert H. Hayden, who preached at the Methodist church in Madison. She had many chores there, but primarily she was hired to watch the two children while Mr. Hayden's wife, Rosa, taught school in Rockland. And she was a welcome companion to Rosa Hayden when her husband had to travel to Madison, which involved overnight stays every day of the week except Friday.

There had been some flirtation between Mr. Hayden and Mary, but nothing of an overt nature had happened until the night of the parish oyster supper on March 20, 1878.[13]

At that time, Mary was no longer working at the Haydens', since Mrs. Hayden had quit her teaching position when she found she was expecting their third child. But when Rosa needed someone to watch the children for the evening, she contacted Mary Stannard. The parsonage in Rockland was having its second oyster supper since January to raise funds for the church, and the Haydens would be attending it to help out.

Mary had long admired the Rev. Hayden, who was young and self-confident, with a sturdy build, dark curly hair, and a charming manner. She thought he was exactly the kind of husband she was looking for, and she envied Rosa—who had become her friend as well as her employer—her good luck.

Once Mary had teasingly asked Rosa whether she thought Mr. Hayden would marry her if Rosa died. Rosa laughed and said, "No, I don't think so!"[14] Mary knew that Rosa had not taken it seriously, but the answer pained her all the same. Maybe she thought Mary wasn't good enough.

On the night of the oyster supper, Mary had put the children—Emma, six, and Lennie, four—to bed and was surprised to see Mr. Hayden back in the house at 10:00 P.M. He explained that he had a headache; he had told his wife he would see that the children were put to bed and would rejoin her when he felt better.

Hayden was more forward than usual, and flirtatious as well. When Mary did not scold him, he pressed his advantage. He sat next to her on the sofa and stroked her neck, laughing as she blushed and became flustered.

At 11:00 P.M. there was a knock at the door, and both jumped up guiltily. Hayden opened it to find Mary's sister, Emogene Stannard, and her half brother, Charles Hawley. They had been at the oyster supper and intended to walk Mary home if she was ready to go. But Hayden told them to go on without her, as Mary's duties for the evening were not finished.[15]

Hayden went back to Mary on the sofa and took her hand. Mary protested at this point, but only weakly. "What if Mrs. Hayden was to come back?" she asked. Hayden responded that his wife was selling tickets for the quilt raffle and wouldn't be able to leave for a while. He got bolder with his attentions and eventually, as Mary told her half sister, Susan Hawley, the following day, he was successful.[16]

As Mary finished telling her story to Mrs. Studley, she began crying again. She had never intended to betray her friend Rosa, she said. Hayden must be made to fix this. It was his idea in the beginning, for she would never have pursued him. He had taken advantage of a poor servant girl, and he would have to protect her honor and her livelihood.

Mary would write the Reverend a letter telling him of her discovery. She would ask him to come down to Guilford and take her to New Haven where she could get an abortion, then bring her back to the Studleys' home in Guilford to recover. Mrs. Studley said yes to this, but the plan disturbed her.[17]

FRIDAY, AUGUST 30, 1878

Mary Stannard was barely literate, and it took her some time to compose the letter to Hayden.[18] When she finished it, she sealed it in an envelope and wrote "Mr. Hayden" across it. Then she wrote another letter to her half sister, Susan Hawley, with instructions to deliver the enclosed letter to Hayden. On one side of the paper, Mary wrote:

Do not let farther see this, I want you to give this letter to Mr. hayden and dont let anybody see it and I will tell you what it is for some day. You give it to him yourself. Dont rede it to farther.

On the other side of the same paper, Mary wrote a more conventional letter, obviously meant to be read to her father, who was illiterate:

August 30, 1878

My Dear Sister: I now take my pencil in hand to let you know that i am well and hope you are the same. I have not felt very well for a day or 2. How is all the folks. I like my place very well and Willie is well. He comes to me asks where you and farther is. Give my love to all and keep a share for yourself. I dont know how long I shall stay. I dont think of any more to write. So good by. Write soon.

From Mary Stanar

The emotions and the effort of writing the two letters had exhausted Mary. She had trouble thinking. She went to Edgar Studley and asked him what to put on the outside of the envelope to get it to her sister in Rockland. Studley took the pencil and wrote the address for her. He assured her his son would mail it that evening.

Sending the letter would go far toward easing Mary's mind and making her feel as if a solution to her problem would be forthcoming. As she watched Edgar Studley's son leave for the post office, she felt lighter and happier than she had all day.

SATURDAY, AUGUST 31, 1878

Jane Studley had not slept well. She arose still fatigued and burdened with worry, not just about Mary's secret, but about the consent she had given her to have Hayden come down to Guilford and help her procure an abortion. This was, after all, not her home, and she had an idea that her son, Edgar, would not be pleased. She decided to tell him before any real damage was done.

Edgar Studley was a middle-aged man with a blunt personality. He didn't always bother to be polite if his anger was aroused, and he was about to tell his mother that he had had enough of Willie Stannard's tantrums and bad behavior ("He is the damndest, ugliest boy I ever saw," he would tell his friends later). Mary would have to take him home; if she wanted to come back without him, that was fine with Edgar; otherwise, he would hire another girl.[19]

When Studley heard the story of Mary's ruin and her abortion plan from his mother, he exploded. "Not in my house!" he raged. "My house will not be connected in any way with immorality. Tell her to get herself ready by tomorrow morning. I'm taking her and her bastard home."[20]

Mary was upset when she heard that she would have to leave the Studleys'. She had hoped to keep her condition hidden from the people in Rockland and had also hoped to keep her position in Guilford.

What would she tell her father about why she was coming home so soon? She did *not* want him to find out about this second pregnancy; when she was expecting Willie, he told her he would throw her out of the house if it ever happened again.

Mrs. Studley had an idea. "You can tell him that Willie was misbehaving, and we asked you to leave on his account." That would work. Mary felt better.

And once in Rockland she could see Hayden herself and make sure he understood that he would have to help her in some way, either by taking her to New Haven or by giving her money so she could go herself.

SUNDAY, SEPTEMBER 1, 1878

The drive to Rockland was a silent one for the first couple of miles, except for Willie's constant chatter. The boy had never been taught that children should be seen and not heard, Studley ruminated as the horse clip-clopped along. He stole a glance at the young woman, and the look of despair on her face caused him to relent a little. Before they left Guilford, his mother had felt Mary's breasts again and found them even larger and harder than they had been on Thursday.

"Who is responsible for your predicament?" he asked, although his mother had already told him. "Is he married or single?"[21]

"He's married," Mary answered. "It's the Reverend Hayden, the preacher at the Methodist church in Madison. He and his family live down the road from us."

"He should be made to stand by you and see you through this," Studley told her. "Will you be talking to him?"

"Yes," Mary assured him. "I'm going to see him as soon as possible to relieve my mind. He might be down in Madison yet, as he don't generally get home until late on Sundays."

"Shall I drive by his house and see if he's at home? I could talk to him about your difficulty if you like."

"I do wish you would, Mr. Studley!" Mary became more animated than she had been at any time on the long trip home.

The farther north they drove, the wilder and rockier the landscape became, choked with briars and thistles. It was like another country, Studley thought, almost like the bleaker parts of England or Scotland. It was hard to believe that this remote wilderness, this almost-frontier, was only a short way from the bustling city of New Haven, the home of Yale College.

"Mr. Hayden's home is just down this road," Mary pointed out as they arrived in Rockland. "If he's at home, his carriage will be under the shed."

But there was no carriage there. Mary sighed in deep disappointment, and Edgar Studley went on to the Stannards' house a half-mile away. Before he dropped Mary and Willie off, he advised her to file a bastardy complaint against Hayden if he refused to help her. Then he headed back to Guilford.

The Stannard home was run-down, unpainted, and too small for the number of occupants. It had only one floor, with an attic or storage area containing a bed. The ground floor consisted of a front room (occupied by Mary, Susan, and little Willie, all in the same bed), a bedroom (occupied by their father, Charlie), and a kitchen. Up until a few months before the murder, the girls' brother, Charles Hawley, was also living there, but he had since got married and moved out.[22]

When their elderly neighbor and benefactor, Benjamin Stevens, stayed overnight, as he frequently did, a lounge was set up in the kitchen for him.

Susan Hawley knew immediately that something was wrong: Mary was back from Guilford too soon. Susan watched her half sister closely as she related Willie's bad behavior to their father, and knew that something else was behind her return. Willie had misbehaved before—he was notorious for it—and Mary had never exhibited emotions stronger than exasperation or frustration. She rarely even got angry, which was one reason Willie was so out of control.

Back in their parlor bedroom, Mary unpacked her and Willie's things and avoided looking directly at Susan. But Susan kept prying until finally Mary collapsed in tears on the bed and confessed the real reason for her early return.

"I'm so ashamed, Susan. And to have the Studleys know about it, especially Mr. Studley—it's awful. I want to die, truly I do!"

Mary told Susan her intention of having Hayden pay for an abortion, either through medicine or an operation.

"I'll see him first thing in the forenoon," she said firmly. "I'll tell Father I'm going over to see Mrs. Hayden's new baby." The Haydens' third child, named Rosa after her mother, had been born a little over a week before Mary left for Guilford, and Mary had not seen her since the middle of August.[23]

Mary fixed herself some tansy tea, hoping it would cause her to abort the fetus.[24] As she drank the tea and discussed her problem with Susan, Charles Hawley and his wife (also named Mary) came in with a letter for Susan from the Durham Post Office. It was the letter Mary had written her from Guilford, which she had completely forgotten about in the midst of all the turmoil.

Susan opened it and read the message to herself, but when she held up the envelope with Hayden's name on it, Mary came over and took it from her.

"This ain't of any use, for I can see him myself, seeing as I have got no home," she said as she burned it in the kitchen stove.[25] Mary felt a wave of depression and helplessness wash over her.

The letter and its contents, which were read by no one after Mary sealed it in Guilford, would be the center of intense controversy at the two trials.

MONDAY, SEPTEMBER 2, 1878

Mary awoke early Monday morning after a restless night. She intended to go over to the Haydens' right away and hoped to be able to see Mr. Hayden alone on some pretext so that she could tell him about her predicament. And in case that wasn't possible, she had written a note to slip to him.[26]

After breakfast, Mary told her father she would be going over to see the new baby. He asked her to borrow a pitchfork while she was there.

Mary made three trips to the Hayden household that day before she was able to see Herbert Hayden.[27] The first one, at 7:00 A.M., lasted only fifteen minutes. She went back at 9:30 A.M. on her way home from Enos Stevens' store, but Hayden was still not back from Madison.

Mary's final trip at 4:00 P.M., to borrow a hayrake, was successful. But by that time, she was so wrought-up over the whole ordeal that she had taken nearly a teaspoonful of laudanum before going over there one more time. (People of the nineteenth century used laudanum, an opium derivative, for a wide variety of ailments, much as we use aspirin. Both opium and laudanum were sold over the counter.[28])

Although both the Haydens would later deny that Mary accompanied the Rev. Hayden into the barn to get the rake, their neighbors testified differently. And when Mary returned home, she told Susan that she had managed to talk to Hayden in the barn and that he had promised to stand by her. He would go into Middletown that week and get some medicine for her or see about a doctor.[29]

As she settled down for the night, Mary felt much calmer and more optimistic. Mr. Hayden would take care of her "trouble" and no one would be the wiser, especially her father.

TUESDAY, SEPTEMBER 3, 1878

When Mary Stannard awoke Tuesday morning, the first thing she thought of was Herbert Hayden's promise to take care of her problem and save her from shame once more. The second thing she remembered was that it was her birthday. She was twenty-two.[30]

The day was more humid than usual and promised rain later on. It would be a welcome break from the relentless heat, but Mary hoped it wouldn't be a thunderstorm: she was deathly afraid of them and often made a perfect fool of herself by clinging to others.[31]

Mary selected one of her better calico dresses to wear. She was not always particular about how she looked or how clean she was, sometimes not even bothering to tame her normally frizzy hair. At times she looked downright unkempt.[32] But today she felt that life was looking up for her. And it was her birthday, after all.

After breakfast the Stannards were visited by their neighbor, Benjamin Stevens, a grizzled, gruff man of sixty-one. Many in Rockland considered "Old Ben" (as he was referred to by adults; children called him "Uncle Ben") to be freeloading off the Stannard family; but, in fact, Stevens was more like a benefactor to them.[33]

Stevens' wife died when he was thirty-four, and he had never remarried. When his father died, he took in his elderly mother and, with the hired help of Susan Hawley, cared for her until she passed away in 1874.[34] He had grown children who would sometimes come over to cook and clean for him (some lived next door and some came to live with him on occasion), but they got on his nerves. Stevens liked to come and go as he pleased and had his own way of doing things. He lived like a poor man, but actually he had quite a bit of money by Rockland standards, with a net worth of around $10,000.[35]

Ben Stevens had known Charlie Stannard since Stannard was a little boy, and there were only seven years' difference in age between them. Charlie always needed money and would do odd jobs on occasion.[36] But what Stevens enjoyed most was being part of the Stannard family: Charlie and his daughters Emogene, Mary, and Isadora, Mary's son Willie, and the Hawley stepchildren, especially Susan. They provided him with a family atmosphere and were glad to include him at mealtimes.

Because Stevens was so much more well-off than the Stannards, he made sure to provide them with food and other things he thought they needed. He usually brought something with him whenever he visited, always careful not to make it seem like charity.

On this day, Mary's birthday, he had a hankering for some fresh butter and eggs for his noon dinner. He was pretty much hung over and exhausted from the barn-raising party he had been to on Monday down at the Smiths' in North Guilford, a party that had lasted all night. He thought the food would do his stomach good. He gave Mary a $5 bill to go down to the store (run by his brother Enos) and purchase the dinner items.[37]

On her way back from the store, at about 9:30 A.M., Mary stopped by the Haydens'. By this time, Hayden had left for Middletown (although he had told his wife he was going to Durham for oats), and his absence seemed to Mary to be a good sign that he was following up on his promise to her. She felt in a more expansive mood than she had on the previous day, and stayed to visit with Rosa Hayden for about an hour.

As she left to go back home with the dinner items, she asked Rosa if she could take the two oldest children with her. They had become quite attached to Mary during the time she took care of them, and were always delighted to see her. Mary thought that, with a new baby, Rosa would be glad to get a break from the older children.[38]

Mary took Emma and Lennie by the hand and walked the brief distance to her house, where the children played with Willie for the next half hour.

At 11:00 A.M. a carriage was heard coming up the road. It stopped outside the Stannard home and the Hayden children ran out, yelling, "Papa!" Reverend Hayden asked if he could get a drink of water and Charles Stannard welcomed him inside.[39]

"The water's warm, though, Reverend," Stannard said. "It'll answer just the same," responded Hayden, as he drank half of a glass. He caught Mary's eye and gave her a signal to meet him outside.

Mary picked up a seven-quart pail and announced that she was going down to the spring for some colder water. Hayden chatted for a few more minutes with Stannard and Ben Stevens, then he and his children climbed into the wagon and headed home.

They met Mary coming back from the spring. Hayden gave the reins to Lennie and got down to take a drink of the well water. "I've just been to see a doctor in Middletown and got me some quick-acting medicine," he told Mary quietly, so the children could not hear. "Can you meet me after dinner today at the Big Rock in the woods?"

As soon as Mary got back in the house, she grabbed Susan and took her into their front bedroom. "He's just come from Middletown and he got the medicine," she told her excitedly. "I saw him on the road to the spring and he told me to meet him after dinner at the Big Rock and I could take the medicine. He said it would act awful quick."

At the noon dinner that day, Mary picked at her food, eating only some of the eggs and passing up the pork.[40] She was nervous and anxious about her meeting with Hayden, but she was also afraid to eat too much before ingesting medicine that would act as quickly as Hayden claimed in causing an abortion.

After dinner was finished and the dishes washed and put away, Mary took a three-pint tin pail and announced to her father and Ben Stevens that she intended to go out for some blackberries to make a pie.[41]

"Me and Charlie saw some the other day near the Big Rock over to Fox Ledge," Ben said helpfully. Mary thought it was funny that he should suggest the very place she intended to go to meet Mr. Hayden! She stifled a giggle and responded that she would look there for the berries.

Back in their room, Mary told Susan she was going to meet Hayden. She gathered together a few things she would need for the abortion—a handkerchief and a linen towel with holes in each corner (called a "woman's" towel because it was used during the menstrual period)—and put them in her pocket. She took a safety pin and two common pins and attached them to the front of her dress. Then she picked out a cheerful sunbonnet to match her mood, and tied it under her chin.[42]

As she was leaving, Mary took Susan's hands and pressed them in her own. "It's going to work, ain't it? I just know it is."

Then she headed out across the road and into the woods with her pail. Father must *never* find out about this. Never. Never.

Chapter 2

THE REVEREND HERBERT H. HAYDEN

You may think, Passer-by, that Fate
Is a pit-fall outside of yourself,
Around which you may walk by the use of foresight
And wisdom.
Thus you believe, viewing the lives of other men,
As one who in God-like fashion bends over an anthill,
Seeing how their difficulties could be avoided.
But pass on into life:
In time you shall see Fate approach you
In the shape of your own image in the mirror . . .

—Edgar Lee Masters, "Lyman King,"
Spoon River Anthology

In March 1878, at the age of twenty-eight, Herbert Hayden was a man
stretched beyond his resources in every area: financially, intellectually, profes-
sionally, and emotionally. Soon, he would be morally bankrupt as well.

Hayden was a man of big schemes and big dreams that never seemed to ma-
terialize. Born in Massachusetts in 1850 of a hardworking family, he watched
his father ply such various trades as shoemaker, toll bridge operator, store
owner, butcher, carpenter, and hotel owner.[1] Young Herbert had participated
in these many ventures to help support the family, but he secretly aspired to a
higher class.

The one profession that seemed attainable to Hayden was that of preacher,
and he set out to accomplish that goal. At 18, he enrolled in a special high
school in Rhode Island run by the Methodists, his late start accounted for by
apprenticeship and work during his early teen years.

Hayden married another Massachusetts native, Rosa C. Shaw, in 1871, and
finished up his course work at the Providence Conference Seminary in 1872.
His plan was to get a college degree and be ordained into the Methodist minis-

try, so he and his new wife moved to Middletown, Connecticut, in 1873, where he enrolled at Wesleyan University.

However, the course of studies at Wesleyan proved to be beyond Hayden's abilities. The required subjects consisted of intensive studies in Latin, Greek, mathematics, English, composition, declamation, rhetoric, logic, and even a unit on land surveying.[2]

Hayden couldn't keep up. In 1875, at the end of his sophomore year, he had completed only two semesters. He blamed this on the typhoid fever he had come down with the summer before entering Wesleyan, which he claimed weakened him during his time at college. One of his Wesleyan professors, however, said that he was simply not a very good student, and Wesleyan advised him not to continue his studies.[3]

By this time, the Haydens had one child (Emma) and a newborn infant (Herbert Leonard, called Lennie). Although Herbert was preaching at the West Rocky Hill church, it was Rosa who was actually the main support of the family. Along with raising two children, she was teaching and taking in boarders. Hayden did occasional carpentry jobs for hire.[4]

Hayden's goal of becoming an ordained minister had been thwarted by his failure at Wesleyan. However, there was still another way he could accomplish this: by serving a sort of apprenticeship as a lay minister, filling in wherever he was needed. Eventually, if Hayden served these posts well, the Bishop might admit him to full ordination.[5] But he would have to prove himself.

The Hayden family moved to Rockland in 1876, where Herbert was appointed to preach in place of the Rev. Joseph W. Gibbs. His yearly salary was $350. Rosa taught school in Rockland, and Hayden took care of the children during the day.[6]

But all was not well with Herbert Hayden. There were personality clashes with some of the parishioners and with the Rev. Gibbs, who was not altogether ready to relinquish his command.[7] And there was the pressure of supporting a growing family on top of buying the clothes that were more befitting a minister.

At the end of that year, Hayden lost his preaching job in Rockland and Reverend Gibbs was reappointed to his old position. The Haydens had to move out of the parsonage.

It is not known whether the departure was voluntary on Hayden's part or the result of action taken by the parishioners, as there were two different accounts at the time of Mary Stannard's murder: one stated that he left the Rockland church "because of unpleasant relations"; the Haydens' version was that the church would not guarantee him the $350 salary he had received the previous year.[8]

Whatever the reason, Hayden was forced to rent a small farm nearby and try to make a living from it. In South Madison (Madison proper) an opportunity arose to fill in for the sick pastor at the Methodist Episcopal church, an appointment which then became permanent when the pastor did not recover right away. Hayden's weekly preaching wage was $5, or $260 for the year—$90 less than what he had earned in Rockland.[9]

Hayden would have been better off staying at the Rockland church even at less pay (if, indeed, he really had a choice in this). He not only had to work his farm in Rockland and preach in Madison, but he also got a teaching job there, which necessitated his being away from his family for the entire week. He would drive back to Rockland on Friday, stay overnight, leave again on Saturday and remain the rest of the week in Madison until Friday came around again.[10] The strain of the commuting and the multiple responsibilities must have been enormous.

To add to the family's difficulties, Rosa became sick while teaching in the spring of 1877. It was at this point that the Haydens were forced to hire someone to help with the children: Mary Stannard, who had been recommended by neighbors.[11]

Mary was not only a "nanny" for the children and a helper with household and farm chores, but also a companion for Mrs. Hayden, who was afraid to be alone at night. Mary lived in the Hayden household during the week, except for the Fridays when Herbert came home. Then she spent the night in the Stannard home a half-mile away.

In December of 1877, Rosa Hayden discovered that she was pregnant with their third child. It was a happy event not unmixed with other concerns: Rosa's preceding two pregnancies had been difficult and the family finances were already strained.

Hayden had been borrowing money from everyone he could, but found himself unable to pay back the notes. He had even gone to Mary Stannard, who told him that her half sister, Susan Hawley, had some money saved up. She intervened on his behalf and Susan loaned him the then-hefty sum of $75 to pay off a prior debt. In the year since he had borrowed this money from Susan, he had not made a single payment.[12]

In March of 1878, then, the time of the parish oyster supper, Herbert Hayden was stretched to the breaking point: He was no closer to his goal of becoming an ordained minister, he was working several jobs and commuting great distances merely to stay in touch with his family, he was heavily in debt, and his wife was four months pregnant.

Hayden needed to feel in control of something, since the rest of his life seemed to be a runaway train headed in the opposite direction from where he wanted to be. With the reappearance of Mary Stannard in the Hayden household, he knew where that area of control could lie.

Herbert Hayden was a short, somewhat stocky, good-looking man with dark, curly hair that he combed low on his forehead and kept "greased" or "oiled."[13] He liked wearing nice clothes when he had the opportunity, and was particular about his appearance. He was charming and gracious and liked being the center of attention. No doubt he was aware of Mary Stannard's positive appraisal of his attributes.

At 10:00 on the night of the oyster supper, Hayden told Rosa he had a headache and was going back to the house to take something for it.[14] He would return when he felt better, he said.

"Check on the children while you're there," Rosa said to him. "Make sure they're in bed."

Hayden said he would do so, but he knew he would not have to do any child care; Mary was very efficient, and the children minded her well.

In the four months of Rosa's pregnancy, the Haydens' sex life had been gradually diminishing until it was practically nonexistent. The prevailing morality in the Victorian era considered the purpose of sex to be reproduction only; anything beyond this was "marital excess." Once a woman was pregnant, therefore, sex was no longer necessary until after the child was born. Men who felt otherwise were made to feel unnatural by the prevailing literature, as were women who enjoyed sex.[15]

Herbert Hayden's seduction of Mary Stannard, seen in this light, was a fall from grace that was fairly predictable from our twenty-first-century vantage point. However, there were clues that Hayden had indulged in extra-marital affairs before this: rumors of other women and of fights with Rosa about them. And Hayden had shocked the somewhat priggish Rev. Gibbs by his "filthy" talk.[16]

After the night of the oyster supper, Hayden continued his affair with Mary, whom he considered little better than a prostitute. She was of a class even lower than his own, to say nothing of the one he aspired to; and she was already a "fallen woman" with an illegitimate child. With her he could feel superior and dominant, as he could not in other areas of his life.

Mary was easily influenced by Hayden, and he could have her whenever he wanted. He must have felt that, if she ever told anyone about the affair, he had only to deny it. Surely, his word as a man of the cloth was worth more than that of a lower-class servant with a child born out of wedlock.

Herbert and Mary met often at the spring shared by both properties. Hayden's cow always wandered away and had to be fetched every evening. Mary timed her trips to the spring for water to coincide with Hayden's daily rounding up of his cow.[17]

Hayden got careless at times, going for walks with her in a nearby meadow or taking her for rides in his buggy, where they were observed more than once by neighbors. Rumors began to float around Rockland about the minister and Mary Stannard.[18]

By summer, however, the affair seems to have ended. Rosa had her baby in early August, and Mary went off to Guilford to work for the Studleys. So, when

Hayden came back from Madison that Monday, September 2, 1878, he was not prepared for Mary's announcement.

Hayden had arrived home about 3:00 that afternoon, and at 4:00 Mary came to the house to ask if her father could borrow a rake.[19]

"Of course," Hayden responded. "Come on out to the barn with me and I'll get it for you."

When they got to the barn, Mary lit into him with a furious passion. She was pregnant, she said, and wanted him to help her out. He *must* help her out, either with medicine or money. She would need at least $50 for an abortion, and she fully intended to get one rather than be disgraced again. If he refused to help her, she told him, she intended to file a bastardy complaint against him.

Hayden was stunned. He could see his entire world come crashing down around him: his career, his family, his reputation . . . everything. And she might as well have asked for $1,000 as $50, for he could not have gotten his hands on either sum.

"Are you sure?" he asked her.

"Yes, I'm sure," Mary answered. "I've been down this road before, ain't I?" She was on the verge of tears.

"How far along are you?" Hayden asked. He was stalling for time now, desperately searching his mind for a solution to his problem. *His* problem. He had no thought about hers. "When did your monthly troubles stop?"

"They haven't stopped," Mary told him. "I have them right now."

"Well, then," Hayden said, relieved. "You must be mistaken."

"No, Mr. Hayden," Mary said miserably, "I'm not mistaken. And I had someone else check me over, too. Don't you remember when Rosa was having Lennie and she still had her troubles? So that don't mean it can't happen. The signs say I'm along about five months, and soon everyone else will see that, too!"

Mary's voice was rising now and Hayden needed to settle her down before Rosa came out to see what was going on. Besides, they had been in the barn a little too long for just getting a rake.

"I'll stick by you, Mary," Hayden said quickly. "Don't say anything to anyone. I'll get some medicine for you this week. Keep up good courage."

They left the barn, Mary first carrying the rake and Hayden following. On the porch stood the ever-vigilant Rosa holding the baby and watching them.

The rest of the day was a nightmare for Hayden. He went about his chores almost by rote, while the back of his mind was busy looking for a way out of this mess without anyone being the wiser.

The next morning, Tuesday, September 3, he rose early and told Rosa he would be driving into Durham, seven miles north of Rockland, to get oats for his horse and some other supplies. Rosa asked him to get molasses and sugar for preserving the pears he had brought home from Madison the day before and also some fuller's earth for the baby's chafing problem.[20]

As Hayden was hitching his horse and getting his carriage ready, Mary's father came into the yard. For a moment, the minister's heart leaped into his throat, thinking Stannard was coming to confront him about Mary's condition. But Charlie only wanted help with his haying later that day. Charlie was always wanting help with something.[21]

"I'm sorry, Charlie," Hayden said. "I've got to get supplies right now and afterward I have some chores to do."

Hayden's plan was to get to Middletown, another eight miles north of Durham. There he hoped to consult with Dr. Leonard Bailey, a homeopathic physician who had attended Rosa when she was expecting Lennie.[22] Dr. Bailey had been so attentive and so helpful during that very difficult pregnancy that the Haydens named their son after him.

Dr. Bailey would know of Rosa's problems during and after pregnancy and Hayden thought he could come up with a plausible enough story so that the doctor would give him a prescription for abortion medicine. And if that didn't work, well . . . he had a backup plan.

Hayden's first stop in Middletown was at the home of Lafayette Burton, a carpenter. The preceding winter Burton had agreed to make some tools in exchange for produce from Hayden's farm. The produce had been delivered, but Hayden had yet to collect the tools. Every time he came to Middletown, Burton was somewhere else.[23]

It had come to be a sore spot with the Haydens. The original deal was for a wagon in exchange for the produce. But when the months passed and the wagon was not forthcoming, even though Hayden had already delivered the produce, Rosa bought her husband a farm wagon out of her teaching wages. They needed the wagon, and Burton didn't seem to ever get around to it.

Now he was pulling the same stunt with the tools. Hayden had been up to Middletown four times to collect them, and each time he was told they'd be ready the next time. Between the wagon and the tools, this whole thing had been dragging on since March of 1877.

Today it did not really matter. Hayden's real purpose in calling on Burton was to provide a reason for going to Middletown in case that should ever come out—especially when he had told his wife he was going to Durham. He would say he thought of it on the way to Durham and decided to keep on going so he could collect his tools.[24]

Once again, Burton was not home. Mrs. Burton told Hayden that her husband was over at the Industrial School. Hayden never went there, however, and would later claim that he did not know where it was, even though the school was distinctly visible from the back window of the house he had lived in for two years while in Middletown.[25]

Hayden's next stop was Tyler's Drugstore. There, he purchased an ounce of arsenic ("for rats," he told the clerk) and his wife's fuller's earth. The clerk, George Tyler, took the arsenic from the jar behind the shelf, wrapped it in paper and then put another paper wrapper on top of that on which he wrote "Arsenic, poison." He tied the whole package with string.[26]

As Hayden was leaving Tyler's Drugstore, he couldn't believe his luck: there on the street was Dr. Bailey! The two men greeted each other and Dr. Bailey, as Hayden knew he would, asked after his wife. This was his opening.

Hayden related the difficulties Rosa was experiencing from the birth of their third child, born two weeks previously.[27] She was practically bedridden with pain and had some discharge. And now, he embellished, it seemed that she thought she was in a family way once again. Did Dr. Bailey know of anything that could stop this latest pregnancy? Hayden was worried about his wife's health and didn't think she could survive another one, especially so soon.

Dr. Bailey was surprised at the question and shocked at Hayden's suggestion of inducing an abortion. He didn't think Rosa would know of a new pregnancy quite so soon. He told Hayden of some remedies that might relieve her present pain, but did not give him a recommendation or prescription for abortion medicine.

Hayden then recalled to Bailey the problem Rosa had experienced when pregnant with Lennie: having regular periods for most of the nine months. He asked the doctor if he had ever seen that before. Was it an unusual condition or could it be expected in a fair percentage of the population?

Once again, Dr. Bailey was surprised at the question. But he told Hayden that, although the condition was unusual, it was not unheard of. Had Rosa had that trouble with the latest child? Hayden told him she hadn't, that he was just curious about the problem.

Hayden headed back to Rockland, discouraged. He had really hoped to obtain enough information from Dr. Bailey so that he could purchase the right abortion medicine, or be given a prescription for it.

Now he would have to go to his backup plan, which he was most reluctant to do. But he would do it if necessary. A bastardy complaint would ruin his chances of ever becoming ordained in the Methodist church, his chances of moving up to a professional class, and his chances of ever being able to escape the necessity of earning a living with his hands.

When Hayden got to Durham on the way home, he picked up the supplies he had originally said he would get there. Then, instead of going back by way of the New Durham Road, as he had done in the morning, he chose the Old Durham Road, which went right by the Stannards' house.

By late morning on Tuesday, September 3, 1878, the temperature had already climbed past the eighty-degree mark on its way to a humid ninety degrees later in the day. As Herbert Hayden approached the Stannard home, he thought it would be only natural that he should stop and ask for a drink of water. This would give him a chance to signal Mary to meet him so he could talk to her about a plan.

Hayden, however, wasn't thinking clearly in his desperation. Or, perhaps he arrogantly thought that no one would be smart enough to wonder why a man only two hundred yards from a cold spring and less than half a mile from his own home would stop where any water on hand was likely to be tepid.

He pulled his carriage to a stop and, to his immense surprise, his little girl, Emma, ran out to meet him.

"Papa! Papa!" she shouted, overjoyed to see him. Four-year-old Lennie followed closely on her heels.

Oh, no! Hayden thought. Was Rosa here, too? Surely, she didn't walk over in her condition! And if she *was* here, how would he give a signal to Mary? How could he talk to her about meeting him later?

Hayden got out of the wagon, smiling stiffly, his mind a jumble of anxious confusion. Charlie Stannard came out of his side door and raised his hand in greeting.

"It's been a long, hot drive, Charlie. How about a glass of water?" Hayden asked.

"Sure thing, Reverend," Stannard said and led him in the front door. Immediately, and to his immense relief, Hayden could see that Rosa was not there after all.

In the front room where Mary, Susan, and Willie slept, Mary and old Ben Stevens were sitting on the bed while Mary counted money out to him. There were no chairs in the room; the only place to sit was the bed.[28]

Good God, how these people lived! thought Hayden, shuddering inwardly. What had he gotten himself into by involving himself with Mary Stannard?

Out in the kitchen, Charlie poured water from a jug into a glass tumbler and gave it to Hayden.

"The water's warm, though, Reverend," Stannard said.

"It'll answer just the same," Hayden told him as he emptied the glass.

By then Mary had come into the kitchen and caught Hayden's eye. He rolled his eyes in the direction of the spring, and Mary caught the hint immediately. Taking up a tin seven-quart pail, she announced she would be going down to the spring to get some cold water.

Hayden loaded his two children into the buggy, arranged them around the large sacks of oats and other supplies, and headed down the road toward the spring. They met Mary on her way back with a full pail of water. Handing the reins to Lennie, Hayden got down from the carriage.

They conversed in low tones as he drank the fresh water.[29]

"Mary, has anything happened since yesterday that might make you think you don't really have a problem?" Hayden asked.

"I wish it wasn't true, Mr. Hayden, but it surely is!" Mary exclaimed. She was beginning to get hysterical again.

"All right, Mary. I just wanted to make sure. I've just been to see a doctor in Middletown and got some quick-acting medicine. Can you meet me after dinner today at the Big Rock in the woods?"

"Why can't you just give it to me now and I'll take it later?" she asked.

Hayden hadn't thought of that. Of course, it made sense. And if he really did have abortion medicine, it would be the best thing for him to do: distance himself as much as possible from her when she took it. He tried to find a plausible reason why he couldn't just hand her the packet, which was in his pocket and still covered by the warning wrapper.

"What if you take it and there's a problem?" Hayden asked. "You don't want your father to find out. Best to take it somewhere very private so I can be there to stand by you."

Mary accepted his explanation and agreed to meet him after dinner that day. She would go on a pretext of picking blackberries, she told him.

"I may not be able to get there until 2:00 or maybe even later," Hayden told her. "If I run right off after dinner it will look suspicious. But don't worry; I'll be there."[30]

Hayden continued on his way home and Mary went back to her house with the water. Her heart was lighter after their talk, but his was considerably heavier because of what he had to do, what she was *forcing* him to do. She had left him no choice.

It was now 11:30 A.M. Back home, Hayden unloaded the supplies, then unharnessed the horse and took him into the barn. There, unseen from the house, he took the arsenic package from his pocket, removed the string and both wrappers from it. He poured the powder into an empty pepper tin and put it in his coat pocket, then threw the wrappers and string into a barrel of items to be burned later.[31]

Hayden changed his clothes from his good ones to those more suitable for work: a brown-striped shirt, brown pants, military-style brogans, and a straw hat. He transferred the spice tin containing the arsenic from the coat to his front pants pocket.

Then he sat down in the yard with his jackknife to shuck the oysters he had brought home Monday. Rosa fixed the oysters for dinner, but because of the baby they could not eat together. She fed Herbert, Emma, and Lennie, and then Herbert held the baby while she ate.

Because Rosa had been weak and nauseous since the baby's birth, Hayden helped out with the usual household chores. On this Tuesday, he made the beds and emptied the chamber pots (a task that would undoubtedly have increased her nausea). Then he smoked a pipe and played with the two oldest children.

Despite his occasional philandering ways, Herbert Hayden was an extremely devoted family man. He loved his wife and doted on his children. In an era when many men were distant from their offspring except in matters of punishment, Hayden enjoyed spending time with them. He played with them nearly every day when he was home, and tucked them in bed every night.

At about 2:00 P.M. Hayden told Rosa he would be going to the woodlot to "throw out" some firewood. The woodlot, he said, was too swampy to get a horse and carriage in there right then. He would walk over, do the work, and then collect the wood at a later time.

In fact, the woodlot, while somewhat moist in places, was nowhere near being swampy.[32] But Hayden needed both an excuse to leave and a reason to go without the horse and carriage, which would have made stealth impossible.

Emma and Lennie followed their father out to the fork in the road, where he then shooed them back to their mother. He turned right and proceeded a few feet in the direction of the woodlot until he could no longer be seen from the house. Then he doubled back, going down an overgrown path toward the spring where he had met Mary that morning.[33]

Hayden had to cross the Old Durham Road at the end of the path where it met the spring, and this would be his only chance of being spotted. As he started to cross, a carriage was approaching the fork, just south of New Durham Road. Quickly, he darted back into the weedy overgrowth until it had turned the corner in the direction of Durham.

He avoided traveled roads in his route to Big Rock where Mary was waiting, and arrived there just about 2:30. As he crossed the final footpath, he could see her sitting on a large, flat rock, her pail next to her. She jumped up when she saw him and knocked over the pail. There was nothing in it.[34]

"Oh, I knew you'd come!" Mary exclaimed. "I was a little worried for a time, but I knew you'd come."

She wore a calico dress and a pretty, checked sunbonnet. Her hands were stained a little from eating blackberries while she was waiting for him. She had been too nervous to do anything else and hadn't thought ahead as to how she would explain coming home after all that time with an empty pail. Mary didn't always think ahead, especially when it came to guile.

"How long do you think this medicine will take before it works?" she asked Hayden. "I'll have to get home before too long."

"It should happen within moments," he told her. "You'll be back before you're missed."

Hayden knew that a fatal dose of arsenic was only a few grains, and he naively thought that a large dose of ninety grains (the whole ounce) would knock her out almost immediately and kill her painlessly.[35] Her system would simply shut down before she felt any real pain, he reasoned to himself, and he could get back to his woodlot and work on his alibi in case he needed it.

Mary had a habit of saying she would kill herself whenever she was distressed. She tended to be emotional and histrionic, especially when she was menstruating, and Hayden counted on people's remembering this.[36] After she was dead, he would arrange her body as if she had taken the arsenic and then lay down to die. No one would doubt that it was suicide, especially when she was found to be pregnant once again.

He pulled out the pepper tin, all associations with arsenic having been removed, and handed it to her.

"You'll need some water to swallow this down," he said. "I'll take your pail and get some." There was another spring at Big Rock, and he went there now and put a little water in the bottom.

Mary opened the spice tin and looked at the white powder inside.

"Well," she said in trepidation, "I had best do it sooner as later." She emptied the powder into the pail, swished it around in the water, and drank the mixture down.

It was now 2:45.

Mary sat down on the flat rock to wait for the "medicine" to work. Hayden stood anxiously nearby, not really knowing what to expect, but thinking it would happen quickly. The minutes ticked by. When would the infernal stuff kick in? The longer it took, the greater the chance of someone coming by, perhaps to pick the very blackberries Mary had supposedly come for.

They conversed very little, both preoccupied with their own thoughts as to what would come next.

After several minutes, Mary felt her heart race madly.[37] It was uncomfortable, but she felt that meant the medicine would soon be working and her troubles would be over. She leaned forward and put her head down to keep from passing out.

It was now 3:00.

More minutes passed. Suddenly, Mary stood up, clutching her stomach. She found it hard to breathe and she felt as if her insides were on fire. The pain was intolerable, and she screamed in agony. Perhaps realizing Hayden's intent, she ran toward the path that led to her house.

It was now 3:15.

When Mary began to scream and run, Hayden reacted instinctively. She must be stopped before someone heard her and came to see what was happening. He grabbed a club-like piece of wood lying on the ground and struck her on the right side of the head.[38] The blow opened her scalp, but did not penetrate the bone.

Mary stopped screaming abruptly, but instead of falling over, as Hayden had hoped, she stood looking at him, dazed. She put her right hand to her head to feel the wound just as he raised the club to strike again. The second blow fell on the back of her hand, and this time she went down.[39]

Hayden was rattled by this turn of events. Could he still make it look like suicide? Maybe the blow to the head would be attributed to a fall, and he could still pull it off. But he would have to work quickly before someone came along. He could only hope no one had heard the scream.

He put the pepper tin back in his pocket and took out his jackknife. The large blade was nicked and dull, but the smaller one, two inches in length, was sharp as a razor.

Hayden knelt behind Mary, whose breathing was very feeble and practically nonexistent as a result of the ninety grains of arsenic and the two blows to the head. He wanted the ordeal to be over with, for her as well as for himself; he had never intended her to die in such agony, but to slip quietly into a peaceful sleep.

He lifted up her head and untied her sunbonnet from under her chin. Then he held her by the hair, stuck the knife into the left side of her throat, and pulled across a few inches. He had killed enough pigs and other animals to know where the vital arteries were. He sliced through the jugular, the first major vein the blade met, then drew the knife up, partially severing the carotid further in, and nicking the larynx under it.

The rapid heartbeat Mary had first experienced as the arsenic set out to do its work was then replaced by a slowing down of the heart and the entire system. By the time Hayden cut her throat, the heartbeat was so thready and feeble that there was no great spurting of blood. Rather, it was more like a trickle. Also, by kneeling *behind* her, he avoided getting any blood on his clothes, as he well knew from his butchering days.

Hayden quickly washed his knife and his hands in the spring. Then he came back to the body, placed it in a peaceful reclining position with hands folded on top, lifted up the head and placed the sunbonnet underneath as a sort of pillow. It was the best he could do for a spur-of-the-moment plan.

Anyone coming on the scene would be struck by the peaceful repose of the dead girl. The only violence to attend her death would seem to have been caused by her own hand. An attacker bent on "outrage" (the Victorian euphemism for rape) would have left her clothes disheveled and torn. No, it would look like suicide, all right.

There was only one problem: a weapon. Hayden could not leave his own knife, as it was the only one he owned. It might be traced to him, and he would have to explain its loss to Rosa, who sometimes used it herself when she needed a sharp knife to cut meat with.

The solution he came up with was to come back later and plant a knife near Mary. He did not think she would be discovered very soon. She was, after all, an independent woman. And, although she presently lived with her father, she could come and go as she pleased. Hayden didn't think they would even come looking for her before morning.

It was now 3:30.

Hayden left the scene, taking with him the now-bloody club he had used on Mary. He quickly retraced his steps along the same route by which he had arrived, hiding the club in the thick, twisted underbrush along the way. There was no time to go to the woodlot now; he had been gone too long.

The minister had left his property from the north end, ostensibly to go to the woodlot in that direction. Now he arrived from the south. (He would later claim that he walked around so he could check on his corn.) Stopping in his potato patch, he called to his six-year-old daughter to bring a container for potatoes. In the end, he had to get it himself, but he needed a little more time to collect himself before going inside.

It was now 4:00.

As thunder rumbled around him and raindrops fell, lightly at first and then gathering strength, Hayden dug a peck of potatoes from his garden, chopped some kindling, and picked up wood chips. Now, at last, he was ready to go in—or, at least as ready as he'd ever be.

As he entered the back door, Hayden took his jackknife out of his pocket and quietly placed it on the shelf above the woodbox in the pantry where it lay when not in use. He hoped Rosa would not notice that it had not been there, but if she had he could always say he had needed it to free the wood from the brambles in the woodlot.

Hayden's striped shirt was sweaty with fear and exertion. He changed into a white one and put the dirty one in the laundry pile.[40] Then he did some chores and sat down to write a letter concerning his mother-in-law's estate.

As he wrote, another part of his mind was preoccupied with going over what he had done and what he still needed to do to distance himself from Mary Stannard's death.

First, he would have to find a knife to place near her body, and that would have to be done that night after dark. He couldn't risk being seen in the area where her body would eventually be discovered. His son, Lennie, was crazy about knives and had two of them. He would take one of those.

Next, he would have to make up for the work he should have accomplished in the woodlot that afternoon. Early in the morning, then, he would have to get out there and work like the devil to pile up enough wood to make it look as if he had done it the previous afternoon. There was some piled wood he had thrown out before this, and he could use that in his alibi as well.[41]

Hayden mulled over these plans and tried to concentrate on his letter for the estate. He prayed that Mary's body would not be found before he had finished what he had to do.

It was now 6:00.

The thunderstorm had been violent, but brief. The late summer evening, cooled off after the rain, was peaceful and pleasant.

Suddenly, a raucous, excited voice shattered the stillness. "Mary Stannard's dead out by Big Rock!" shouted thirteen-year-old Burton Mills as he raced into the yard. "And she's cut her throat, or someone has done it for her!"[42]

Chapter 3

THE STANNARD-HAWLEY CLAN

How could I till my forty acres
Not to speak of getting more,
With a medley of horns, bassoons and piccolos
Stirred in my brain by crows and robins . . . ?
And I never started to plow in my life
That someone did not stop in the road
And take me away to a dance or a picnic.

—Edgar Lee Masters, "Fiddler Jones,"
Spoon River Anthology

If there was ever a prototype for the 1950s movie character Pa Kettle, it was Mary's father, Charles Sylvester Stannard. Lazy, illiterate, and completely devoid of either education or ambition, he was nonetheless affable and inoffensive. In a community of poor farmers, Charlie Stannard was at the bottom of the economic and social strata.[1]

Charlie did odd jobs for other people, hayed his own land, and grew some vegetables to sell. Yet, he did not possess even the most essential of work tools, contenting himself instead with borrowing from his neighbors. His house was run-down and unpainted and the yard overgrown with brush. There was little furniture in the house, no carpet on the floors, and the interior best described as "dilapidated."[2]

And it wasn't even Charlie's house. Somewhere around 1850, at the age of twenty-six, Charlie moved into the home of thirty-year-old Horace Hawley, possibly as a hired hand but more likely as a co-worker in the local charcoal industry. In the Hawley household at the time were Horace's twenty-nine-year-old wife, Charlotte, and their children: Fanny, ten; Dayton, seven; Harriet (Hattie), three; Sylvester, two; and Charles, six months. Susan came along in November 1852.[3]

Charlotte Hawley was fed up with Horace, who was shiftless and abusive. In contrast, Charlie Stannard was gentle and kind. Charlotte fell in love with him and decided to get a divorce from Hawley.

Late in 1852 or early in 1853, Charlie and Charlotte went to Madison to see a lawyer, Probate Judge Edward R. Landon. Landon was in a hurry, so he continued to shave while Charlotte spilled out her plea for a divorce.

"I'll do the best I can," Landon told her. He indicated Charlie with his straight razor. "Is this a relative?"

"No, sir," Charlotte blushed. "But if I get the divorce, I hope to make him one."[4]

The Hawleys' divorce was granted in April of 1853, and Charlie and Charlotte married that November. The divorce decree said that Horace had deserted Charlotte, but he may have done this because of her adulterous alliance with Charlie.[5]

Charlie Stannard supplanted his predecessor. He had, in the words of defense counsel at the trial, "[gone] into the family and [taken] house, wife, and all."[6]

Charlie and Charlotte went on to have four children of their own: Emogene in 1854; Mary Elizabeth in 1856; Isadora in 1859; and Charlie in 1861. (Little Charlie died tragically of burns at the age of three.[7])

The younger Hawley children stayed with their mother until old enough to "work out," then occasionally came back to the homestead to live for a while.

But Charlie was no better a provider than Horace Hawley had been. Along with raising her family, Charlotte was forced to take housekeeping jobs in order to support them. She was so overworked that at one point, around 1871, she had a physical and mental breakdown that incapacitated her for a few months. The breakdown, however, may have been exacerbated by the cancer that killed her in early December 1873, and may have also been associated with menopause.[8]

At the trial, Hayden's defense team jumped on a rumor (presented by Hayden himself) that insanity ran in Mary's family because her mother and grandmother had gone crazy. But, seen from today's perspective, these women were undoubtedly just reacting to the incredible stresses brought on by constant childbearing, childrearing, housekeeping, and the necessity of working outside the home.

Mary herself was thought of as "simple" and easily influenced, possibly even somewhat retarded. And she may have been. Ben Stevens said she was a "good, smart girl,"[9] but he was probably being protective of an extended family member, as there is little other evidence that the term "smart" could ever have been applied to Mary.

On the other hand, lack of education was often perceived as stupidity by the community and the newspapers of the nineteenth century, so it is difficult to assess Mary's abilities accurately—or, for that matter, those of any of the Stannards and Hawleys. Anyone who had difficulty understanding a question because of a lack of vocabulary (or even, as in the case of Charlie Stannard, because of being hard of hearing) was termed "dull of comprehension" or "slow-witted."[10]

But, whether it was due to genetic insufficiency or a lack of education, none of the Stannard-Hawley clan had the mental skills to come off well on the stand when pitted against defense attorneys trying to trip them up. Charles and Sylvester Hawley were presented as simple buffoons. The attorneys and spectators laughed at them, and the newspapers made fun of them.

And, to add to the general impression given by the Stannards and Hawleys as shiftless and stupid, came the death of thirty-six-year-old Dayton Hawley during the second trial. Hawley, possibly drunk, stood on a railroad track while a train approached from over a mile behind him. He never turned around, despite the frantic whistles and bells sounded by the conductor.[11]

Of all the Stannards and Hawleys, however, the most capable seems to have been Susan. She was intensely dedicated to her family, even sacrificing her chances at a life of her own to care for them.

When Mary became pregnant in 1875, Susan left her position as Ben Stevens' housekeeper to take care of her half sister. After the baby was born, Mary and Susan alternated work and childcare chores. At the time of Mary's death, Susan was Willie's primary caretaker and was also attending to her father's needs.[12]

Despite her lack of education, Susan Fowler Hawley was shrewder and savvier than her siblings or her parents. She managed to save money from the small portion of the already-meager earnings that she kept for herself, and was even able to loan $75 to Herbert Hayden in 1877. She was never characterized as "slow-witted" by either the defense or the press, as were other members of her family.

Susan must have been aware of the shortcomings of her family, as she was fiercely protective of them against what she saw as the machinations of the larger world. At the trial, her shrewdness and protectiveness would be used against her and hinder the cause she fought so hard for: justice for her dead sister.

When his wife died in 1873, Charlie Stannard simply stayed in the house that had belonged to Horace Hawley, while Hawley lived in the homes of his various employers.[13] By the time of their mother's death, all of the Hawley and Stannard children were old enough to work out of the home, and Mary had already been doing so for a few years. Susan Hawley and the Stannard girls contributed a portion of their incomes to support Charlie, since his own income was so meager and sporadic.

Charlie Stannard could not read or write, add or subtract, and possibly had difficulty telling time. That some of his children and stepchildren could do so to a slightly greater extent was probably due to Charlotte's influence. But despite his failure as a role model of respectability, the Stannard and Hawley children, as well as his Rockland neighbors, seemed genuinely fond of him. His children supported him and his neighbors gave him food and loaned him tools.[14]

The defense referred to Charlie in their closing argument as "this stupid, clever man,"[15] a strange combination of adjectives. Perhaps the statement reflects Charlie's ability to survive despite his lack of education and drive.

But the defense theory that Stannard had anything to do with his daughter's death is preposterous for several reasons: Not only was he very fond of her, but much of Mary's income went to his support; it would have been like killing the goose that laid the golden egg. Moreover, the violence, the energy, and the sophistication with which the murder was carried out were all beyond Charlie's capabilities and inclinations.

By the summer of 1878, five years after the death of his wife, fifty-four-year-old Charlie Stannard's life had settled into a somewhat stable routine. He had his occasional odd jobs, mostly for his friend Ben Stevens, who took pity on him and provided him with as much work as he could. His humiliation over Mary's illegitimate pregnancy had passed and he was enjoying his grandson, two-year-old Willie. Mary was getting regular employment and Susan was taking care of the family by cooking, cleaning, and watching Willie.

When Mary came home from Guilford at the end of August, Charlie had no idea that she thought she was pregnant again. True, he had told her last time that he would kick her out if it happened again, but he probably would not have done it.[16]

Charlie had felt shame over his daughter's first pregnancy because of what the community must have said about the Stannards as "poor white trash" and did not want a recurrence of it. His stepson, Charles Hawley, had told him in the spring of 1878 that Rockland was buzzing with rumors of Mary and Reverend Hayden and argued hotly that Charlie should "kick her out of doors"[17] to protect the family's reputation. Stannard could never have brought himself to do that, so he chose not to believe the rumors.

In the days following her return home, Mary seemed restless and fidgety ("hazing around," in Rockland vernacular).[18] She came to Charlie again and again, saying she was going for a walk or to see the Haydens' new baby, and asking if he needed any errands run. He was getting ready to do some haying, so he had her borrow some tools from Herbert Hayden: first a hayrake, then a pitchfork. Ben Stevens sent her out for butter, and Charlie himself went to get some pork from a neighbor for their noon meal on September 3.

Early on the morning of September 3, Charlie walked over to the Haydens' to see if he could get Herbert to help him with raking and stacking the hay.

Stannard was adept at getting others to help him, and they invariably ended up doing most of the work. But Hayden was getting ready to go for supplies and said he had his own chores to do later.

Never one to hurry where work was concerned, Charlie didn't get to the haying until after dinner that day.[19] He dawdled all morning, chatting with Ben Stevens, and later Herbert Hayden, then had dinner with the family at noon. After dinner, he went to a neighbor's and was away for a half-hour. When he came back home at 1:30, Susan was visiting with Eliza Mills, a neighbor who had come by to see if Mary could do some sewing for her.

Charlie told Mrs. Mills that Mary had gone to the Fox Ledge area to pick blackberries for a pie and urged her to wait around and try some. He stayed talking with Susan and Eliza Mills and playing with Willie until 2:00, then headed out for his fields. Little Willie toddled right behind, but Charlie brought him back. "Willie can't go with Grandpa," he told him gently.

Charlie spent two hours in the hot sun that Tuesday, which was as much continuous work as he could stand. Besides, it was about to rain, and this gave him a good excuse to stop. At 4:00 he trudged across the field and into his back door just as rain was starting to fall and thunder could be heard in the distance. He was surprised to find that Mary was still not home, especially as she was terrified of thunderstorms.

Susan, who knew where Mary had gone and why, was even more concerned at her sister's prolonged absence. Maybe something had gone wrong with the "quick medicine" Hayden had purchased. Maybe Mary was in need of help. And now the storm was coming on faster.

"Father," Susan said in a worried tone, "I wish you'd go see what's keeping Mary. Maybe she's lost her way in the woods like she did with Mrs. Mills that time."

Charlie headed down the path toward Fox Ledge, but stopped about fifty yards short of the rock. No sense walking more than he had to: if Mary was around, she'd hear him. Besides, the bushes were wet.

"Hallooo!" he shouted. "Mary!" There was no answer to his calls, although Charlie was quite deaf and probably wouldn't have heard it anyway.

He went back to his house, thinking Mary must have gone home by another route. By now it was raining very hard. Charlie stopped to gather some wood for cooking supper and draw some water from the spring. As he approached the house, he saw Susan heading across the road and toward the woods.

"I'm just going to see if I can find Mary," Susan told him. "She hasn't come back yet, and I can't think what's happened to her."

"Don't you go getting yourself wet and catching your death," Charlie said. "She'll fetch around pretty soon, you just watch. And if she hasn't come back by the time I finish with these chores, I'll go back up there myself."

Susan said nothing about Mary's real purpose in going to the woods, and had no intention of doing so unless it became absolutely necessary. What if, in her worry, she blurted it out to Father and then Mary came along, cured of her problem? Mary would never forgive her. No, she would bide her time for the moment.

Charlie did his chores in his usual leisurely fashion. Susan wanted to yell at him to hurry it up, but couldn't very well do so without saying why she was so worried. So she bit her tongue and grew more and more agitated at his nonchalance. Finally, half an hour later, he was ready to go back to Fox Ledge.

This time, infected with Susan's obvious concern and feeling a sense of uneasiness at his daughter's absence, Charlie went all the way up to Fox Ledge and walked down the old roadway to Whippoorwill (Big) Rock. He was about ten yards away when he saw Mary's body lying partially in the roadway. She lay on her back, leaning slightly on her right side. Her hands were placed on her stomach as if she were laid out for burial. He could see that her throat was cut.

"Mary!" Charlie cried out in agony. He put the back of his hand on her hands and face and felt how cold she was, even on that hot, humid day. He knew she was dead, but he couldn't begin to comprehend it. Leaving her just as she was he ran, sobbing and pulling at his hair, to the nearest house: the home of Francis and Eliza Mills.

Chapter 4

DISCOVERY: THE ROCKLAND COMMUNITY TAKES OVER

Passer-by, sin beyond any sin
Is the sin of blindness of souls to other souls.
And joy beyond any joy is the joy
Of having the good in you seen, and seeing the good
At the miraculous moment!

—Edgar Lee Masters, "Jeremy Carlisle,"
Spoon River Anthology

Eliza Mills had waited for Mary Stannard as long as she could. At 3:00 she began walking back to her home, where she lived with her husband, Francis (twenty-one years older than the forty-eight-year-old Eliza) and their sons Burton, thirteen, and Freddie, twelve. Along the way she was joined by Freddie.[1]

Eliza Mills was a woman who lived at a high emotional pitch. She thrived on drama and tended to react somewhat histrionically to events, especially when she could put herself in the midst of them.[2] She was a good-hearted, generous woman, was Mrs. Mills, but she dearly loved a "crisis" from which she could derive the maximum of dramatic effect. These crises served to enliven the humdrum routine of her daily life.

Currently, Eliza Mills claimed to be affected by a nervous condition caused by the recent Wallingford tornado.[3] It was her way of prolonging the most exciting event to hit the area in common memory, an event that would only be surpassed by the murder of Mary Stannard.

The quaint little town of Wallingford, only ten miles from Rockland in a direct line, had been the scene of a devastating tornado on August 9, 1878, the same day the Haydens' third child was born and less than a month before Mary Stannard would be found at Big Rock with her throat cut.[4] Houses and barns had been tossed into the air and even brick buildings, notably the new high school and a factory, were leveled.

Wallingford residents were picked up and hurled into trees and fields, while houses and buildings fell on others. Thirty-two people died and forty-one were injured. In some cases, entire families were wiped out or—even more tragically—only one member was left alive.

The dead were gathered, some with horribly disfiguring wounds, and laid out in a schoolhouse. In the two days following the tornado, an estimated 10,000 people came to Wallingford from New Haven and surrounding areas to view the devastation and see the dead bodies in the school gymnasium. The *New York Times* estimated that about two-thirds of those visitors lifted up the sheets to see the wounds.

The Wallingford tornado incident illustrates the degree to which people in the nineteenth century intruded themselves into sensational events, even—or especially—if those events were full of tragedy, grief, and disgusting sights. The same thing would happen in the Stannard case and, three years later, in the Jennie Cramer case.

Although the Wallingford tornado did not touch Rockland, Eliza Mills was thrilled and horrified by the closeness of the event and claimed a nervous debilitation as a result of it. She would never have admitted it, but she was thoroughly enjoying the Wallingford tornado and wasn't ready to let it be forgotten.

As Mrs. Mills and her son walked toward their home and past the intersection where the old abandoned Haddam Road came in, she heard a shrill, bloodcurdling scream that was cut off quickly. She stopped and said "Hark!" to Freddie, but the sound never came again. Freddie thought it might have been a rooster. "Had I thought at that time it was a human voice," Eliza Mills would say later as she testified in what the newspapers called "a thrilling manner," "I should have gone directly there, weak as I was."[5]

They arrived home about fifteen minutes later and Eliza looked at the clock, which was twenty minutes fast; it was 3:35.

At 6:00, as the Millses were getting ready for supper (or what Rocklanders called "tea" in the British tradition), Charlie Stannard burst in, distraught and nearly incoherent. He had gone looking for Mary, he said, and found her up by the Big Rock, dead, with her throat cut. He needed help carrying her back to his house.

Eliza Mills remembered the scream. "That was Mary's voice I heard!" she said now. "It was her last scream." Francis sent the boys out to tell the neighbors and bring them back to help with the body. Freddie ran toward Nehemiah Burr's house and Burton went to tell Herbert Hayden and Luzerne Stevens. Francis Mills accompanied Charlie Stannard down the road to where Mary lay, while Eliza went back to the Stannard home to break the news to Susan and wait for the body to arrive.

The men were soon joined by Herbert Hayden, Luzerne Stevens, and some of the other neighbors roused by the boys. At Big Rock, they stood looking at the body, laid out so peacefully and with no sign of attempted "outrage" (rape). Perhaps Mary had cut her own throat, and this was discussed for a while. The men spoke in low tones out of respect for the dead girl and her father.

But if Mary had cut her throat, where was the knife? It was beginning to get dark now and a search was made for the knife or some other weapon that might have been used. They looked in the bushes and all around the area but could find nothing. They decided to come back the next day to look when it was light. In the meantime, they needed to get Mary back home and notify the authorities.[6]

The men searched the former charcoal-burning area and found a wide, flat board, which they placed next to the body. Positioning themselves around the dead woman (Hayden at her head), they carefully lifted her onto the board. They noticed her pretty checked sunbonnet, bloody now, folded neatly where her head had lain. Had she removed it herself? Underneath her a large pool of blood had sunk into the ground.[7]

About a dozen men had gathered at the Big Rock site, and six of these now acted as pallbearers in carrying the body back to her home: Nehemiah Burr, a young farmer and peddler whose barn would become important because of its proximity to Hayden's woodlot; Luzerne Stevens, who lived across the road from the Haydens and was their closest neighbor; Sylvester Hawley, Susan's brother and Mary's half brother; Fillmore Scranton, another young farmer who lived near the Haydens; Charles Scranton, a roommate of Sylvester and Charles Hawley; and Herbert Hayden.[8]

Arriving at the Stannard home, the men carrying the dead body of Mary Stannard were met by the women: Susan Hawley, Eliza Mills, Louisa (Mrs. Luzerne) Stevens, and Cornelia (Mrs. Loren) Stevens. Cornelia was the wife of the local undertaker and frequently helped with the cleaning and laying out of the dead.[9]

Louisa Stevens had hurried over to the Stannards' when Burton Mills brought the news of the death to her husband, Luzerne, and the Haydens. Ten years younger than her thirty-nine-year-old husband, Mrs. Stevens had already perfected the arts of snooping and gossip. She was a busybody pure and simple, and her entire family seems to have been afflicted with this disease.

Louisa spent much of her time looking out her windows and keeping track of the comings and goings of her neighbors, especially the Haydens. She did not entirely approve of the Haydens. What kind of mother would let a toddler play with a sharp knife, especially after he had cut himself more than once? Louisa had taken it upon herself to scold Mrs. Hayden for letting Lennie play with knives. And then there were the rumors of Reverend Hayden and other women, including Mary Stannard.[10]

But the thing that finally alienated Louisa Stevens from Rosa Hayden was the latter's decision to call in Mary Davis instead of Louisa as her nurse during her confinement before and after her baby was born. After all, Louisa only lived across the road, whereas Mary Davis lived two miles away. Rachel Stevens, Luzerne's mother, had served as Rosa's midwife for this birth, and Louisa just naturally assumed that she herself would be her nurse.[11]

The Stevenses looked on the selection of Mary Davis as a personal slight against Louisa, although the truth of the matter was that Rosa Hayden felt more comfortable with Mrs. Davis, who was her close friend. Nearly a month after the baby's birth, Mrs. Stevens had still not gone over to see her. In a community like Rockland, the failure to perform this simple, neighborly gesture sent a message loud and clear.[12]

On Monday, September 2, the day before the murder, Louisa Stevens was watching out her windows as usual, aided in this regard by her husband, his mother (Rachel Stevens), and his sister (Henrietta Young).[13] She saw Mary at 8:00 A.M. going into the Haydens' house, then coming out about fifteen minutes later to get Rosa some water from their well. A few minutes after that, Mrs. Stevens saw Mary go toward her home.

Two hours later this vigilant neighbor saw Mary coming down the hill from her home and, forty-five minutes after that, come out of Haydens' house and go back up the hill carrying a three-pint tin pail. At 3:30 or 4:00, Mary was back at the Haydens' again and headed back home with a rake in her hand. And later she saw old George Davis come by to talk with Mr. Hayden.

Rachel Stevens and her daughter were sitting by the kitchen window for Mary's 4:00 visit. They watched as Hayden went into the barn, followed by Mary, and then saw both emerge about five minutes later. Mary was carrying a rake.

"Sure enough!" Henrietta Young clucked triumphantly.[14] She and her mother had heard the rumors about Hayden and Mary, and this seemed to give substance to those rumors: the two had been in the barn *much* too long just to get a rake. Rosa Hayden seemed to think so, too, as she had come out onto the porch holding her baby, looking anxiously toward the barn.

The next morning at 6:00, Louisa Stevens looked out her bedroom window and saw Herbert Hayden drive out of his yard in his top carriage. Later, she saw Mary Stannard coming out of the Haydens' gate between 7:00 and 8:00 A.M., then at 11:00 watched her come back toward the Haydens' where she heard her talking to the children. A few minutes after that, she saw Mary and the Hayden children walk in the direction of the Stannards' house.

Although Louisa Stevens was supposed to be helping her husband put up wallpaper that Tuesday, she still found time for her self-imposed duty of keeping tabs on the neighbors. She noticed that Hayden came back in his carriage at 11:30 and that the children were riding with him; she watched him play with Emma and Lennie after dinner, and saw him again at 4:30 coming through his potato patch.

Nor was her husband, Luzerne, entirely immune to the lure of window-watching. He testified that he, too, had witnessed some of these same comings and goings of his neighbors. Both Louisa and Luzerne seemed oblivious to what their trial testimony revealed about them as neighbors, and the defense sarcastically referred to their household as "the Rockland Watchtower."[15]

However, if after the news of Mary's horrible death Louisa Stevens rushed over to the Stannard home to find out more gossip, she was nonetheless a big help to Susan Hawley and Charlie Stannard.

The men carrying the dead body of Mary Stannard set the pallet down in the yard across a couple of sawhorses. From there they proceeded to notify the local coroner, Henry Stone, and to round up an inquest jury.[16] Someone went to get Dr. Rufus Matthewson and his son, Earle, still in medical school at New York City's College of Physicians and Surgeons.

Since an autopsy was to be performed, the women could not clean and dress the body as they might have for a normal wake and funeral. Instead, they removed Mary's clothing and prepared her for the autopsy. There was so much caked blood that it was necessary to cut through the dress and the sleeves of the chemise (a one-piece undergarment) in order to remove them. Then they wrapped an old bed quilt around her naked body until the doctors should arrive.[17]

In setting aside Mary's clothing, the women discovered the feminine towel and other articles in her pockets. Since Mary's period was finished for that month, it seemed strange that she would have a menstrual rag with her.[18]

When the Doctors Matthewson arrived around 3:00 A.M., the body was carried into the front parlor that had served as bedroom for Mary, Susan, and Willie. Susan had told Eliza Mills and Louisa Stevens about Mary's supposed pregnancy (without, however, mentioning Hayden's name), and so the doctors were alerted to watch for a fetus of approximately five months' gestation.[19]

The light was poor in the Stannards' front parlor, but the autopsy proceeded nonetheless. The doctors found a scalp wound that did not penetrate the skull, a bruise on the right hand, and a cut in the throat. But they did not find any evidence of rape, pregnancy, or even of recent sexual intercourse.[20]

After the autopsy, the undertaker's wife, Cornelia Stevens (who was married to "Uncle" Ben's brother), washed the body. She noticed that there were blood spots on the left side of the face, and on the right side and back, but none on Mary's hands (which would have been there if she had committed suicide). She rewrapped her in the bed quilt and put coins on her eyelids as fare for her passageway to the other world.

By this time the inquest jury had arrived and situated itself in the Stannard kitchen, ready to hear what evidence there was. When local coroner Henry Stone arrived at the residence that night, he was so overcome by the sight of the dead girl that he fainted.[21]

Susan testified first, telling them what Mary had told her about her supposed pregnancy. On the other side of the swinging door, Eliza Mills, Louisa Stevens, and Cornelia Stevens hovered close by to eavesdrop. For the first time, they heard the name of Mary's lover: the Reverend Herbert Hayden.[22]

Early on Wednesday morning, Herbert Hayden rose early, hitched his seventeen-year-old horse to a wagon, and headed out to the woodlot where he claimed to have been the preceding day.[23] Working quickly, he threw wood into piles and then loaded his wagon. He made two trips for some of this wood, but made sure to leave several piles there as "evidence" of his activity on Tuesday. Prior to the day of the murder, he had been in the woodlot and piled up some of the wood for when he should need it next. This he took, leaving the newer piles behind.

On his way back home he met Andrew Hazlett, a local resident, who told him that it had been pretty much decided by the inquest jury that Mary Stannard had been murdered. The previous night they had gone to the scene with lanterns to look for the weapon. While they failed to turn up the knife, they did find a large stone with what looked like blood on it and which was probably used by the murderer to knock Mary down.

"Do they suspect anyone?" Hayden asked.

"Well, yes, they do," answered Hazlett. He was surprised because it was Hayden himself whose name was being mentioned. But Hayden quickly drove off without asking who it was. To Hazlett's way of thinking, this was the act of a guilty man.[24]

Later that morning, Hayden met two other residents, who asked him what he thought about what had happened to poor Mary Stannard. Hayden, who fully expected the autopsy to reveal a five-month fetus, replied that it seemed Mary had gone off and gotten herself pregnant. Then, not wanting to endure the shame of a second illegitimate child, she had killed herself.[25]

Back home, Hayden unloaded the wood and noted that Mary Davis, the wife of his friend Talcott Davis, and their daughter Etta, were visiting Rosa. As he entered the kitchen, he asked loudly, "Wife, where's my knife?" Rosa told him it was on the shelf over the woodbox.[26]

But Hayden didn't really need his knife for anything. He had merely wanted the Davises to witness his getting it from the shelf, as if it had been there all along. He began to clean his fingernails with it and Rosa scolded him, "Oh, Herbert, don't use the knife on your nails!"[27]

At 10:00 that morning, Hayden took his son's knife to the murder site to plant it there.[28] Once it was discovered, it would distract the inquest jury and the sheriff and possibly divert suspicion from himself. And, if he were discovered at the scene, he only needed to say he was looking for a murder weapon.

To Hayden's immense surprise and disappointment, he found Ben Stevens at Fox Ledge. Stevens had gone to search the brush for a weapon that might have been used to cut Mary's throat.

Immediately, Hayden began talking to Ben about the insanity in Mary's family and how that meant she was probably insane, too. Stevens greatly resented this diagnosis. Mary was not insane, he told Hayden heatedly, but was "the likeliest of girls" (a phrase that meant she had great possibilities of success). Nor was Mary's mother really insane, either. She had had some difficulties around the time of her menopause, but many women do. They took her to a place in Hartford, and once her physical problems cleared up, her mental ones did, too.

But with Ben Stevens there, Hayden had no opportunity to plant the knife. He made a brief show of looking for one and then returned home.

After dinner that afternoon, Hayden went back over to Stannards' house, where he had heard he was wanted by the inquest jury. He was the first witness for the afternoon and, to his horror, discovered that Mary had told Susan Hawley everything. The jury members grilled him thoroughly on his relations with Mary as well as his movements on the day before and the day of the murder.

In the midst of his testimony, Hayden made an odd statement: he said he hoped that would be the end of his questioning because he had to go to town the next day to get help for his wife, who was ill.[29]

Several times during the jury's deliberations, Hayden anxiously asked Grand Juror Edward Stannard (no relation to Mary) if a verdict had been reached.

Instead of going back home, Hayden stayed around talking with the others who were there. Now that he knew the results of the autopsy, he told them Mary couldn't possibly have thought she was pregnant, as she had just had her period the previous month.[30] It seemed a highly personal piece of information for a man to have about a woman who was not his wife.

The Stannard household had never seen such activity as it now experienced on Wednesday and Thursday, September 4 and 5. The jury was still holding its questioning on Wednesday while at the same time curious villagers stopped by under the auspices of offering condolences. And the family was trying to prepare for the funeral, which would be held on Thursday at the Rockland Methodist Church.

The two Stevens women, Mrs. Loren and Mrs. Luzerne, had sat up all Tuesday night with the body, as was the custom.[31] Early on Wednesday, Susan Hawley's sister, Hattie Smith, came to the house to help wash her half sister's bloody clothes and prepare her for burial.

Instead of being dressed, Mary was wrapped in a shroud. The clothes she was wearing when she was murdered would be needed for examination, and in a poor family like the Stannards, it wouldn't do to bury someone in clothes that could be used by another family member. Mary's shoes (more like work boots than shoes) were almost new, and Susan took these for herself.[32]

Ben Stevens arrived Wednesday morning after hearing the tragic news from his brother. When his initial shock wore off, he assumed the role of a man in charge. Charlie Stannard was incapable of doing so, as his grief drove him to occupy himself with odd chores outside, such as fussing with the woodpile.[33]

Ben liked playing the patriarch. When anyone asked to see the body, he solemnly took them into the front parlor and lifted the covering from Mary's face. And when he noticed Susan Hawley wearing an old dress, he tapped her on the shoulder with his cane and said, "Sus', come here a minute." He took her into the pantry off the kitchen and told her she should change into a better dress, as lots of folks would be coming by that day.[34]

Among the watchers that Wednesday night was Mary Davis, the Haydens' good friend.[35]

On Thursday, nearly the entire Rockland community went to what the papers called "the humble home of Charles Stannard" to accompany Mary's body to the church. Eliza Mills placed herself in charge of lifting the shroud from the dead woman's face so the curious could see.[36]

By now the name of Herbert Hayden was on everyone's lips as the prime suspect, and there were few who doubted his guilt. As the service began, then, they were surprised to see the subject of their gossip take his place in the congregation. Mrs. Hayden was not with him.

After the funeral, Hayden approached Charlie to offer his condolences.

"You know I've always been a friend to your family, Charlie," he said. "There have never been hard feelings between us."

"Yes, that's true, Reverend," Charlie responded without looking directly at him. "Up until now, that is."[37]

Hayden had been before the inquest jury and he had also heard the gossip around Rockland. He knew it was only a matter of time before he would be arrested and he needed to get Rosa on his side and shore up the weak places in his alibi.

Rosa Hayden was a competent woman, a good wife, and an excellent mother. She was a graduate of the State Normal School of Massachusetts where she received her teaching certificate,[38] and she had done more than her share to support her husband and children when Herbert could not find enough work.

But she was also a traditional woman by Victorian standards, and that meant an uneasiness when it came to sex. Men were different, she felt, and if at times Herbert needed to find his pleasure elsewhere, she chose to pretend it wasn't happening.

Rosa had no intention of letting another woman ruin her home, however, and so she kept as tight a rein on her husband as she thought she could get away with.[39] She kept track of his comings and goings, and if there was another woman around, such as Mary Stannard, she did her best to be present when they were together and not provide an opportunity for the devil to do his work. At times, she and her husband had had arguments over these other women.

Rosa Hayden was also a nervous, sensitive woman. She was afraid to be alone, for example, and was often in ill health. Her three pregnancies had not been easy, either, and it took her a long time to recuperate from each one. When Herbert could not be with her, she insisted on a companion, even if it was just little nine-year-old Jennie Stevens from across the way.

On Thursday morning as her husband was getting ready to go to Mary Stannard's funeral, Rosa found him lying face down on the bed, weeping. Herbert almost never wept, and it frightened her.

"Why, Herbert, what's the matter?" she cried. She could not have been prepared for his answer.

"They suspect me of Mary Stannard's murder, and I think I'll be arrested soon," he told her.[40]

Rosa became hysterical, inconsolable. She had heard the rumors about her husband's intimacy with Mary, and had seen some hints of it herself, but murder? It just wasn't possible.

By the time Hayden returned from the funeral, Rosa had calmed down enough to have a discussion about the situation.[41] The truth would look very bad for him, he said, and she must help save his life—not only for his sake, but for hers and the children's as well. The authorities would ask her questions about where he had been and what he had done, and he needed her to be very clear about those things.

When he stopped at the spring on Tuesday, the day of Mary's death, he *had* talked with her. She was distraught, upset about becoming a mother again and the disgrace that would result. She wanted his advice as a minister of God as to what she should do, as she was meeting the young man later that day.

Hayden couldn't very well have this conversation with his two children in the wagon, so he arranged to meet her at a secluded spot later. He was afraid she would commit suicide or undergo an abortion unless he counseled her, and both of those would be sins against God's holy commandments. Surely, Rosa could see that he had a duty to meet with that poor girl and do the best he could to make her see God's will for her. Surely, she could never suspect him of what the town thought he had done. She *must* believe him, *must* stand by him.

Rosa listened silently as he went on, her face pale with fear and shock.

Hayden said he had gone to the woodlot just as he said, but later had taken the back way to meet Mary. Neighbors talk, he said, and he didn't want any gossip about their very innocent meeting. But when he got there, she was already dead. He thought she had committed suicide out of despair, and he wanted no connection with it. He knew if he stayed there or sounded the alarm that he would be in exactly the position he was in now, so he had come back home without saying a word. He had not told Rosa, he claimed, for fear of upsetting her when she was so unwell.

Rosa Hayden did not really believe that her husband was capable of murder. Intimacy with other women? Yes, she could believe that. But not murder. She saw down the long, long road of the future with her three children, her ill health, and no husband to help support them, and said: "What do you want me to do, Herbert?"

Hayden told her she would need to provide him with alibis that distanced him from the crime and everything connected with it. That horrible Susan Hawley had made up stories, or Mary had, about his fathering her child. She would need to laugh at the idea that they were ever intimate or ever had a chance to meet about Mary's supposed pregnancy.

Rosa could do that with no hesitation: hadn't Mary herself told her about having her period just last month? How could she have thought herself pregnant for the past five months then? In her anxiety to help her husband and prove him innocent, Rosa conveniently forgot about her own monthly troubles when she had been pregnant with Lennie.

"They'll say I met with her in the barn on Monday," Hayden told her, "then again on Tuesday at the spring. You must tell them I was never in the barn with her, and that you saw me at the spring from your window."

And so together they outlined their plan for Rosa's perjury: where she was sitting, why and at what time she was sitting there, what she had seen on Monday and Tuesday.

He would need an alibi for the knife, too, he told her, since it was exactly the kind of knife used to slit Mary's throat. She could say she used it to cut up the pears he had brought her.

"But I didn't cut those until Wednesday," she told him, "and Mary Davis knows that."

"It doesn't matter," he said. "Tell them you asked me to leave my knife with you on Tuesday in case you wanted to cut up the pears. You can say Lennie used the knife on Tuesday and that's how you know it was there."

Lennie *had* used a knife on Tuesday, to cut up pumpkins and sticks, but it was his own knife.[42] Still, the authorities would not know that if the Haydens claimed he had used his father's. Louisa Stevens could be a witness that Lennie had often used that knife. Hadn't she reprimanded Rosa for letting him play with it when he got cut one time?

Rosa had cut up the pears with a different knife on Wednesday, but she agreed to say that she had used her husband's knife instead, and that it was right on the shelf where she had put it on Tuesday.

"And," she added excitedly, "remember when I scolded you for using the knife to clean your fingernails with? It was on the shelf then and Mary Davis saw you take it down!"

Her misgivings about her husband's involvement with the crime were melting away now. She would stand by him, and God would understand and forgive. He was a good husband to her, and he loved his children dearly. There was nothing he wouldn't do for any of them. How could such a man be a murderer? No, it was impossible and she would not let him hang for it. She would not let her children bear the stigma of having a father who was a murderer.

The Haydens rehearsed their parts until they practically had them memorized. It was important, he told her, that their stories meshed in every particular. What jury would believe the trashy Susan Hawley instead of the elegant and demure Rosa Hayden?

But Hayden never told his wife that he had been to Middletown, that he had talked to Dr. Bailey, or that he had purchased arsenic on that Tuesday. She would not find it out until she read it in the newspaper four days after his arrest.[43]

The Haydens were none too soon with getting their stories down. They would not have another chance, as the sheriff arrived early Friday morning to arrest Herbert and take him to Madison for trial.

After Hayden's arrest, the entire town of Rockland became detectives. They swarmed over the woodlot and the murder site, timing themselves as they duplicated what Hayden said he did and how long it had taken him. They peered in the windows of the Stannards, the Haydens, the Stevenses, and other witnesses, and prowled around in the dark. Families were frightened at this nighttime activity and the sheriff told them to stop.[44]

Edward Stannard, the grand juror, consulted a clairvoyant and found out from her that Hayden had, indeed, committed the murder. The spirits had told her so. In a wildly sarcastic editorial, the *New York Times* wondered why the medium relied on anonymous spirits from beyond, who may or may not know anything about it, instead of going "right to headquarters": the murdered girl herself. Think what a breakthrough this could be in future murder trials, the article went on, to have the spirit of the victim as a witness. Think how much time and trouble this could save![45]

The day before Hayden's arrest, Silas Y. Ives (who owned the house Charles Hawley was renting) came to tell Hayden "as a friend" that he was about to be arrested and had better not try to run away. The day after the arrest, this same man helped his daughter sue Hayden for $5 he owed her, then sued him himself for the same amount![46]

On Saturday, the Rev. Joseph W. Gibbs, whom Hayden had replaced in Rockland and who then took back the position when Hayden went to Madison, came by with his wife to offer their support to Rosa Hayden. But his real mission was to validate what he believed to be Hayden's guilt. He cross-examined Rosa so extensively as to what time her husband had done various things that she wept uncontrollably for several minutes. Her brother, Jesse Shaw of Fall River, Massachusetts (a city that Lizzie Borden would make famous fourteen years later), took Reverend Gibbs on a walk just to get him away from a distraught Rosa.[47]

Nor was this intrusive detective activity confined to Rockland residents. Men came up from Madison and interviewed witnesses just out of curiosity. One of these, named William Perry, eventually earned the nickname "Pinkerton" Perry and was hired by Hayden's father to help with his son's defense.[48]

Before he was hired by the elder Mr. Hayden, Perry and one of the grand jurors, Sherman Buell, decided to try and trip up Mrs. Ward, the deaf woman who claimed to have seen a man in the bushes near the spring. They so confused her with their questions (some of which she probably could not hear very well) that she ended up by saying she couldn't even be sure it was a man she saw.

Mrs. Ward's daughter was at the end of her patience with the two would-be private eyes. "I guess my mother has seen enough men to know one," she snapped. But Perry and Buell were convinced they had compromised Mrs. Ward's eye-witness testimony, and gave each other the nineteenth-century equivalent of "high fives" when they left her house.[49]

Reverend Gibbs should probably have stayed neutral in the matter, since Hayden was a brother Methodist minister. But Gibbs had often heard Hayden's sexual innuendoes and his smutty jokes and was convinced he was guilty. If it had not been for that kind of talk, he told some of his friends, he would have thought Hayden incapable of either the intimacy or the murder.[50]

So, while the Methodist hierarchy in Hartford was busy scrambling around to find a top criminal lawyer to represent Hayden (and, by extension, the Methodist church), Reverend Gibbs was telling his congregation that anyone who thought Hayden innocent was a Judas. Mrs. Elizur Stevens, who had publicly proclaimed her belief in Hayden's innocence, took this remark personally and was quite put out by it.

Then Gibbs switched his metaphor and applied the Judas title to Hayden himself, saying that Judas at least had spared the community an expensive trial by going out and hanging himself.[51]

Young Frank Bartlett, who would later marry the Talcott Davises' daughter, Etta, shocked his companions by stating that Mary Stannard got what she deserved for telling stories about Hayden. If anyone did that to him, he declared, he would "kill her or any other damned woman."[52]

In South Madison, where Hayden preached every Sunday, the general feeling was that he was innocent. In Rockland, where he lived, the prevailing belief was in his guilt.[53]

And so the communities, and the families within those communities, took sides with impassioned feelings. Few were neutral. It would be the main topic of discussion among them for the next sixteen months.

Chapter 5

JUSTICE COURT TRIAL: PRELUDE TO "THE GREAT CASE"

They were trying Dr. Duval
For the murder of Zora Clemens,
And I sat in the court two weeks
Listening to every witness.
It was clear he had got her in a family way;
And to let the child be born
Would not do.
Well, how about me with eight children,
And one coming, and the farm
Mortgaged to Thomas Rhodes?

—Edgar Lee Masters, "Barry Holden,"
Spoon River Anthology

Herbert Hayden's trial in front of the Justice Court opened on Tuesday, September 10, in the basement of the First Congregational Church in Madison. The day began hot and would only get hotter in the dark, stuffy, airless basement filled with a "motley crowd"[1] of five hundred Rocklanders and Madisonites. This makeshift setting was made necessary by the lack of a courtroom facility in Madison.

Presiding over the trial was fifty-seven-year-old Henry B. Wilcox, the town's justice of the peace and also its registrar of vital statistics. Wilcox had signed the death certificate for Mary Stannard's mother, Charlotte; had signed the birth certificate when Willie was born (carefully noting that he was "illegitimate"); and only a few days before the trial had signed Mary's own death certificate.[2]

Wilcox was himself a Congregationalist, which was no doubt why that church was chosen for the trial. However, even though not a member of Hayden's Methodist congregation, he was a fellow Mason and held the minister in high esteem. Wilcox was greatly disturbed about both the murder and the accusations against Hayden, so disturbed that he had difficulty sleeping. And when they came to him to sign Hayden's arrest warrant, he flatly refused, saying he would rather sign his own death warrant.[3]

With so much official and personal involvement in the case, Wilcox should have recused himself as having a conflict of interest. Moreover, he was not an attorney and had no legal background apart from what he might have picked up in the course of his duties. He did have some "courtesy justices" from Madison available to him, but Wilcox must have felt out of his league in this very high-profile case.

There was a great deal of interest in the trial, with reporters coming from all over Connecticut and even from New York City. The Hartford papers declared that "there has not been an event of greater importance in the criminal annals of the State."[4]

With so many spectators and reporters present, not to mention the vast number of witnesses to be called, the little church basement became nearly intolerable in the late summer heat. The sheriff opened the screenless windows to let in air, but the space was immediately filled up with young boys intent on hearing the gory details of the proceedings. Deputies tried their best to keep the windows cleared of boys, to no avail. On top of that, so little light entered the basement that the lamps had to be kept lit all day.

The trial of Herbert Hayden was rapidly becoming the most exciting event in the state, besting even the recent Wallingford tornado. Even so, it would pale in comparison with the proceedings in New Haven the following year.

Everyone wanted to get a look at the man accused of such a horrendous murder and reporters watched him carefully to satisfy the curiosity of their readers. "Does he look like a murderer?" those readers would want to know, and the newspapers endeavored to answer that question. It didn't seem possible that this "fresh, vigorous young man"[5] could have done what he was accused of.

Herbert Hayden made the mistake of many guilty people in assuming that an innocent person would act carefree and confident, indifferent even, whereas a guilty one would show nervousness and anxiety. In reality, a truly innocent person is never carefree and indifferent, but anxious about his fate and voluble about his lack of involvement.[6]

Throughout his trial, Hayden appeared relaxed, smiling, and confident. He came to court carrying a bouquet of flowers and frequently smelled it during the proceedings. He chatted with his friends and his attorneys, and spent his out-of-court moments smoking cigars supplied him by sympathizers. In contrast, his wife was anxious and distraught, frequently shedding tears both on and off the witness stand.[7]

The role of the newspapers in judicial proceedings in the late nineteenth century cannot be underestimated. Bound by no gag orders or evidentiary rules, newspapers routinely interspersed editorial opinions on the guilt or innocence of the accused in factual reports. They quoted verbatim from the testimony, so that even witnesses excluded from the courtroom could read what others had said before them. And they disclosed evidence that had been excluded as inadmissible by the court, thereby making it more likely that members of the jury would hear about it from others or read it themselves.

Hayden's first trial, in the Justice Court according to Connecticut law, was more in the nature of a preliminary hearing, so there was no jury impaneled. However, since the likelihood of a second trial was strong, especially if Hayden were found guilty, the newspaper reports undoubtedly influenced future jurors, particularly with regard to the testimony of the Haydens and Mary Stannard's family.

The prosecution was led by forty-year-old H. Lynde Harrison, a judge with the New Haven County Court of Common Pleas and an extremely able advocate. Assisting him were two "lesser lights,"[8] James I. Hayes and Edmund Zacher, both of New Haven.

Head counsel for Herbert Hayden's team, Samuel F. Jones of Hartford, already enjoyed a statewide reputation as a criminal defense attorney. He had been hired by Hartford's Methodists, who were alarmed at the possible anti-Methodist ramifications of the case. The Methodist church had been established in Madison for the past forty years, but only after overcoming "bitter and strong hostility" on the part of the Congregationalists. The hierarchy in Hartford did not want the Hayden case to lose the church its hard-won stronghold in the area.[9]

With Samuel Jones on the defense team were L. M. Hubbard of Wallingford and Tilton E. Doolittle of Madison.

Shortly before her death, Mary Stannard happened to hear of an autopsy performed on a neighbor who had died suddenly. "If I died," she told her friend Rosa Hayden, "I wouldn't want anyone cutting me up."[10] By the time of the second trial in 1879, her body would be exhumed four times and dissected so much that there was almost nothing left to put back in the coffin.

At the beginning of the Justice Court trial, the prosecution let it be known that it wanted to exhume Mary's body for another autopsy. The Middletown *Sentinel* had published a report that Hayden had purchased poison in a drugstore there, and the state wanted to look for abortion medicine or poison. Since testing for poison was costly ($300–$400), the prosecution was waiting for the druggist to return from out of state to tell them precisely what poison to be looking for.[11] (This was the first intimation Hayden would have had that the arsenic would be discovered in Mary's stomach and he had not yet mentioned his purchase of it to anyone.)

Accordingly, on September 11, Mary's grave was opened and her body exhumed. Boys were let out of school so they could watch, and they formed a very eager audience at the cemetery. Not so eager were Mary's sisters, Susan and Emogene, who were very upset to hear that her body would be coming back to the house. They went to stay with someone for the next few days so they would not have to witness it.[12]

This second autopsy was attended by Dr. Earle Matthewson, who had assisted at the first one with his father; Dr. Pliny Jewett and his son, Thomas, who would graduate from Yale Medical College that spring; and Dr. Moses White of Yale, who was also the New Haven city coroner.

Susan and Emogene would not have wanted to be in attendance at this autopsy, as it was a thorough and gruesome one indeed. Dr. White removed most of Mary's organs, putting them into new, clean glass jars which he sealed up to take back to his laboratory at Yale before turning them over to Dr. Samuel W. Johnson for examination.

(One citizen wondered why this circus-like atmosphere could not have been avoided by setting up a tarp in a secluded part of the cemetery instead of parading the body through town on the way back to the Stannard home.[13])

When Hayden was arrested, his knife was taken from him for examination by Dr. Moses White for evidence of blood. White was also given the bloody stone found at the scene and which was supposed to have been used to knock Mary down.

A reliable test for distinguishing between animal and human blood would not be discovered until 1901.[14] Until that time, scientists relied on the guaiacum test (which used tree resin to determine the presence of blood)[15] and microscopy, to determine the shape, size, and number of corpuscles. Microscopic examination could eliminate certain mammals from consideration and narrow down to a probability whether the blood were animal or human. However, it could not determine this with absolute certainty.

Dr. White had taken Hayden's knife apart and found material in the thumbnail groove that he later determined to be blood corpuscles, probably human. He had also examined the wound in Mary's neck and thought that the smaller of the two blades in Hayden's knife was exactly the kind it could have been made with. White, moreover, had "no doubt" that the blood on the stone was human because it was of the same kind as that found on the knife and on Mary's sunbonnet.[16]

Naturally, this testimony caused great sensation in the courtroom as the first piece of real, solid evidence against Hayden. The defense wanted Dr. White to enter the knife into evidence so they could examine it also, but here the prosecution thundered a resounding "No!"

The battle that ensued gives the first insight into a theme that would be repeated throughout both trials: the fear that the other side would tamper with or destroy the evidence. Both Hayes and Harrison shouted loudly to Professor White, telling him not to let the knife out of his hands, not even for a moment.

Jones was incensed and roared his objection to the court. He had a right to look at the knife, he insisted, and Wilcox meekly said it would seem as if he should be able to. Harrison did not care who looked at it, as long as it did not leave Professor White's hands.

"You can't scare me!" Jones shouted at Harrison. "I've seen boys before."

"And I've seen bullies before," Harrison retorted.

"I've seen blackguards before," Jones shot back.

But Harrison stood his ground and refused to allow anyone else to handle the knife. He wanted no higher court to say that there had been an occasion for tampering. Jones responded that anyone who could even hint at such a thing was not beyond planting a little blood on the knife himself.[17]

White finally settled the matter by telling the court that he wasn't finished with his examination yet: he still needed to take the handle apart and could not risk any disturbance of the evidence.

The defense had its own turn to play keep-away when the prosecution demanded that they turn over Hayden's clothing for examination. Jones gave the state a taste of its own medicine, saying that defense experts had not finished their own tests. They would deliver the clothing at the proper time. A heated argument followed, with the judge rapping vainly for order.[18]

Harrison asked the court to issue an order for the production of the clothing, but Wilcox said he didn't think an order would do any good, as the defense would not relinquish the clothes. (Wilcox seemed unaware of the nature of a court order, the disobedience of which is grounds for arrest.)

Today, courtroom etiquette forbids opposing counsel to speak to each other directly. Instead, they must address their objections to the court. Shouting matches such as the one just described was one of the factors causing overlong trials in the Victorian era and would be grounds for contempt of court charges today.

To counter the state's blood testimony, the defense asked Dr. White whether a deep cut from the knife, a cut that went down to the very bone, would produce the human blood corpuscles found in the thumbnail groove. White acknowledged that it would. Well, Jones went on, Hayden had suffered just such a cut only a couple of months before the murder and the fresh scar was still evident.[19]

Ultimately, though, the blood testimony was worthless. Even if there had been a way to determine that the blood on the knife was human, there was still no way to connect it to Mary Stannard's murder. A man who used a knife often was bound to get cut by it occasionally, and there was the testimony from Louisa Stevens that four-year-old Lennie had also gotten cut on his father's knife. And Hayden had helped carry Mary back to her home, so any blood on his clothes could be explained away.

The technology that could have isolated Mary Stannard's blood from Hayden's knife blade, blood which he had attempted to clean off at the Big Rock spring but which had stuck in the thumbnail groove, was over a hundred years away: DNA fingerprinting. Finding Mary's DNA in the blood on the knife would have proved Hayden's guilt beyond the shadow of a doubt.[20]

Much of the lay testimony at the Justice Court trial consisted of the self-styled detectives coming forward to narrate the results of their walking, running, or wood-throwing experiments. Those testifying for the state (including Mary Stannard's brother) had gone as fast as they could over the route, of less than a half mile, supposedly followed by Hayden from the woodlot to the Fox Ledge area, and had completed it in times ranging from five to fifteen minutes. Those testifying for the defense had taken their time—as long as forty minutes—and did not always use the shortest route.

Similarly, in the woodlot experiments, the state's witnesses said the amount of wood Hayden said he had thrown out of the "swamp" from 2:00 to 4:00 on Tuesday afternoon could have been stacked in ten minutes on Wednesday morning. Defense witnesses said it would easily take an hour and a half because of the brambles. But James Hill noticed that some of the piles Hayden said he had thrown up for gathering looked as if they had lain there a while.[21]

Other witnesses, primarily Hayden's Rockland neighbors, testified to where and when they had seen him, what he had said, and how he had acted in the days before and after the murder, often contradicting each other.

Although Henrietta Young would testify at the second trial that she had seen Hayden and Mary enter and leave the barn together, she said nothing of it at the Madison trial. And, although both Luzerne Stevens and his wife, Louisa, would testify in New Haven that they had not seen Hayden between 11:30 A.M. and 4:00 P.M. on the day of the murder, Luzerne now testified that he had seen him at 2:00 that afternoon.[22]

Dr. Leonard Bailey of Middletown was a reluctant witness and at first tried to use the physician-patient privilege. Eventually, he would say that he and Hayden had spoken only of Mrs. Hayden's current illness, but he would tell a different story to a colleague outside of court.[23]

In other words, witnesses were creative with the truth, according to where their beliefs lay about Hayden's innocence or guilt. They would make statements outside of court that would inevitably get back to the prosecution or the defense. Confronted on the stand about these, they would deny them or say they didn't remember whether they had made them or not.

At the second trial in New Haven the following year, this problem of perjury was compounded by Connecticut's almost backward refusal to provide court stenographers for trials. Sometimes the defense or prosecution would hire a stenographer for some or all of the testimony, and of course the newspaper reporters jotted much of it down. But there was no independent, disinterested stenographer available to take down *all* of the testimony, word for word, of every witness.[24]

Not only did this allow witnesses to change their testimony the second time around, but it took up valuable court time while attorneys asked for brief "time outs" so they could write down what was being said. And cross-examinations took longer as attorneys desperately tried to get witnesses to admit they had said something entirely different when they had testified the year before.

Crucial to the prosecution's case was the testimony of Jane Studley and Susan Hawley as to what Mary told them about her supposed pregnancy, who was responsible for it, and whom she was going to meet the day she died.

And there was the letter Mary had written to Hayden and burned herself, along with the statements she had made to Susan about it, as well as her letter to Susan asking her to deliver the enclosed (with "Mr. Hayden" written on it) to the defendant.

It was damaging evidence of Hayden's intimacy with Mary and also provided a motive, and the defense fought furiously to keep it out by claiming that it was hearsay.

Hearsay is defined as any statement offered by someone other than the one who made it to prove the truth of that statement.[25] This is to prevent a defendant from being convicted on the word of someone who might have a grudge against him, and also to support the theory that an accused has the right to confront and cross-examine any witnesses against him.

Hearsay usually occurs when the person who made the statement is unavailable and Mary Stannard was just about as unavailable as a witness can get. Although a "dying declaration" can be admissible as an exception to the hearsay rule, the law states that the declarant must know she is dying when she makes it—which, of course, Mary did not.

Hayden had not been present when any of these statements were made, Jones now argued, and even the prosecution admitted he had not read the letter supposedly addressed to him. The prosecution countered that the letter to Susan instructing her to deliver the enclosed letter to Hayden showed that she was intimate enough with him to write to him.

Wilcox knew that he needed help with this knotty problem. He told both sides he would consult with judicial experts. As it turned out, the two judges Wilcox called on were out of town, and so he turned to another prominent New Haven attorney: George H. Watrous, who would later be hired by Hayden's defense for the Superior Court trial.

Watrous' impression was that, although it was remote on the question of motive, the letter to Susan tended to show an intimacy between Mary and Hayden and therefore both the letter and the statement surrounding it should be admitted.[26] Watrous did not have enough time to consider the statements Mary made to Susan and Mrs. Studley (having been dragged out of bed by Wilcox when the justices couldn't be found); hence, they were never admitted. It was a devastating blow to the prosecution.

However, all the excluded evidence was duly reported in great detail by the newspapers[27] so that everyone could read exactly what Mary had said to both Jane Studley and to Susan. Had there been a jury in this trial, the jurors would have been able to read about it, too.

From the outset of the Justice Court trial, it was evident from both the newspaper coverage and the defense's cross-examination that the Stannards, the Hawleys, and Ben Stevens would be presented as buffoons at best and murderers at worst. This portrayal would only increase with the Superior Court trial the following year.

Charlie Stannard was depicted as "a farmer of the lowest class" by the *New York Times* and Ben Stevens as "another low-class farmer," even though he was worth more than most others in Rockland. The *Times* reported as fact the false rumor that Stevens was the father of Mary's illegitimate son, Willie.[28]

Ben was referred to more than once as a "Solon Shingle." This is an allusion that is lost today, but it probably was meant to call to readers' minds a fictitious yokel whose humorous exploits in practicing law were recounted in the daily newspapers.[29] These little character sketches served the same purpose as the comics would later in the century.

Stevens had a quaint way of talking (as did many of the Rocklanders), was bluntly outspoken, and enjoyed his liquor. After all, the night before the murder, he had been up all night dancing and drinking at a barn-raising party. Reporters from the cities provided their readers with many laughs at old Ben Stevens' expense.

The defense tried to shed doubt on Hayden's guilt by showing that Stevens was a much more likely candidate. Accordingly, they subpoenaed his clothing and his knife for examination. (The knife turned out to be dull and in poor shape, and Stevens gave the courtroom a good laugh when he admonished the sheriff not to ruin his knife in the examination process.[30])

Yet, when asked on the witness stand whether he had ever heard of or seen any intimacy between Mary Stannard and Herbert Hayden, Stevens—who could have helped himself immensely by saying he had—said he had not. And he defended Mary's family against the accusation of insanity, which could have tended to show that Mary had committed suicide.[31]

When Susan Hawley was finally able to testify concerning the two letters, she was cross-examined minutely as to her recognition of Mary's handwriting. Because Edgar Studley had addressed the outside envelope and because Susan had originally said it was Mary's handwriting, the defense tried to show that her testimony was suspect and that Susan was a liar.

The legal process involved in the prosecution and defense of an accused on trial for murder was completely unfamiliar to the untutored Susan Hawley. She took the desperate attempts of the defense personally, and as a result became increasingly sullen and hostile on the stand.

In the second trial, this was nearly Susan's undoing, as she would be portrayed as the evil nemesis of the innocent Reverend Hayden. But for now she was merely the ignorant half sister of the murdered girl, a member of a laughable tribe of lowlifes.

When Rosa Hayden, weak and ill from complications of childbirth, took the stand (in the form of a rocking chair to accommodate her discomfort), she proved to be the most powerful weapon in the defense arsenal. As she gave her testimony, many who had previously believed in Hayden's guilt changed their minds on the basis of her demeanor as a witness.[32]

Mrs. Hayden started with a summary of their lives together from the time of their marriage: their struggles, their many jobs, and their children, all in all presenting "a pleasant picture of a happy family."[33]

Then she went into the specifics of the case, claiming that she had asked her husband to let her use the knife while he went to the woodpile. While he was gone, their son Lennie had used that very knife to cut up some pumpkins and sticks.

Mrs. Hayden's testimony was subdued, straightforward, and convincing. She frequently burst into tears when asked about her husband's faithfulness to her, stating that she was sure he was. She related the details of the oyster supper and said that it was she who asked her husband to go home and put the children to bed, and that he was not gone more than ten minutes.

On the day of the murder, she had sat by the window and watched Herbert go down the lane toward the woodpile. When he scooted the children back to her, he turned and blew her a kiss . . . from a quarter-mile away. Prior to that idyllic scene, she had, from that same window, seen his carriage stop briefly at the spring for no more than a minute—certainly not long enough to have a conversation with Mary Stannard.

And Rosa Hayden threw yet another suspect into the pot: Edgar Studley, whom she claimed she had seen on the day of the murder. In a bit of hearsay that Justice Wilcox did not hesitate to allow, she told the court that Mary gave Edgar Studley as her reason for coming home early: Mrs. Studley had promised that her son would not be in the house when she went down to Guilford, but he was. Mary was afraid he would force his attentions on her, so she had come home early.[34]

And when she took the stand again the following day, Rosa added something she had "forgotten" before: she had watched her husband walk down the road toward the woodlot until he reached the stile near Nehemiah Burr's barn, when she could no longer see him. The implication was that he had, indeed, gone to the woodlot and not to the Big Rock to murder Mary Stannard.

Mrs. Hayden's testimony was an incredible feat for a woman who was afraid to stay in the house by herself. But she must have felt that she, too, was on trial for her life and that she needed to "screw her courage to the sticking-place."[35]

Herbert Hayden also took the stand in his own defense, and gave an account that was almost word for word the same as his wife's. He even added to the theme of Edgar Studley as suspect by saying he had heard that Mary had "a beau in Guilford."[36]

In fact, the Haydens' accounts have a rehearsed quality about them, as they no doubt were. They are *too* pat, *too* mutually corroborative. But the articulate, educated, respectable Haydens came across much better on the stand than the ignorant, slovenly Stannard clan, and their performance at the trial caused many people to change their minds about Herbert Hayden's guilt.

The end of the Justice Court trial came faster than anyone could have anticipated.[37] The defense rested its case after the morning session on September 25, and the usual recess was called until after the noon meal.

The prosecution had asked for a continuance of at least one day so their expert could finish up the testing of Mary's organs for poison. But Justice Wilcox, who had never believed Hayden guilty, agreed with the defense that the state had had its chances and that to prolong the trial was unfair to the defendant.

When the afternoon proceedings were about to begin, then, only one member of the prosecution team was present: James I. Hayes. Where was Judge Harrison? Wilcox wanted to know. Hayes stood up to explain that the state would be withdrawing from the case at this point since the necessary continuance was not granted. Hayes had only returned out of courtesy, to explain this to the court.

Samuel Jones was secretly delighted at this turn of events. He stood up and gave what he had undoubtedly planned to give as his summation, pointing out that Hayden did not look in the least like a murderer. He accused the prosecution of bad manners: Judge Harrison had lost his temper and his failure to return was an insult to the court. Then he asked Wilcox for a decision.

Although he could not have anticipated the end of the trial to come so soon, Wilcox was curiously well-prepared with an opinion. He pulled out a sheaf of papers and reviewed the testimony against Hayden, then granted a discharge based on four major points:

1. The uncontradicted evidence of three witnesses as to Hayden's absence from the oyster supper for no more than ten minutes [Two of these witnesses, however, were the Haydens.]
2. The lack of evidence as to an intimacy between Hayden and Mary [This was a puzzle, in that there was certainly no lack of rumor concerning it. Supposedly, Loren Stevens was supposed to testify about this, but he doesn't seem to have been asked about it. The prosecution would attempt to rectify this for the next trial.]
3. The lack of evidence that Hayden had acted guilty after the murder [In light of what we know today about criminal behavior, this is an incredibly naive statement.]
4. The truthfulness of Mrs. Hayden's testimony [Wilcox said he didn't doubt a word of it.]

Summing up, Wilcox reached a pitch of dramatic intensity, "If I were as sure of heaven and eternal happiness as I am that Rev. Herbert H. Hayden is guiltless of killing Mary Stannard, I should rest content. Sheriff, discharge the prisoner."

At these words, the courtroom erupted in applause as well-wishers and the curious crowded around Hayden to congratulate him. Many wanted to carry him out on their shoulders, but he had the good taste to refuse this.

Rosa, weak from sickness and a headache after her testimony, had not come back after dinner. Mindful of the adoring throng who would overhear him, Jones told Hayden, "Go to your noble wife and tell her at once."

But in the end, Jones went himself to the home where Mrs. Hayden was staying. She came down the staircase, pale and distraught, and Jones told her the news. Witnesses said she turned even paler and then, without saying a word, passed out.

Herbert Hayden announced his plans to move his family from Rockland (where most of the residents thought him guilty) to Madison (where most thought him innocent), resume his preaching that very Sunday, and teach in the school again on Monday.

In the meantime, the state's expert, Professor Samuel Johnson of the Yale Medical College, was about to make a discovery that would shed a whole new light on the case: ninety grains of arsenic distributed throughout Mary's organs. The Justice Court trial, sensational as it was, would prove to have been nothing more than a preliminary rehearsal for what would be called The Great Case.

Chapter 6

Interim: Preparing for "The Great Case"

On Sunday, September 29, 1878, Herbert Hayden preached the most important sermon of his life. Returning to his home in Rockland following his discharge by Justice Wilcox the preceding Wednesday, Hayden found himself lionized by a mostly adoring public. (Others, not so kindly disposed, hinted that they would lynch him if he didn't get out of town.[1])

Never had so many come to the little Methodist church in Madison, but come they did, from other towns and from miles away. They crowded the aisles and spilled out into the street just to hear the preacher who had so recently been on trial for murder. The church, in anticipation of the hoopla, was decorated with festive bouquets and symbolic anchors.[2]

Hayden's seat on the altar was surrounded by chairs for visiting dignitaries: Justice Henry Wilcox, who had presided at his trial, on his right; another Wilcox, the reputedly wealthy Alvah, on his left; yet another Wilcox, Deacon Hiram; and eighty-five-year-old Ichabod Scranton, who was always described as "the oldest man in town."

The Wilcoxes and Scranton belonged to the Congregationalist church, but wished to make a visible statement of support for Hayden. And the presence of Grand Juror Sherman Buell reinforced even further the bias of the Madison legal mechanism in favor of Hayden.

Hayden made his entrance in dramatic fashion, waiting until everyone was seated and then immediately dropping to his knees in silent prayer. Aware of the audience and also of the great number of reporters in attendance, he chatted briefly with sixty-six-year-old Reverend Henry Latham, smiling all the while. Latham would be the presiding minister for this day's service.

Hayden had been advised not to make any direct reference to the trial in his sermon,[3] but the scripture texts he chose were obviously intended to convey a message. In Psalm 27 the psalmist prays for God's help in his affliction, but also asks Him to smite his enemies:

Drag me not away with sinners and with those who commit crimes, who speak of peace with their neighbors, but have evil in their minds. Reward them according to their works and according to the malice of their crimes. Give to them according to the works of their hands, render to them their due.[4]

Matthew 5 contains the Beatitudes and Hayden read this next. No doubt he felt that verses 10 and 11 applied to him:

Blessed are they who suffer persecution for justice' sake, for theirs is the kingdom of heaven. Blessed are you when men reproach you, and persecute you, and, speaking falsely, say all manner of evil against you, for my sake.[5]

The sermon itself was a meditation on John 8:31–32: "[Y]ou shall know the truth and the truth shall make you free." However, according to the *New York Times* correspondent in attendance, Hayden was "not a powerful preacher."[6]

Hayden must have enjoyed himself tremendously as the center of so much adulation. And it must have been close to what he had in mind when he envisioned a successful preaching career. At that moment, the possibility of re-arrest was very far away, a distant speck on the horizon.

Hayden also had the support of Reverend William T. Hill, the presiding elder of the New Haven District of the Methodist Church. In a letter to the *Christian Advocate*, a Methodist paper published in New York City, Hill reported Hayden's "triumphant acquittal." He went on to say that the case had gained much notoriety because of the eagerness of the newspapers to focus the spotlight of guilt on a minister.

Not content with touting the sanctity of "Brother Hayden," Hill blamed the minister's ordeal on Susan Hawley, calling her the "disreputable sister of the murdered girl" and stating that her testimony "would not hang together."[7]

The Methodists of Madison, in drafting a series of resolutions in favor of Hayden, also played the game of Pin the Blame on Susan and took it a step further by hinting that she had committed the crime herself.[8]

The Resolutions criticized the "ungentlemanly, unscrupulous, and inhuman course" followed by the district attorney in bringing the case and insinuated that the "criminally frivolous" charges against Hayden were merely the "wicked designs of evil men," not in the least substantiated by any evidence. The whole thing was nothing but a "filthy scandal."

But not all clergymen were as pleased with Hayden's acquittal and as outraged at the charges against him as Reverend Hill and the Madison Methodists. The Resolutions had also thanked a Bishop Williams and other Episcopal clergymen for their support of Hayden. However, one such minister immediately responded in the *Times* and said that the statement discredited him and his fellow Episcopal clergymen. He strongly doubted that Bishop Williams would want his name mentioned in connection with it, either.[9]

Moreover, the main publication of the Methodist church, the aforementioned *Christian Advocate*, had refused to take a stand in support of Hayden. This refusal was criticized in the Madison Resolutions as "turning a cold shoulder on Brother Hayden in this his great hour of trial."[10]

Then there was the Rev. Joseph Gibbs, Hayden's predecessor in Rockland, who could never be convinced of his innocence, even though he was reluctant to testify against him. After the Justice Court trial, Gibbs enthusiastically distributed a pamphlet whose long title reflects the sensationalism prevalent in Victorian literature: *Poor Mary Stannard! A Full and Thrilling Story of the Circumstances Connected with Her Murder.*[11]

Gibbs would later act surprised when asked if he knew that the booklet, which had been put together by a New Haven newspaper reporter, supported Hayden's guilt. He said he thought it exonerated him, but he certainly must have known it did not. And, after Gibbs sold the copies he had, he went back and ordered more!

At any rate, Hayden's moment of triumph was short-lived. By Tuesday, October 8, the state had procured a new arrest warrant based on the findings of Professors White and Johnson that Mary Stannard had ingested enough arsenic "to have killed everyone in Rockland."[12] Sheriff Byxbee of New Haven went to South Madison, where Hayden had moved his family after the Justice Court trial.

Byxbee reached Hayden's home around the supper hour. Hayden's parents, Hiram and Sarah, had just closed their Island House hotel on Martha's Vineyard for the season and were visiting their son and his family when the sheriff arrived to arrest him. Rosa was nearly hysterical at this new turn of events, and Hayden's parents were upset, too. In fact, everyone seems to have been shocked except for Hayden himself, who was calm, cool, and cheerful.[13]

Sheriff Byxbee let Hayden finish supper with his family before taking him back to New Haven. This time the prisoner would not be staying in the home of a parishioner, as he had during the Madison trial, but in a real jail. Nonetheless, Hayden was a veritable chatterbox all the way down, smoking a cigar and talking nonstop with Byxbee about all sorts of topics. He listened without comment to the sheriff's account of the discovery of arsenic in Mary's body.

The Haydens had always maintained that they held Mary in the highest regard and knew of nothing against her character except her illegitimate child. Both of them had testified to this on the stand, and had said the same to everyone who questioned them before Hayden's first arrest. Yet now, on his way to jail in New Haven, Hayden badmouthed Mary Stannard.

He told Byxbee that Mary was simpleminded and a loose woman. He had only hired her, he said, because he felt sorry for her (although the family line had always been that Rosa had done the hiring of Mary whenever she was needed). Mary was "drifting toward a life of shame," and he thought he could rescue her by bringing her into his home. He and his wife had done everything they could to reform her. The insinuation was that, not only had the rehabilitation attempt failed, but this was the thanks he got for his good intentions.[14]

At the jail, Hayden was shown to his cell, Number 4. At the entrance to the cell area there was a sign written in Latin: "Dum Spiro, Spero," or "While there is life, there is hope." It is an easily translatable sentence, but all his Latin courses at Wesleyan were of no avail: someone had to tell him what it meant.[15]

Meanwhile, the prosecution reported that, after a thorough search of Hayden's barn, no arsenic could be found. Samuel Jones, the Hartford attorney, said that the defense had the tin spice box containing exactly one ounce of arsenic. When Hayden told them where he had put it, Jones had sent someone to the barn to get it. The man he sent was Hayden's best friend, Talcott Davis.[16]

Herbert Hayden was next brought before the New Haven County Grand Jury to see if there was cause to proceed with an indictment and a trial. The jurors needed to hear from only ten of the state's thirty witnesses before coming to the conclusion that there was probable cause. A true bill was returned for two counts: first, that Hayden had killed Mary Stannard by means of arsenic, and second, that he had killed her by cutting her throat (in case the state could not prove one of these beyond a reasonable doubt).[17]

While the prosecution was busy examining the new evidence and shoring up its case against Hayden, the defense took to the airwaves of gossip and rumor to undermine that case. Their main theme was that Hayden was being set up to take the blame for the murder of Mary Stannard by people, as Samuel Jones put it, "whose names I need not mention."[18]

First, they claimed that the arsenic discovered in Mary's body had actually been planted there by the state. Next, they attempted to point accusatory fingers at Ben Stevens by circulating a rumor regarding a pair of bloody pants he was supposed to have given to his daughter-in-law to wash right after the murder. Sickened by the blood they contained, she reportedly passed out twice and shortly after that gave birth prematurely.[19] (Apparently, no one had thought to question the illogicality of a murderer's getting someone *else* to wash his blood-stained pants.)

The bloody pants rumor was later discovered to be false, and both Ben Stevens and his son (the husband of the woman in the story) threatened to sue for slander. The rumor had been started by the defense and fostered by a threat made by Grand Juror Buell to Mrs. Stevens' mother: if Mrs. Stevens would not say that there was blood on Ben's pants, he would have her arrested.[20]

Most people recognized the absurdity of trying to create a suspect out of Old Ben Stevens. One New Haven resident, signing himself "Church Member," wrote a letter to the editor of the *Register* complaining about the so-called Christians who were labeling those who believed in Hayden's guilt as "enemies of the church." These same people, the writer continued, were more than ready to point the finger of blame at Ben Stevens even though holding to the opinion that "God has forbidden us to condemn a man before we know he is worthy of condemnation."[21]

But Ben Stevens was an attractive suspect for the Hayden supporters, who called themselves "the Friends of Justice" and thought of the minister as "an innocent and godly man" being framed by an "infamous and skillfully-constructed conspiracy." They were determined to find evidence against Stevens (who had been characterized in the press as a "dissipated widower"),[22] and to that end they hired two detectives to see what they could turn up. The ubiquitous "Pinkerton" Perry and his cohort Phelps (a resident of Hartford and therefore probably procured by Samuel Jones) took to hanging around the Stevens residence late at night, peeking in windows and questioning neighbors.[23]

The Stevens women and their neighbors were frightened to death by this nighttime skulking. Finally, some deputy sheriffs had to threaten Perry and Phelps with arrest if they didn't stop. The Friends of Justice group was indignant at the interference of the deputies.

These self-styled detectives were only wasting their time. Ben Stevens had been too preoccupied to notice, but he actually had an eyewitness who could give him an alibi for the time of the murder: Mrs. DeForest Ward, who had seen a man dart back into the bushes down at the crossroads at 2:20. Mrs. Ward didn't know Hayden, but she *did* know Ben Stevens, and she had seen him on the road to his house a half-hour before she spotted the man at the crossroads.[24]

And Ben was also seen by his next-door neighbors, Edgar Stevens (no relation) and his son George, arriving home at about 3:00—approximately fifteen minutes before Eliza Mills was to hear Mary's death-scream two miles away.[25]

In October 1878, while Hayden was still waiting for his trial and the Friends of Justice were busy gathering exculpatory evidence, some picnickers at Big Rock made an astonishing discovery.

Mary Stannard's murder site had become popular with tourists from surrounding areas, and thousands had visited it to look for clues, have a picnic, or merely stand and stare. On one such occasion, a young woman got her dress caught on some brambles. As she attempted to free herself, she noticed a knife in the brush. She called her fiancé and her father over, and they extracted the two-bladed knife (thereafter referred to as "the found knife").[26]

The Friends of Justice wanted the knife turned over to them, but the picnickers insisted that they would only relinquish it to an officer. Undaunted, the Hayden support group sent Talcott Davis and Justice Wilcox (the judge in the first trial and now a member of the Friends of Justice) to get it.

Wilcox introduced himself as "Sheriff" Wilcox and almost succeeded in getting the knife before Frazer (now the husband of the woman who found it) remembered that the Madison sheriff's name was Hull. Wilcox sheepishly had to admit who he was, and the real sheriff quickly came around to claim the knife. For a while after that, the Justice was teasingly referred to by townspeople as "Sheriff" Wilcox.[27]

Before arsenic had been discovered in Mary Stannard, the well-meaning Justice Henry Wilcox set himself up for yet another faux pas. Sheriff Byxbee had gone up to Madison to get from Wilcox the letter that Mary had written to Susan Hawley and also Lennie Hayden's knife for testing.

Wilcox stated his belief in Hayden's innocence in no uncertain terms, and even repeated his famous line from the Justice Court trial: "If I were as certain of heaven and eternal happiness as I am that Herbert Hayden is guiltless of killing Mary Stannard, I should rest content." Byxbee responded that Hayden might, indeed, be innocent, but he'd like to know the analysis of the contents of Mary's stomach. Maybe there was arsenic in there.

Wilcox was shocked at this suggestion. He looked Byxbee in the eye and said: "John, that stomach is just as clean as yours or mine. I tell you if there is a single grain of arsenic found in her stomach, I will take back all I said about Mr. Hayden's innocence and say that he is guilty!"[28]

Wilcox's dedication to Herbert Hayden seemed to be getting him into all sorts of trouble.

Sheriff Hull served an order on Talcott Davis for the surrender of the arsenic in the spice tin, which had been somewhat symbolically wrapped in a copy of *The Christian Advocate*, and turned it over to Professor Johnson of Yale. Then, on orders from the state's attorneys, the sheriff bought an ounce of arsenic from several drugstores throughout Connecticut for comparison purposes.[29]

In the meantime, an important piece of evidence had unraveled for the state. Professor Moses White, who had been "morally certain" that the blood on the stone found at Big Rock was not only human but matched that on Mary's sunbonnet, now made the embarrassing discovery that it was not blood at all. The rust-colored algae on the stone looked like blood and mimicked the appearance of human corpuscles under the microscope. On closer inspection, however, Professor White could see his mistake.[30]

Not only was this a disappointing loss of evidence, but it meant that Professor White, even though he discovered the mistake himself, had lost his credibility as an expert witness with regard to blood. Another scientist would have to be found for the knife testimony.

But if the state suffered a setback with the blood, it gained an advantage in the fortuitous discovery of a walnut-sized tumor on one of Mary Stannard's ovaries. This could account for her symptoms of pregnancy and would undermine the defense theory that she was either making these up or imagining them.[31]

During this interim period, Mary's body was exhumed three more times (once to make sure it had not been stolen, disturbed, or tampered with). Dr. White cut her head off below the knife wound, put it in a clean, new pail and sealed it over with rubber. He sent the brain, which was by then a mass of smelly putrefaction, to Dr. Samuel Johnson for examination.[32]

Between waiting for court terms to begin and end, and the defense's reluctance to go to trial immediately, New Haven would have to wait an entire year for The Great Case.

And what of Hayden during this year? He had the time of his life. For once he did not have to be concerned with earning a living through constant labor. He was the center of a great deal of attention, spent time writing his autobiography, and got fat on jail food. Supporters sent him cigars, fruit, and other gifts. He had a steady stream of visitors. And his jailers allowed him an unusual amount of freedom, letting him wander around the halls at will.[33] (Three years later the defendants in the Jennie Cramer case would complain that Hayden's privileges were not extended to them.[34])

Hayden's family, however, was not having the vacation that Herbert was. Rosa had to sell their furniture and other belongings in order to survive and was forced to rely, Blanche DuBois–like, on the kindness of strangers. Reverend Hill appealed to all Methodist church members to come forward in support of Mrs. Hayden and her children, whether with donations of money and food, or with offers of hospitality.[35]

Hayden did not want his children to visit him in jail, and so for almost a year and a half they did not see their father at all.[36]

Then, shortly before the trial was to begin, an ominous note was struck with the death of Loren Stevens, the Rockland undertaker who was to have testified to direct knowledge of the intimacy between Mary Stannard and Herbert Hayden. His loss was another blow to the state's case.[37]

Finally, however, everyone was as ready as they could be, and the curtain was about to rise on the trial of *Connecticut v. Hayden*. Hayden had been arrested on Tuesday, October 8, 1878, and his trial would begin in New Haven on Tuesday, October 7, 1879.

The Great Case was under way at last.

Chapter 7

THE GREAT CASE

*Talk about the endurance of Rowell,
the pluck of Bibby, or the skill of Hanlan,
what are all these to the long-suffering
forbearance of the Hayden jury. If any
men deserve gate money and belts, they do.*

—New York Commercial Advertiser, 1879

In October of 1879, the presidency of Rutherford Birchard Hayes was coming to a close. The post–Civil War Reconstruction of the South was over, and America was entering a new era of Progress and Prosperity, symbolized by the invention of the cash register that same year.[1]

1879 also saw the invention of the incandescent lamp by Thomas Edison, who had introduced the phonograph two years earlier. Americans were ten years away from aspirin and fifty years from penicillin, but they already had the telephone, the typewriter, and the microphone.[2]

Drugstores advertised "Rock & Rye," a mixture of white rock candy and whiskey, as a cure for coughs and colds. Lydia Pinkham promoted her vegetable compound for women's ailments.[3]

In entertainment, there were two current crazes: *Pinafore* and pedestrianism. Gilbert and Sullivan's comic opera *H.M.S. Pinafore* had taken America by storm in late spring of 1878 and was being performed by every kind of group imaginable, even a Boston Sunday School's Junior Pinafore Group.[4] Newspaper reports, including those of the Hayden trial, were peppered with quotes from *Pinafore*. (A modern theater director has described Gilbert and Sullivan's works as "Monty Python set to music."[5])

Pedestrianism was a fad involving marathon walking events. Individuals or groups would post belts, cash, and other prizes for the greatest number of miles walked or jogged around an indoor track in twenty-four hours or more. There were even "multiple-day-go-as-you-please" events where entrants (called "pedestrians" or "walkists") competed for upwards of twelve hours a day.[6] The most famous of the walkists was Charles Rowell of England.

Even women got involved in this sport, completing their laps in garments that retained femininity and decorum, yet were comfortable: loose dresses that went between the knee and the ankle, with bloomers or "*zouave* pants" underneath.[7]

Ned Hanlan of Canada, the handsome Olympic rowing champion who revolutionized the sport, was another popular icon of the day. He frequently came to the United States to challenge comers and always drew a lot of publicity.[8] (The 1986 Nicolas Cage movie, *The Boy in Blue*, details Hanlan's career.)

This, then, was life in 1879 America. And when the Hayden trial opened in October, a new entertainment item was added to the menu of the inhabitants of Connecticut.

A rumor had gone abroad that tickets would be issued for entrance to the trial, and hordes of locals (mostly women) swarmed upon Sheriff Byxbee's office to claim them. However, the tickets were only to be issued to lawyers and reporters. The remaining seats, numbering about seventy-five or so, would be available to the public on a first-come, first-served basis.[9]

Accordingly, the lines formed early every morning for the 8:55 opening of the doors. People pushed, shoved, and trampled each other to get in and the deputies had quite a time of it to close the doors on the hundreds who were unsuccessful. The courtroom was cleared each noon for the lunch break and so the same scene was repeated for the reopening at 1:55.[10]

The newspapers made a point of reporting the numbers of women each day, always exhibiting surprise at their presence for particularly gory testimony.

During the three months of the trial, many notable figures attended along with the throngs of more commonplace viewers. Former U.S. Representative Origen Storrs Seymour sat in as a guest of the bench at least twice. Charles Dudley Warner, who had co-authored *The Gilded Age* with Mark Twain in 1873, stopped by when he was in town, as did U.S. Senator William Wallace Eaton and former Governor Richard Dudley Hubbard. District attorneys from other cities and states made it a point to attend on occasion. And the papers couldn't keep track of all the New Haven high society members who showed up.

All of these, the notable and the obscure, had come not only to hear the details of a sensational case, but to view for themselves the principals they had read so much about since September 3, 1878.

Herbert Hayden, the defendant, was looking healthier than ever after his year of leisure in jail. He had gained fifteen pounds, grown a stylish goatee, and usually dressed in ministerial black with a white tie. As in 1878, his extreme and unusual indifference to his fate would be commented upon by all, and his face was said to have a "plaster cast" appearance. He always seemed cheerful, chatting and laughing with friends and relatives.[11]

Rosa Hayden, whose "devotion convinces many that Hayden is innocent," sat behind her husband nearly every day, in full sight of the jury, dressed plainly but in tasteful elegance. "She has a noble face," said one report. In contrast to her husband, Mrs. Hayden never smiled.[12]

Susan Hawley came every day as well, usually with her half sisters Emogene and Isadora, and brought little Willie Stannard with her. She always dressed in black and went back home to Rockland each night on the train.[13]

Mary's little blond, blue-eyed boy, now three, was a big hit with the court attendees, charming everyone with his friendliness. During the noon recess, when Susan took him for a walk, people would stop to greet him and shake his hand. Ignorant of the true nature of the proceedings, Willie had a wonderful time as the center of attention.[14]

Nearly all the inhabitants of Rockland were present in the courtroom as well, either as witnesses or curious spectators. Mary was one of their own in ways that Hayden was not, and they missed her terribly. One resident spoke for all when he told a reporter:

She is greatly missed here, and we never shall have another girl hereabouts who can fill her place. She was one of the best girls I ever knew, and her awful death ought to bring an equally terrible one to the person who killed her, whether it was Mr. Hayden or someone else.[15]

Rocklanders loved Mary, whom they considered a "good-hearted, honest, and straightforward girl." And almost all of them considered Hayden to be her murderer, because he alone had a motive and an opportunity to kill her.

The judges sitting on the case would be Chief Justice John D. Park of the State Supreme Court, whose long, flowing beard made him look like an Old Testament patriarch; and Judge Edward I. Sanford, the presiding judge.[16]

The lawyers for the State of Connecticut were Judge Lynde Harrison and Edmund Zacher, as before, now joined by Thomas McDonald Waller, known as "the silver-tongued orator." Hayden's defense team of Samuel Jones and L. M. Hubbard had added the flamboyant and successful George H. Watrous, the attorney whom Wilcox had consulted on the admissibility of Mary's letter to Susan.[17]

Not even Opening Day of the trial, projected to be dull with its procedure and jury selection, was without drama. Samuel Jones addressed the court, saying that the prisoner was poor and needed to pay for witnesses and experts in order to defend himself against the State's evidence. It was a time before public defenders and court-appointed attorneys, so the State agreed to foot the discovery bills for Hayden.[18]

Next, Jones threw down the gauntlet and gave an inkling of what at least part of the defense would be. He asked that their own experts be allowed to examine Mary's letter to Susan, as they suspected it was a forgery. But Harrison gave the same reply he had given in Madison concerning the knife testimony: your experts can examine it, but it doesn't leave the custody of the sheriff. Needless to say, fireworks followed this announcement.

Next came the reading of the indictment, which Hayden would have to plead to. "Wait a minute!" yelled Jones when it was finished. "That's not right!" No one else had noticed that the second count—that Hayden had killed Mary by means of arsenic—named the victim as "Mary H. Hayden." The first count—that he had killed her by means of a knife—stated her name correctly.

"That's just a clerical error," said Waller dismissively. "It's obvious that the pleading meant 'Stannard' and not 'Hayden.' "

But Jones would not be mollified. In actuality, he wanted the second count *removed*, as it allowed the State to bring in evidence that would not have been admissible under the first count alone. Its removal would weaken the State's case considerably, and he was trying to force the prosecution to drop the "murder-by-arsenic" count by his stubborn refusal to give in. The defect meant that the whole grand jury hearing and indictment would have to be done over, and Jones was hoping the prosecution wouldn't want to bother with it.

The State offered to amend the second count, but the defense refused to consent to an amendment. The court said it would research the issue and make a decision the following day.

In thinking over the matter, Jones must have deeply regretted his calling attention to the defect. Had he kept his mouth shut, a conviction against Hayden could have been overturned by a reference to the indictment. In fact, the following day, the defense and the prosecution seem to have reversed their stances: the State (they had probably figured out the consequences) said an amendment wouldn't do, while the defense was now willing to consent to one.[19]

Unfortunately, Harrison explained, it wasn't amendable even if Hayden waived his right and gave his consent. Now Jones, who was originally unwilling to proceed when compromises were offered the preceding day, whined that it wasn't fair for the State to take all this extra time when his client had already spent a year in jail. (He had conveniently forgotten the biggest reason for the one-year delay: the defense had not been ready to proceed.)

So, back to the drawing board they went. A new grand jury had to be convened and testimony heard once more. Witnesses went over their stories yet again.

It took three days for the new grand jury to hear the evidence. The Rockland witnesses, frustrated at having to go through it one more time and impatient with waiting around while chores needed to be done back home, were constantly begging Harrison to let them go next. It took all his skills of diplomacy to convince them to stay.[20]

During Susan Hawley's testimony, Hayden showed his nonchalance (and most likely his contempt) by leaning back in his chair and putting his feet up on the table in front of him. Normally, he took notes in a little red notebook, but not this time.[21]

One of the grand jurors brought bunches of Concord grapes for everyone, including Hayden.[22] Meanwhile, bets were made among reporters as to whether this grand jury would come in with a true bill. Most thought it would, so the odds were long against it.

Eventually, however, an indictment was brought in, and this time the prosecution had included *four* counts instead of the original two: that Hayden had killed Mary by means of arsenic, arsenic and a stone, a knife, and all three combined.[23]

The jury pool consisted of farmers and tradesmen from New Haven County. The *Register* stated unkindly that some of them didn't look competent enough to try one of the "cow cases" of that fictional rube lawyer, Solon Shingle.[24] Reporters freely commented on individual veniremen (prospective jurors), whose names and addresses were published in the paper with obvious disregard for either tampering or retaliation.

Only two questions were initially asked of prospective jurors, then follow-up questions as needed:

1. Do you have any problem with capital punishment?
2. Do you have an opinion on this case?

One man was excused because he didn't understand the word "argument." The *New York Times* reporter said that meant he probably wasn't smart enough to deal with the case.

Another man claimed it was possible he had *expressed* an opinion, but he was positively sure he had never actually *formed* one.

A venireman had stated his opinion on Mrs. Hayden's evidence as "the clearest and nicest piece of testimony I ever read." A grocery store owner had heard the case "tried" many times in his store. And a "well-dressed young man" never read the newspapers, but preferred the story papers, the precursor of the dime novel.[25] All of these were excused.

In all, there were sixty-nine men examined. The State challenged seventeen, the defense challenged sixteen, and the court excused twenty-four for cause.

The resultant jury was composed of six farmers, two retired merchants, a hoe manufacturer, a sanitary inspector, a carpet dealer, and a well driver.

During the three months of the trial, the jurors were never sequestered until deliberations. Although they were warned by the judge not to read the newspapers, it was widely assumed that they did anyway.

At last, testimony in the case of the *State of Connecticut v. Herbert H. Hayden* was ready to get under way.

The first segment of the trial centered on the fact of the murder and the chain of control over the body and its various organs, to counteract the claim of the defense as to tampering or substitution. The standard-bearer for the state in this regard would be Dr. Moses C. White.

Dr. White, sixty, was a professor in the Yale Medical College. He had practiced medicine for thirty-two years and performed over one hundred autopsies during that time.[26] Like all scientists, he was exact, seldom able to bring himself to a definite pronouncement without myriad qualifications. But White carried this tendency to another level entirely.

On direct examination, Dr. White detailed the three autopsies of Mary Stannard, which he had participated in: that of September 11, 1878, when the body had been carried back to the house; that of October 7, 1878, when he cut off the head and took it away; and that of March 1, 1879, when Dr. William Hotchkiss removed the remaining kidney and other organs not previously taken for examination.

The cross-examination of Dr. White by George Watrous was a torture for both of them and a delight for the crowd, which found the constant "sparring" (as the newspapers termed it) highly entertaining. Watrous continually tried to get a definitive answer out of White, who was reluctant to state anything baldly. (At one point when White finally answered a question with a decided "I do not know," Watrous drily responded, "You admit that. Well, let us stick a pin there.")

At the same time, Dr. White was angered and frustrated by Watrous' incessant badgering. The attorney asked question after question, picking at the most minute details in an attempt to cast doubt on the professor's statements and to lay bare the possibility of tampering with the evidence.

For example, when questioning Dr. White about what he observed Dr. Hotchkiss do at the March exhumation, Watrous asked pointed questions about the latter's hands. He was trying to show that Dr. Hotchkiss could have brought an arsenic-laden kidney and planted it in Mary's body, or that he could have put arsenic in his hands and then stuffed the poison into the kidney:

Watrous: Did you look at the inside of his hands, to see if anything was in either of them when he put them into the body?

White: I saw both of his hands plainly and I know, absolutely, that he had nothing in
them.

Watrous: Now, what was your object in looking at his hands? Did you suspect anything?
Why did you look to see if there was anything in his hands?

Hours passed with this kind of exchange, and finally Dr. White was merci-
fully released at the end of the first day of testimony.

At the beginning of the second day, the normally affable Dr. White bore a
decidedly pained look as he took the witness stand for more cross-examination
by George Watrous. The audience, bored by the extensively scientific testimony, nonetheless was highly entertained by the conflict between the lawyer
and the witness.

Dr. White did score a point, though, when Watrous asked him how long it
would take arsenic to travel to the kidneys. The gadfly attorney had snapped a
quick "How do you know?" at White's answer that it would take under fifteen
minutes, whereupon White smugly replied that he had done an experiment on
himself. He had ingested a tiny amount of arsenic in the presence of two other
professors, then emptied his bladder. Fifteen minutes later he emptied his bladder again and tested the results: the arsenic showed up in the urine.

Watrous then questioned Dr. White on the second autopsy, when Mary's
body had been taken back to her home and placed on boards in the dooryard.
He was attempting to show that Susan Hawley could have tampered with the
results by placing arsenic in the water used to rinse the jar that Mary's organs
were placed in.

Watrous tried to get Dr. White to say that a woman had brought him the
water, or that a woman would have had time to go to the well to get the water,
slip the arsenic in it, and bring it back to him. The women had been sent away
from the premises and Dr. White had already said he had not seen them
around, but the defense attorney wouldn't let it go. The exchange was a lively
one and gave everyone a good laugh:

Watrous: Will you swear that after you called for water a woman did not go to the spring
down the road after it?

White: I know positively that no woman could have done so.

Watrous: Or some man?

White (testily): A man did not do it, nor did a horse for that matter.

Dr. White had stated on direct examination that he had locked the jar containing Mary's stomach and liver in his strongbox, which he had purchased
from a safe manufacturer. The strongbox was then put in a closet in his office at

Yale. He kept the keys to the strongbox with him always, and amused the courtroom by stating that he had *never* lost a bunch of keys in his life!

In his cross-examination on this point, George Watrous tried to demonstrate that someone, somehow, might have been able to access the stomach and liver and tamper with them. He spent one half-hour on this point alone, by the end of which Dr. White was a quivering mass of helpless, nervous rage.

Thus ended Dr. Moses White's first turn on the stand. To his eventual consternation and the audience's delight, he would be recalled later in the trial. The White-Watrous confrontation had only just begun. It was a preview of the way the defense would treat all of the State's expert witnesses in an attempt to discredit their testimony in the eyes of the jury.

In the meantime, not to be outdone by their Rockland neighbors, the playfully sarcastic reporters from the New Haven *Register* consulted a clairvoyant to find out who killed Mary Stannard. Mary herself came forth this time and told the reporters, through the medium, that Hayden had *not* been the one who killed her. She was very upset, she said, that he was being hounded in this way, as she had cared for him very much during her life. However, Mary neglected to say who *was* responsible for her death.[27]

The State suffered two more blows in the early stages of the trial. While waiting to give her testimony, Jane Studley, the stout elderly matron who had done a gynecological check on Mary, suffered a massive stroke after climbing the courthouse steps to claim her grand jury witness fees.[28]

Mrs. Studley lingered for just under a week and died, without ever regaining consciousness, on November 3, 1879. She was so obese that a special casket had to be made for her. There were two funeral services, one in New Haven (attended by many curiosity-seekers) and one in Hartford where she was buried next to her husband, Daniel.[29]

The second blow was the discovery that another prime witness, Ben Stevens, was near death from dysentery, the plague of the nineteenth century. At one point he recovered slightly, only to suffer another relapse. However, he sent word in October that he might be able to drag himself down to New Haven around April . . . if he were needed that early![30]

A New Haven Methodist minister, the Rev. Mr. McAlister, was also doing his part to undermine the State's case by preaching about the "evil-minded" attorneys who were seeking to get a conviction against Hayden. Each week this was his topic, and each week his pews were filled to capacity. The Rev. McAlister did not hesitate to name Harrison, Zacher, and Waller in his diatribes.[31]

And so the Hayden trial—The Great Case—ground on, each week causing a new estimate as to when it would end: now by Thanksgiving, now by Christmas, now by the New Year. Perhaps Ben Stevens' prediction wasn't off the mark, after all.

The linch-pin of the State's case, which would take three weeks of testimony in itself, was the item that had nearly been eliminated in the argument over the defective indictment: the analysis of the arsenic in Mary's stomach and that found in Hayden's barn.

The expert testimony presented by the prosecution on the subject of the arsenic was the most forensically sophisticated that had ever been presented in a courtroom. The problem was whether the jury would be able to understand it.

Chapter 8

ARSENIC AT CENTER STAGE

Few spectacles, it might be said, can be more absurd and incongruous than that of a jury composed of twelve persons who, without any previous scientific knowledge or training, are suddenly called upon to adjudicate in controversies in which the most eminent scientific men flatly contradict each other's assertions. How, it might be asked, can ordinary tradesmen and farmers, who have never been accustomed to give sustained attention to any subject whatever for an hour together, be expected to weigh evidence, the delivery of which occupies many days, and which bears upon subjects which can only be described in language altogether new and foreign to their understanding?

—quoted in Francis L. Wellman's
The Art of Cross-Examination (1903)

In the nineteenth century, and even into the twentieth century, arsenic in its purest commercial form was cheap and accessible. No prescription was needed, and many times the customer was not even asked what it was to be used for.[1]

Druggists dispensed two kinds of arsenic: as a liquid called Fowler's Solution (primarily for internal use) and as a white powder. In 1878 white powder arsenic cost ten cents an ounce, and druggists could purchase it wholesale for around eight cents a *pound*. In fact, it was so cheap and so plentiful that most druggists did not bother to measure it out exactly, so that often the purchaser received more than an ounce (the typical amount requested).[2]

Arsenic had both practical and medicinal uses. It was an efficient insecticide and rodent killer (sometimes called ratsbane; a popular commercial brand was "Rough on Rats").[3]

The beneficial effects of arsenic were to stimulate the nervous system and to improve appetite and digestion. It was routinely used in the treatment of St. Vitus' Dance (known today as Huntington's Chorea) because of its effect on the nervous system.[4]

The use of arsenic for cosmetic purposes became something of a fad among young women of the Victorian era. Since a hallmark of feminine beauty at that time was a pale and delicate complexion, these "arsenic eaters," as they were called, would gradually increase their consumption until they were able to take a dosage that would have been fatal for anyone else. It was the price they paid to achieve pallor.[5]

Druggists bought arsenic powder in packages of approximately five or ten pounds, which they kept in a storage area, and then used a jar or bottle for dispensing it to customers. When the druggist or his clerk sold a quantity of arsenic, he sometimes (but not always) asked the purpose of it, and sometimes (but not always) wrote the purchaser's name and amount in a tally book. Then he put the powder in a paper, wrapped it, and usually put a second paper around that (and sometimes even a third) upon which he wrote "Arsenic, poison."[6]

When Herbert Hayden purchased an ounce of arsenic from David Tyler's drugstore in Middletown on September 3, 1878, he said he wanted to kill some rats. George Tyler, the druggist's clerk and also his cousin, waited on Hayden that day and noted the amount and reason for the purchase in a tally book. However, although neither of the Tylers knew the Rev. Hayden, the clerk neglected to ask his name.

Mary had been given over ninety grains of arsenic in white powder form, approximately a teaspoonful. (A fatal dose is considered to be two to four grains.) Throughout the second trial, physicians emphasized how much suffering such a large dose must have caused her. In spite of the stabbing and bludgeoning she also endured, the cause of death was determined to be arsenical poisoning.

Hayden said he had taken the ounce that he purchased, unwrapped it (including the outer layer with the words "Arsenic, poison" on it), emptied it into a tin spice box and hid it on top of a support beam (or "stringer") in his barn. He did this, he said, because poison in the house made his wife nervous and he didn't want his children to find it while playing in the barn. Why he took off the warning wrapper and why he used the kind of box that his children would have considered harmless was not explained. Nor did Hayden explain why he did not use any of the high shelves in the house's locked closets.[7]

At the time of Hayden's first arrest, sheriff's deputies had thoroughly searched his house and barn for evidence of any communication with Mary Stannard, as well as bloody clothes he may have hid there. Although they were not specifically looking for arsenic at that time, none of the deputies came across the tin spice box. As soon as Hayden testified at the inquest that he had purchased arsenic, the prosecution sent deputies back to the barn to look for it. It was nowhere to be found.[8]

Where was the missing arsenic?

Hayden was a free man for two weeks before his re-arrest on October 8. The following day, defense head counsel Samuel Jones told the press that the reason the prosecution couldn't find the arsenic was that, right after Hayden testified to having purchased it, the defense had sent Hayden's good friend Talcott Davis to the barn to get it. He found it with no difficulty, Jones told the reporters, right where Hayden said it would be. And it was exactly one ounce.[9]

Once arsenic was established as the cause of death, and Hayden, by his own admission, connected to a purchase on the very day of the murder, the poison took center stage as the major controversy of the trial and was responsible for some of the most sophisticated forensic evidence ever presented in a criminal court up to that time. This was made possible by the ready availability of Yale professors, who were at the forefront of their professions in the worldwide scientific community.

The defense claimed that, since an ounce of arsenic had been found in the barn, and since that was the amount that Hayden had purchased in Middletown, he had not poisoned Mary Stannard. Moreover, they said, the arsenic in Mary's stomach had been placed there *after death* by the doctors on instructions from the prosecutors, who were hell-bent to convict Hayden.

Consequently, the State's case-in-chief consisted of two main areas of evidence regarding the arsenic: first, that the arsenic had been introduced into Mary's body while she was still alive; and second, that the arsenic found in Hayden's barn was *not* the same that he had purchased in Middletown.

The arsenic testimony, including the defense's cross-examination, took three weeks in a trial that lasted three and a half months. During this time the scholarly presentations of the Yale professors and other scientists stood in stark contrast to the uneducated, lower-middle-class farmers and tradesmen who comprised the jury. Although most of the expert witnesses made every attempt to explain their experiments and conclusions in lay terms, the testimony simply overwhelmed the jurors.

And George Watrous knew it.

George Watrous' addition to the defense team for the second trial can only be termed, in hindsight, a stroke of genius. At fifty, Watrous, president of the New York, New Haven, and Hartford Railway Company, was an intensely energetic, quick-witted attorney. Throughout the 1879 Superior Court trial, he intimidated the State's witnesses with sarcasm, hostile questions, insults, and direct attacks (as has already been seen with his treatment of Dr. White). He challenged *everything* and wore everyone down with his badgering. He insinuated, or stated outright, a belief in perjury or evidence tampering on the part of the witnesses.

As a result of this unrelenting "in-your-face" approach, witnesses easily became confused and contradicted themselves. Many of them were reduced to tears. And not even opposing counsel were spared his scathing remarks.

With the expert witnesses, Watrous took advantage of the typical scientist's reluctance to state anything as an absolute, as black or white, or as incapable of occurrence. Since scientists deal daily with a world wherein the seemingly impossible often becomes possible, they were particularly susceptible to his tactics.

Watrous would concoct bizarre scenarios and then ask the witness whether these could ever, under any circumstances, occur. The expert would be brought to a point of admitting that, although his reading and experience said that they could *not* occur, he would not be willing to state that it was absolutely *impossible* for them to occur. In this way Watrous defused the effect of the expert testimony which, had it been understood by the jury, would have been decisive.

The first witness concerning the presence of arsenic in Mary Stannard's body was Professor Samuel W. Johnson, who held the chair of analytical chemistry at Yale and was also a professor of theoretical and agricultural chemistry there. He had had a long and distinguished career as a Yale scholar and as a forensic expert at trials.[10]

Dr. Johnson was a small, neat, fussy man with glasses, almost the prototypical science professor. He came to court with an exhibit that reflected the results of his findings: thirty-three little glass tubes lined up in a black walnut box which opened like a portable chess game. Tubes 1–14 contained various segments taken from Mary Stannard's stomach and mixed with certain chemicals to determine the presence of arsenic; tubes 15–33 contained the results of experiments used to determine the *amount* of arsenic in the entire body.

Johnson had received Mary's stomach, liver, brain, diaphragm, gullet, intestines, lungs, and one kidney a week after the first hearing in 1878. In the stomach he found about two tablespoons of liquid (probably water) and some partially digested food which he identified as being most likely egg whites and blackberries.

Along with the food items in the stomach, Johnson discovered a teaspoon of a heavy, gritty white powder which he analyzed as arsenic, and some flakes of arsenious sulphide, or yellow arsenic. The yellow arsenic, he explained, was the result of the white arsenic coming into contact with the gas that is released in the decomposition of the body. There were over sixty grains of arsenic in the stomach.

An analysis of the liver revealed more than twenty-three grains. The brain had disintegrated and swam in gray lumps that Professor Johnson said resembled German noodle soup, but he was able to use the Marsh test on these particles and determine the presence of arsenic there, too. Marsh tests also revealed arsenic in the kidney and lungs. Since the arsenic had permeated the body, he concluded that it had entered the victim while she was still alive.

For all his fussiness and exactness, Professor Johnson was not without his sense of the dramatic. He had measured out ninety grains of arsenic—the total amount determined to have been ingested by Mary Stannard—and put it in a vial to show the jury. In another vial he put the two to four grains that is considered fatal.

George Watrous began his cross-examination with the central question: had the arsenic been put in the body before or after death? Johnson replied that it was before death because the dissolving had begun immediately. In a dead stomach solution would take place but only if there were liquids present. Dead bodies do not secrete the gastric juices that speed up the process.

But, Watrous pressed, what if an ounce of arsenic were put in the stomach after death, then the body was buried, dug up, buried again, dug up again, and different parts taken away: couldn't you have arsenic in some of these parts? Johnson replied that there might be arsenic in the parts of the body that were placed adjacent to the stomach because it would spread by diffusion. In a live body, arsenic spreads by absorption.

Arsenic placed in the stomach after death could conceivably penetrate the brain eventually, but the obstacles were so great that it was highly unlikely. Before the arsenic could diffuse from the stomach to the brain, it would encounter the hydrosulphide gas produced by decomposition. Once this happened, an insoluble combination would result, so the arsenic would never reach the brain. However, in a live body, the circulation would take it there in minutes.

In fact, Professor Johnson had been ready for this very question and had performed an experiment whose results would be ready later in the trial. He and several other professors had taken two freshly dead human stomachs and, on September 25, 1879, placed arsenic in them in the amount of seventy-four grains in the first and ninety in the second. They washed the contents of both before putting in the arsenic and placed the first stomach in a clean glass jar next to the liver from the same body (which is how Mary's organs had been placed after removal). They put the second stomach in alcohol to determine whether that might facilitate diffusion of the arsenic.

At the end of a month, the professors would open the stomachs in Johnson's lab at Yale and report the findings to the court. Johnson expected that the results would show that the dead stomachs did *not* have engorged blood vessels such as they had found in the autopsy of Mary Stannard.

After the first trial resulted in the revelation of the arsenic connection to Mary's death, the State began to suspect that Hayden—or someone on his behalf—had planted the ounce of arsenic in his barn. Prosecutors commissioned

Sheriff Hull and Sheriff Stevens to make purchases of arsenic from thirty-six drugstores around the state and turn them over to Professor Johnson, along with the tin box found in Hayden's barn.

Johnson was also the recipient of arsenic purchased at Tyler's by Allen Colegrove, a Middletown farmer, on October 1, 1878. He had bought it for his hired hand to use in killing rats and three-fourths of it had been used for that purpose. Colegrove turned the rest of the package over to Johnson in its original wrappings. (It is interesting to note that the Colegrove arsenic was used with wrappings intact so as to preserve the warning label, whereas Hayden said he immediately removed those warning wrappers and put the powder in a spice box.)

Colegrove had also made a purchase from Tyler's about a month *prior* to the murder. All three purchases—Colegrove's two and Hayden's one—came from the same bottle. In fact, Colegrove's October 1 purchase was not quite an ounce because it was at the very end of the bottle that Hayden's arsenic had come from.

Professor Johnson took all of these samples, made another of arsenic taken from Mary's stomach, and turned them all over to another professor, Edward Salisbury Dana of the mineralogy department. Prior to giving them to Dana, he kept them locked up in a private closet in his private room within his private laboratory.

On cross-examination, Watrous spent *one-half hour* trying to show that the packages weren't so secure after all, and that someone could have tampered with them. He went on past the usual hour for ending the daily session and it grew dark in the courtroom. The janitor came in and lit the gas lamps, but still Watrous continued with his questions.

The next day Watrous continued his cross-examination of Professor Johnson and tried to break down the chain of control over the packages. His position was that, in passing through so many hands, the packages could have gotten mixed up. Johnson brought in several of the packages and pointed out his notations on the top of each wrapper (Watrous derisively called them Johnson's "hieroglyphics") indicating what he had done with each one and the date on which he had done it.

As Johnson unwrapped package after package of arsenic, with Watrous closely supervising, white powder flew around the courtroom, settling on desks and lawbooks. Wrappers were passed to the jury and Watrous sarcastically noted, "The inner wrapper contains arsenic, you see, which you are respectfully requested not to swallow or inhale—at least until you are through with this case."

At one point, the Judge told Watrous to be careful with this demonstration or he would mix up the packages. Watrous was delighted at this unsolicited help from the bench: "If we do," he retorted, "we shall undesignedly illustrate what others may have undesignedly done."

Watrous pointed out one package and asked Professor Johnson when it had been delivered to him. Johnson told him the date was marked on the package, and then scored a point off the gadfly defense attorney: "It is part of what you called 'hieroglyphics,' but it doesn't require an Egyptian to translate it." Watrous was not so easily squelched, however: "Now, Professor, it wasn't necessary for you to reveal your nationality in that way."

The main witness for the prosecution was the man who had taken all of these packages of arsenic from various sources and analyzed them: Professor Edward Salisbury Dana, who occupied the witness stand for three days of testimony.

Edward Salisbury Dana was only twenty-nine when he testified in the Hayden trial, the same age as the defendant, yet he was already incredibly accomplished. This handsome, boyish-looking scholar had, on the same day he first took the stand, been made a full professor at Yale, at that time the youngest one. When he testified, other Yale professors came to the courtroom to take notes.[11]

Dana's specialty was mineralogy and crystallography. He had studied at the University of Heidelberg and the University of Vienna as well as at Yale, and had been familiar with the use of the microscope from the time he was a teenager. Professor Dana was the son of another eminent Yale scholar, Professor James Dwight Dana of the school of geology (whose textbook is still in use today), and the grandson of yet another Yale legend, Professor Benjamin Silliman.[12]

Edward Dana was the first authority in the United States in crystallography (the study of the geometrical forms of various minerals), and at his death at the age of eighty-three he was called "the foremost American geologist of his time" by the Yale University Corporation.[13] In 1879, at the time of the Hayden trial, he had already published several pamphlets on the subject in both English and German as well as a textbook on mineralogy.

Along with his other noteworthy accomplishments, Dana was the one expert witness who was able to stand up the best to the badgering tactics of George Watrous and not lose his composure. For a young man who had achieved such a high degree of fame in such a short time, he was remarkably humble and amazingly patient.

Before he did any analysis of the arsenic samples given to him, Professor Dana made a trip to England where he visited the two main factories for the manufacture of arsenic: the Great Devons Company in Tavistock, Devonshire, and the Garland Works in Cornwall. There, he became familiar with the methods of making arsenic from the two companies that produced *all* of the arsenic sold in the United States at that time.[14]

Prior to Professor Dana's testimony at the Hayden trial, there had been no publication of the methods of arsenic manufacture, nor of a method by which one might distinguish the products of different works.

Dana brought bottles, which he showed to the jury, containing arsenic samples collected at different stages in the manufacturing process: before and after condensation, and before and after grinding. His conclusion was that the nature of the process lent itself to distinctions being found between ground arsenic made at different times and at different manufacturing plants; and also between batches made at the same plant but at different times. These distinctions could readily be seen in a microscope, but could not be seen with the naked eye.

After condensation and before grinding, arsenic could be found in two distinct patterns: as a fine, floury powder that looked very much like ground arsenic; and as large, coarse lumps of a crystalline substance. Placed under the microscope, the flour-like arsenic, prior to grinding, could be seen as independent crystals in the shape of an octahedron. These crystals were so small (1/1000–1/2000 of an inch) that they were basically unaffected by the grinding process. They went through the mill almost unscathed and, as a result, kept their original polish and brilliance.

However, with the unground lumps, the result was different: these got crushed and broken into ragged, irregular fragments with most of their brilliancy lost. After grinding, both kinds were seen as alike by the naked eye, but the microscope told a different story.

Dana found that the factory at Tavistock seemed to produce a product that consisted mostly of the fine, floury kind with a small percentage of the lumpy kind. From this plant, he obtained ten packages of ground arsenic manufactured over a span of nine years, with the most recent being produced the month he visited.

When he examined these ten samples under a microscope of 200 power, Dana could easily see the difference in some of the samples. However, all of the Tavistock samples contained the general similarity of having a much higher proportion of octahedral crystals to the dull, jagged fragments.

From this, Professor Dana concluded that there was such a difference in white arsenic manufactured at different times at the same works that this difference could often be detected by a microscope. These character differences could be seen in the proportion of the eight-sided crystals to the irregular ones.

When the prosecuting attorney asked Dana to state what caused the different proportions in the same arsenic, the witness declined to do so. He would have to stay in Tavistock a year, he said, before he could give more than just a theory as to why this might happen.

Watrous jumped up at this point and objected to Dana's giving his theory on the grounds that "the life of a man hangs on this case and we can't take up a lot of court time with theories." But he was overruled, and Dana gave his opinion that a basic law of chemistry was probably the reason: the size of any crystals will be large if formed slowly and small if formed quickly.

Dana had also visited the Garland Works and saw its unground arsenic as a more equal combination of the flour-like crystals and the lumps. He was only able to get three samples from this factory: one from the grinding mill, one from an open keg ground the week earlier, and one from a bottle in the office; the latter sample was ten years old. (Although Tavistock produced 200 tons of arsenic a month, the Garland Works could not manufacture nearly this much because it had fewer furnaces.)

When Dana examined the Garland samples under the microscope, he found the first two very much like each other; the third was different, but similar to a sample that had been sent to him by Dr. Squibb of New York City (later of the well-known drug company) and labeled "Garland."

Dana's conclusion was that the arsenic made at each factory had a consistent mineral character; however, he hesitated to state that this was proved beyond question because he had only visited two factories. But he had also received samples of four different brands of commercial arsenic sold on the market and found them to be so distinguishable that he felt confident he could look at 100 unmarked samples of each kind and separate them with no problem.

After a description of a separate kind of manufacturing process, that which yielded something called glassy arsenic (a noncrystalline version), Dana came to the subject of the testing of the samples. This was to be the most important part of his testimony.

Dana had a total of 110 samples, which included those sent to him by Dr. Squibb and those he brought back from England. Some of the samples given to him by Dr. Johnson were actually duplicates of other samples, but he was not told which. This was done as a check on accuracy. He carefully numbered and catalogued each of the 110 samples. Some of these he later split up and sent out to other scientists for validation purposes. On each sample he did chemical and microscope tests to make sure each one was arsenic.

The significant samples were as follows:

#1, 44, 45	Arsenic from the tin in Hayden's barn, referred to as "barn arsenic"
#5, 46	McKee arsenic, purchased from the druggist across the street from Tyler's in Middletown (Tyler had run out

of arsenic and purchased some from McKee; this is what was sold to Colegrove and Hayden.)

#8, 39, 110	Colegrove arsenic (purchased at Tyler's)
#3	Arsenic from Mary Stannard's stomach, and referred to as "stomach arsenic"

Between the barn and the Colegrove samples, Dana said, there were many striking differences. His conclusion was that it was "impossible that they could have come from the same source or been manufactured at the same time." As the professor said this, not a sound could be heard in the crowded courtroom. The newspaper noted that it was "still as death."

Dana had prepared fourteen glass slides of the Colegrove arsenic and twenty slides of the barn arsenic for examination under the microscope. In the Colegrove samples, the percentage of crystals to lumps was less than half of the whole amount. In the barn arsenic, however, this percentage jumped to three-fourths of the whole. The barn arsenic crystals were small, whereas the Colegrove crystals were three to four times larger than those in the barn samples.

Nor did the differences end there. The Colegrove crystals were dull and contained more dust-like material, while the barn crystals had kept their brilliance.

Next, Dana compared these samples to the stomach arsenic. As an aside, he stated that he had prepared one of the stomach samples with Dammar varnish, but didn't use that one in making his conclusions because the surface had been unprotected. He wanted to make this clear up front, he said, "to avoid any pointless and unnecessary questions in the future."

Everyone in the courtroom knew he referred to the defense tactics of George Watrous, and laughter broke out. The newspapers looked forward to Dana's cross-examination. It might just be that the formidable Watrous had met his match. At any rate, the confrontation would not be dull.

When Dana compared the Colegrove and stomach arsenics, he found them *exactly alike* except for two things: the crystal surfaces in the stomach arsenic had a sort of etching effect that might have resulted from being eaten away by something; and there were some fragments of the yellow arsenic produced by the decomposition process as the gases met the white powder.

Dana found no differences between ten slides of McKee arsenic and the Colegrove, and the McKee was essentially the same as the stomach arsenic. This made sense, since Tyler had purchased some arsenic from McKee and that was what he had sold to Colegrove.

Then Professor Dana spent a half-hour describing how a microscope was used. He set up diagrams that represented what he had seen under the microscope with the Colegrove and barn samples. The differences were obvious.

Then he set up two more diagrams, to illustrate the solvent action in the stomach arsenic versus the appearance of uningested arsenic from a package.

The final two charts were larger, more magnified blowups of the barn arsenic next to the Colegrove. Once again, the differences were easily seen. (See illustration in essay after p. 123.)

Herbert Hayden wore glasses in court that day for the first time since his trial had begun. Usually vain about his appearance (he came to court every day with his hair "oiled" and with a flower in his buttonhole), he could not afford to miss this important evidence against him. He took copious notes.

Professor Dana explained that in his experiments he had grouped the different arsenic samples (some known to him and some not) by their characteristics. After he made his conclusions, he took twelve slides each of the barn, Colegrove, and McKee arsenics and marked them. Then he mixed them up and, without looking at the marks, examined them under the microscope. *Every single time* he was able to separate the barn slides from the Colegrove and McKee slides with ease.

Dana's testimony had done considerable damage to the defense, and now Watrous set out to destroy it—or, at least, to confuse the issues. One of the first questions he asked was whether the State had paid for the trip to England. Although this question is standard in criminal trials today, it was a novelty in 1879. Its purpose, of course, was to show that the expert had a specific agenda and therefore would testify to whatever would help the "sponsor's" case.

Professor Dana, however, was a true scientist and a true gentleman. His testimony could not be purchased, and if his conclusions had not been favorable to the State, they would not have dared put him on the stand. As it happened, Dana paid for his passage over and traveled alone. He charged the State only for his out-of-pocket expenses while over there, and not for his time. The total amounted to $200, none of which had been paid to him at the time of the trial.

Watrous asked interminable questions concerning the various stages of the manufacturing processes at the English arsenic works. He even tried to get Dana to say at what angle each of the Tavistock chambers lay along the hillside, but Dana couldn't be accurate about this and refused to make a guess. Watrous kept at him, however, until finally Dana took a pencil and moved it in an angle from 80 degrees to 10 degrees in illustration of the approximate range. Watrous was disconcerted for once, and everyone laughed.

In his cross-examination of Dana, Watrous attempted to show the possibility of discrepancies in the formation of crystals, and that any given batch could look like any other given batch. In other words, that this was *not* an exact science of prediction and no one could state with accuracy that two samples were similar or dissimilar.

To achieve this, Watrous came up with a far-fetched hypothetical situation in which a factory worker would put a shovelful of the fine crystals into the mill, wait for it to be ground, then put in a shovelful of the large crystals. After each of these had been put in, he said, suppose that the end product was put into two separate bottles: wouldn't you have two very different samples from the same batch at the same works? Dana admitted that, in the improbable situation of each shovelful being ground separately and not commingled with any of the others, that might be the case.

Watrous then asked a long series of questions regarding hypothetical situations of different packages sent to different retailers at different times. Dana continued to qualify his answers, but never contradicted himself. He insisted that he would never base a conclusion on anything slight, whether it was a similarity or a difference. The conclusions he made in the samples he tested resulted from large, verifiable differences.

However, Watrous had scored major points for his side. Trial lawyers who heard him said it was a masterpiece of cross-examination and that it would be hard to estimate the force of Dana's testimony on the mind of the average juror. In fact, what Watrous really did was to force Dana into so many qualifications based on improbable scenarios that the jurors were no doubt confused by it all. The newspapers noted that the boring scientific testimony affected everyone in the courtroom, and this must have included the jurors as well.

Dana testified that he had given fourteen samples of arsenic to Professor William H. Brewer for verification of his results. He told him that numbers 3, 8, 44, and 46 had special importance, but he did not give him their names or histories. He also gave eleven samples to Professor Wormley of the University of Pennsylvania.

After Professor Brewer had completed his investigations, Dana told him a little about the results of his own experiments. Watrous was indignant at this: why didn't he keep his discoveries to himself? Dana responded that Brewer was independent in his main points and that he never said anything until after Brewer had completed his examination.

But Watrous wouldn't let it go. "Why say anything to him about your discoveries?" The ever-patient Professor Dana answered quietly, "I suppose it was because I wasn't sharp enough to see that the matter might be put to me this way."

Dana's findings were substantiated by both Professors Brewer and Wormley. Brewer had been chair of the department of agriculture at Yale's Sheffield Scientific School for fourteen years, had used a microscope for thirty-one years, and had taught its use in his classes.[15]

Professor Brewer did not know the names of any of the fourteen samples given him by Dana until after he reported his findings. In a group characterized by crystals that were larger in size, he placed the stomach sample, the two Cole-grove samples, the Garland, and the McKee. In a group characterized by smaller, more brilliant crystals, he placed the two barn samples, the Drayton (the brand name of Tavistock arsenic), and a sample purchased at Talcott Brothers in Hartford.

Significantly, Professor Brewer found *no* difference between the two barn slides (#44 and #45) and the sample from Talcott Brothers (#29), while there were slight differences among the others in that same grouping.

And, although Brewer mixed all the slides up time and again, he never failed to group them correctly because they were so distinguishable.

Professor Theodore G. Wormley, professor of chemistry in the medical department of the University of Pennsylvania, corroborated both Dana and Brewer in yet another independent examination of the arsenic samples.[16]

When the experiment performed by Professor Johnson on the two dead stomachs had been completed and observed by several scientists, the State began calling the doctors as witnesses. They saw no signs of inflammation in either of the stomachs, and no enlarged or engorged blood vessels. This would indicate that, if a stomach *did* exhibit these characteristics at autopsy (as Mary's had), the arsenic had been taken in prior to death.

Dr. Hotchkiss showed the jury a diagram of how they had washed the dead stomach by attaching it to a water faucet before putting the arsenic in it. Watrous said that the witness had probably washed out the gastric juices, too, and also that he didn't know if what he found in it was sugar, salt, or arsenic. Harrison, the prosecutor, yelled out, "We'll give you some of it, if you want it."[17]

But the dead stomach experiment was to die its own death because of the tenacity and stubbornness of George Watrous. Dr. Moses White, who had procured the stomachs from the families of the two deceased, was asked the particulars by Watrous: names of the dead people, the causes of death, when they had died, what had been in their stomachs at the time of death, and the chain of control over the stomachs from death to their placement in Johnson's laboratory.

Today, organ donation is universally practiced and universally lauded. However, in 1879, there were negative feelings about disturbing the dead, and families who made donations to science did so with the stipulation that no one find out about it. Dr. White refused to give these details in court, not only because it would violate the promise of secrecy he had made, but also because future donations would be jeopardized.

Dr. White offered to *write out* the answers to the questions for the judge and jury to see, but said emphatically that he would *not* answer in open court. White was always nervous when being cross-examined by Watrous, and this new confrontation brought him near hysteria.

Watrous continued to insist that Dr. White answer in open court, and refused the offer of the writing. Neither man would budge in his position.

At this point, the prosecution made an amazing announcement: it would *withdraw* all evidence regarding the stomachs so as to avoid putting Dr. White in the position of having to violate the secrecy of their owners. And so the great stomach experiment was removed from the trial and the jurors admonished to disregard all testimony they had heard regarding it.

Watrous questioned Dr. White about the autopsy of Mary Stannard, which he had attended with Dr. Johnson when the body was exhumed in order to test for arsenic. He hammered away at his old theme: Did Dr. White know whether arsenic was put into the body after death? And White, whose main problem on the stand was that he was painfully literal, stated that he hadn't seen any put there.

"Answer the question," Watrous insisted, and White, after a metaphysical discussion of the concept of "knowing," finally admitted indignantly that he "did not absolutely know." He was insulted at Watrous' insinuation that he or Dr. Johnson or any other physician would be so unethical as to plant arsenic in a dead body in order to aid the prosecution. (Watrous and White had already been around the block on this subject with regard to Dr. Hotchkiss.)

The remainder of the arsenic testimony came from the druggists David Tyler and Addison McKee and Tyler's clerk George Tyler, regarding the purchase and dispensing of arsenic: when purchases had been made and from whom, how much had been purchased, how and when it was transferred from the larger package to the dispensing jar, and so forth.[18]

Nothing dramatic was revealed in this testimony except that Watrous managed to get the witnesses to state that they didn't know for sure whether different purchases from different sources had been mixed in the dispensing jar at the same time.

What, then, is the story behind the arsenic found in Hayden's barn?

First of all, it must be stated at the outset that, although perjury laws existed in 1878, violations were rarely prosecuted except to gain some other advantage (as will be seen in the Cramer-Malley case). People of the time seem to have had a different view of perjury than we do today. They thought nothing of lying on the stand or tampering with evidence if they thought it could help someone they truly believed was innocent or if, in their opinion, the information appeared to be incriminating but was irrelevant to the case.

That said, let us go back to the question of the arsenic in Hayden's barn. Hayden, of course, had used the arsenic he purchased in killing Mary Stannard, so there *was* none in the barn.

But the Middletown *Sentinel* had published a report that the druggist McKee had sold some poison to a minister. When the prosecution tried to follow this up, it was discovered that McKee was out of the state. They were wait-ing for him to come back so they could find out what kind of poison they should be testing for. However, it turned out that the druggist was mistaken: the arsenic he had sold was to another minister, not Hayden.[19]

Hayden had been seen talking to Dr. Bailey outside Tyler's Drugstore in Middletown and when this was reported, the druggist's clerk, George Tyler, came forward: he did not know Hayden, he said, but he had sold an ounce of arsenic on the date of the murder to a man whom he later saw in the street talk-ing with Dr. Bailey.[20] This is how Hayden became connected with the arsenic purchase, since he had never told anyone except Mary Stannard—including his wife—that he had gone to Middletown or bought anything there.

In preparing Hayden for his testimony at the inquest, his attorneys would have questioned him about this and he would have to admit that, yes, he had bought arsenic at Tyler's Drugstore in Middletown. Jones and Hubbard knew the state was looking for some kind of poison or abortion medicine in Mary's body. When they heard Hayden tell about the arsenic purchased on the very day of the murder, they must have known they were in trouble.

Where had he put it? they would have asked. And Hayden told them he had thrown it out as soon as he knew he was suspected of Mary's murder. Only when it was too late did he realize that it was a stupid thing to do, that he should have kept it as proof of his innocence. (This very same hypothetical situation was outlined by George Watrous in his summation for the defense.[21])

Hayden could not have purchased arsenic anywhere in the state after the first trial without being recognized, and besides, his daily actions for those two weeks were closely scrutinized by neighbors and by the sheriff. But Jones, his chief attorney, had his offices in Hartford, forty miles away. It was he who probably sent someone to Talcott's Drug Store to make the purchase that would save his client.[22]

Jones then would have removed the wrappings that identified it as coming from somewhere other than Tyler's in Middletown, put the arsenic in a tin spice box—perhaps the very same pepper box used by Hayden—hid it in Hay-den's barn, and then sent the local dupe (Talcott Davis) to go "find" it. The ar-senic had to be discovered by someone not in on the plan so that the story would have the ring of truth when it was told in town and on the stand.

Did Hayden's attorneys believe their client was innocent? Most likely they did. It is hard to imagine that they would have planted evidence had they thought he was really guilty. In their minds, the failure to find the arsenic in the barn was something that would hurt an innocent man, whereas their creative sleight of hand would hurt no one.

No one, that is, except Mary Stannard.

Chapter 9

EXPERTS ON PARADE

The Hayden trial is in its fifth week, and it is thought the jury will have some trouble in deciding whether to hang Hayden or the medical experts who have prolonged the case.
—*The Norristown [PA] Herald*

Americans in the 1990s were saturated with and disgusted by the interminable trial of football hero O. J. Simpson for the murder of his ex-wife and a restaurant employee. It became a staple of late-night talk shows, stand-up comedians, and daily newspapers. It was The Case That Wouldn't Die.

Americans in 1879 had similar feelings about the Great Hayden Case, which seemed endless by their standards. By December 2, the case had consumed a total of 150 hours of trial time: 44 for the state, and a whopping 106 for the defense, which had yet to present its case in chief.[1]

The longer the Hayden case went on, particularly with regard to expert testimony, the more public sympathy swayed in favor of the man on trial. The *New York Telegram* complained of Connecticut's "persecution" of the Reverend Hayden and the "endless vivisection" of his soul. It compared him to Prometheus and science to the vulture that eternally plucked at his liver. It went on to accuse the Connecticut lawyers of wanting to become part of a case as famous as that of John White Webster, the Harvard professor hanged in 1850 for killing the wealthy and prominent Dr. George Parkman. And, finally, it expressed doubt that Hayden could ever be executed as a result of "all this scientific trash."[2]

The *New York Graphic* referred to the case as "the show" and declared it a nuisance. Instead of endeavoring to find out the guilt or innocence of the accused, the trial seemed instead to "afford an opportunity for certain lawyers and 'experts,' medical and chemical, to gain fictitious notoriety."[3]

And even the *Albany [NY] Law Journal*, which could have been expected to sympathize with the legal proceedings, called the trial a "comedy of errors." The expert testimony seemed useless, it declared, especially when the experts were contradicting each other and indulging in name-calling. Hayden did not seem to be in any particular danger of dying, unless the trial were to last for the rest of his life.[4]

With all the negative reaction to the length of the trial, and particularly the expert testimony, it can be assumed that these feelings pervaded the jury as well. As ordinary citizens in a world where most education left off at grammar school, they would have relied on what they called common sense rather than all this "scientific claptrap."

The arsenic testimony, of course, had taken up a great deal of time. But there were still the specialized areas of blood, photography, and gynecology yet to come, as well as the sensational and controversial "boot heel" testimony.

By 1879, forensic science had only developed to the point of being able to determine the *probability* of a given blood sample's being human. This was done by measuring each corpuscle, coming up with an average, and then comparing the average to the span determined for humans and other animals.

The human average is 1/3200 of an inch, while that of a pig is 1/4200 and a horse is 1/4600. However, the *range* of some animals could overlap: for example, the human range is 1/2700–1/3800, which is overlapped by the dog (1/3200–1/4400), the pig (1/3400–1/5500) and, to a small extent, the ox (1/3800–1/6300). So, at the time of the Hayden trial it could not be determined with precision whether a given blood sample was human.[5]

Four years earlier, in 1875, a German scientist had discovered that there were various types of human blood, but it was not until 1900 that this theory was tested. As a result, we now have the characteristics of blood types A, B, O, and so on. Forensically, of course, this is only helpful if the victim and the killer have different blood types, but it has helped crime detection enormously since 1900.[6]

In 1901, another German doctor discovered the precipitin test to distinguish between human and animal blood, a topic of much cross-examination in New Haven in 1879. Almost fifty years later, a British scientist discovered a distinct component in the white blood cells of women, so that the gender of the person leaving blood behind could be determined. And in 1984 came the great breakthrough of DNA "fingerprinting" for the detection of that unique individual signature that shows up not only in blood, but also in semen and saliva.[7]

None of these later developments were available at the Hayden trial. Consequently, the blood testimony was too inconclusive to be of much use in spite of all the time spent on it by both sides.

Dr. Moses White had begun the blood examination for the state by looking at Hayden's knife and his clothes. However, with the discovery that the "blood" on the stone was actually algae, his credibility as an expert witness on this topic had been seriously damaged. Therefore, the prosecution engaged Dr. Joshua Treadwell of Boston, a Harvard Medical School graduate whose specialties were microscopy and blood.

Treadwell examined the material found in the thumbnail groove of the small blade of Hayden's knife. There were several blood corpuscles (preserved by dirt which prevented rust from forming) and some fatty tissue. The blood corpuscles were well within the range of that of humans: 1/2909–1/3720, with most of them measuring 1/3221.[8]

Dr. Treadwell found no blood on the shirt Hayden supposedly wore on the day of the murder, but did find spatters on the shoulders of another of his shirts. The blood spots on this latter shirt ranged from 1/2909 (the same size as the largest found on the knife) to 1/3555 on the right shoulder, and from 1/2883–1/3368 on the left. On Mary Stannard's sunbonnet were corpuscles measuring from 1/2782–1/4050, with the majority being 1/3207.

Hayden's pants showed evidence of having been washed or otherwise submitted to water, so Treadwell was unable to measure the blood on them accurately. However, they did test positive for blood with the guaiacum test, and the corpuscle measurement seemed to be below 1/4000.

No blood was found on Ben Stevens' clothes or on his knife. There was some human blood on the "found" knife, but as this knife was located in the picnic area rather than in the murder area, the defense was never able to connect it to the case. Hence, it was never admitted into evidence.

Dr. Treadwell had also examined Lennie Hayden's knife and found pumpkin and pear cells, which contradicted Rosa Hayden's statement that Lennie had used his father's knife to cut up pumpkins and that she had used it for the pears.

In all, Dr. Treadwell was on the stand for two days, most of which was taken up by the defense for cross-examination. His testimony was extremely exact, with detailed descriptions of all the experiments he had conducted, explanations of charts and pictures he had brought, and qualifying statements such as that human blood was in the same range as that of the whale, the seal, the sloth, the beaver, the porcupine, the orangutan and the dog-faced baboon. In other words, it was testimony designed to put the spectators to sleep. The audience this was intended for—the jury—was caught yawning several times.[9]

However, there were some entertaining and dramatic incidents along the way in the clashes that inevitably arose when George Watrous was cross-examining an expert. The most notable of these was the "arithmetic mistake."

Dr. Treadwell was already enraged by some of Watrous' antics when the mistake came up. At one point, when the doctor was attempting to answer a question, Watrous dismissively cut him off in the middle with "Well, we'll drop that." Treadwell had had enough and jumped to his feet: "No, sir, we won't!" he exploded angrily. "I shall finish my answer and explain!"

Shortly after this episode, Watrous saw that Treadwell had made a mistake in his averaging of some of the corpuscles. He asked him to repeat the math, which Treadwell did . . . with the same mistake. "Put it on the blackboard," Watrous told him, "and you'll see your mistake."

Treadwell was already furious with the defense attorney and now he could barely see straight. He put the two figures on the board (3,137 and 2,758), added them (5,895), then divided by two and came up with the same wrong answer (2,997). Here is a report of the exchange in the *New Haven Evening Register*:

"That is correct, is it?" asked Mr. Watrous.

"It is," responded the doctor, now a trifle nettled.

"Does 2 go in 9, nine times?" asked Mr. Watrous.

"No," replied the doctor, "but 2 does go in 18 nine times if I ever learned anything at school," and he angrily threw his notebook down on the table in front of the witness stand.

When the doctor went over his math once more, he discovered his mistake. Although embarrassed, he still had the good grace to laugh at himself, as did the entire courtroom. Watrous smugly commented that his intention was to show the jury that experts were fallible.

Dr. Treadwell provided more laughs when he was asked his opinion of the U.S. Army Surgeon, Dr. Joseph Woodward, whom the defense intended to call as its own expert. This was a topic Dr. Treadwell relished, as he had strong opinions of Dr. Woodward, whom he considered "egotistic and assuming."

The problem with Dr. Woodward, Treadwell said, was that he was so busy getting together the two volumes on the medical history of the Civil War that he had no time to keep up his work on the blood, so he was getting behind the times and relying on old information for his opinions. It was obvious to the spectators that Treadwell was finally enjoying himself on the stand as he warmed to his topic.

Watrous decided he had to cut Treadwell off, as he would have gone on forever criticizing Dr. Woodward.

"I wonder if Woodward is as excitable as you are," the lawyer mused.

"Oh, he's more so," Dr. Treadwell said, and everyone roared with laughter.

When Treadwell began to take off on this subject again, Watrous had to remind him that *he* now had the floor. In a good mood at last, Treadwell good-naturedly assented: "Well, what I was about to say is so good that it'll keep."

But the blood testimony, for all its minutia of detail, was useless in the prosecution of Hayden. Not only did the jury find it tedious and incomprehensible, but in the last analysis it could never be determined whose blood was on his knife or his pants.

What could our modern-day forensics have contributed on this subject? Today, criminalists look for evidence of the theory of transfer: every killer leaves something of himself behind and takes something of his victim or the crime scene with him.[10]

A DNA test of the blood and fat particles on Hayden's knife might reveal them to be Mary Stannard's. Fiber analysis might show threads of her calico dress on his clothing, or of his homespun pants on her checked sunbonnet. Fingerprint dusting might indicate that Hayden had touched Mary's berry pail, which was not the same one he had drunk from that morning at the spring. All the eyewitness testimony in the world would not be half as valuable as this scientific proof that could place him at the scene of the crime at the time of Mary's murder.

New Haven photographer Abram DeSilva was hired shortly after the murder to take pictures of the crime scene and the locale. Some of these were retaken prior to the 1879 trial as well.[11]

Mrs. Hayden testified at the 1878 trial that she had watched her husband go past Burr's barn and into the meadow as far as the turnstile, at which point he turned and blew her a kiss. DeSilva's photograph showed the view from a point just south of Burr's barn to Hayden's house, a view completely obstructed by a fence and high bushes.

Then DeSilva took the same shot from Hayden's house from outside the window Mrs. Hayden said she was sitting in when she saw her husband go into the meadow in the direction of the woodlot. No such view could be seen.[12]

Sylvanus Butler, who surveyed the distances between various points, stated that he performed an experiment to see what Mrs. Hayden could have seen looking toward Stannards' spring. She said she had seen the top of her husband's carriage stop for only a few seconds, then proceed homeward, so he couldn't have had a conversation with Mary about where to meet her later.

However, Butler testified that he stood outside the window where Mrs. Hayden said she had been sitting and watched his assistant wave a white handkerchief on a stick all the way to Stannards' house and back. There was only one spot where Butler could see anything, and that was when the carriage had gone about 150 feet below the spring. At that point, he could see the handkerchief, but nothing else.

Someone standing at the spring, Butler said, could see the chimney and part of the roof of Hayden's house. Standing at a stone wall *opposite* the spring, he could make out the upper part of Hayden's windows but not the lower ones where Mrs. Hayden was sitting.[13]

The defense's cross-examination consisted of trying to show that both men had stationed themselves at strategic points that would help the prosecution but that they were not showing the whole picture. DeSilva, they claimed, was "lying" with photographs that didn't show what the eye could see. Waller scoffed that the defense was trying to see "whether this witness has stopped the sun in its course and changed the laws of light."[14]

Mary Stannard thought she was pregnant again, but the autopsy revealed no fetus. In fact, the examining doctors found that she had not been pregnant since she had had Willie two years before. Mary's beliefs in this regard were important as they provided Hayden with a motive for killing her. The defense claimed that not only was she *not* pregnant, but had no reason to think so because of having her menstrual period—hence, no motive.

However, in one of their subsequent examinations, Drs. White and Jewett found a small cyst of about five months' growth and the size of a walnut on Mary's right ovary. They turned it over to Dr. Mitchell Prudden, the medical examiner for New York City. These doctors and several textbook references stated that such a tumor could, in fact, cause a woman to have symptoms of pregnancy.[15]

Because the tumor had not been mentioned in the first trial, pending the examination by Dr. Prudden, the defense tried to show that, like the arsenic, the tumor was an afterthought planted by the prosecution.

Watrous recalled his "old friend" (as he sarcastically referred to Dr. White) to the stand and succeeded in bringing the good doctor to the point of frustrated fury once more. The thrust of his questions was aimed at White's not noticing the tumor right away (so it couldn't have been very noticeable) and his not mentioning it at the first trial (so he couldn't have thought it very significant if, in fact, he had really noticed it at all).

Dr. White insisted that he *had* mentioned it at the first trial when asked about the health of the reproductive organs. However, no newspaper report of the day mentions this, and so he was probably just engaging in the sort of wishful thinking that so many other witnesses did in this trial: I should/shouldn't have said that; therefore, I did/didn't.

Watrous confronted Dr. White with this lack of newspaper proof, but White retorted that he didn't consider the newspapers a valid authority. Undaunted, Watrous snapped back with "Perhaps they return the compliment." And when the doctor said he hadn't wanted to volunteer anything he wasn't asked about, Watrous humiliated him with a reminder of the famous "bloody stone."

White, shaking with rage, got up from the witness seat and grasped the rail in front of him with white-knuckled tension. Since Watrous wanted to push the matter, White would oblige him with a statement he hoped would hurt the defense's case: that his real impression about what he saw on Mary Stannard's ovary was of an ovarian or extra-uterine pregnancy, but that he had not said so before because of not wanting to make Hayden's position worse with a statement that he couldn't back up. The sac had characteristics of both an ovarian tumor and an ovarian pregnancy.

But Watrous was like a bulldog regarding his main points: Why didn't anyone testify about this at the first trial? Why didn't anyone write it up in the many autopsy reports? The Matthewsons never mentioned it, and neither did Dr. Jewett. Why didn't Dr. White call their attention to it? White said it was because he thought it should be looked at under a microscope; besides, they could see it for themselves if they wanted.

Why did Dr. White let Dr. Jewett write in the report that the organs were healthy? Watrous wanted to know. White said he didn't write the minutes.

"But you suffered it to be written," Watrous pressed.

"Suffered, Mr. Watrous!" exclaimed the beleaguered doctor. "I suffer you to do what you please."

After this exchange, Watrous told White to stop scowling because he wasn't afraid of him! It is easy to see why the spectators at the trial relished these confrontations in the midst of so much medical testimony. The White-Watrous sparring matches never failed to disappoint, and the audience paid close attention when the doctor was on the stand. It was possibly the only expert testimony that was really listened to.

In the middle of the trial, rumors began to float around that the state had found more evidence to incriminate the defendant: marks on Mary's face that exactly corresponded with the hobnails on Hayden's boot.[16] The public eagerly looked forward to this particular testimony because of its sensational and gory aspects, as well as its being something definitive that the most uneducated mind could grasp.

The prosecution finally admitted that, yes, the rumors were true. They would be presenting the evidence in due time, but first they had to invite the defense to look at it. Samuel Jones and L. M. Hubbard went to Dr. White's lab with their own medical experts and watched while Mary's face was removed from a jar of alcohol and fitted back over the skull as best as it could be.

As might be expected, the defense claimed to see nothing on the face except some marks that were probably the beginnings of decay, while the State claimed that the holes in the face lined up exactly with the nails on Hayden's boot. The theory was that he stepped on the left side of her face to hold her head still while he slit her throat.

The rounded, or back, part of the heel was pointing toward the ear. One side of the heel lapped over the cheekbone and the other over the lower jaw area in the direction of the chin. Dr. Treadwell, who testified on this matter, said that the marks could not have been made by decay nor could they be remnants of Mary's bout with poison ivy that spring.

The defense was not content with charts and photographs and expert testimony. Jones insisted on having the actual skull and face brought into court and fitted together so the jury could see. (Now, *this* was more like it, the spectators thought!)

The State was reluctant to produce the evidence, ostensibly out of respect for the dead woman, but probably because they suspected it was a weak theory. Finally, after much wrangling between the two sides and the court, the State abandoned the whole notion. It would not present any boot heel testimony for the jury's consideration, and the jury was not to consider what it had already heard. Like Dr. White's stomach experiment, the long-awaited cheek-and-boot-heel evidence came to nothing.

Was there anything to it, though? Probably not. The marks had not appeared prior to this time, and were most likely caused by decomposition. But the most persuasive evidence that the marks were not caused by Hayden's boot heel is the very awkwardness of the position. Anyone who attempts to arrange a boot heel over a subject's face in the same way described by the prosecution (provided a willing subject can be found!) for the purposes of gaining a firm hold to slit the throat from left to right will immediately see the truth of this.

And what of the defense's experts? The defense approach seemed to be to rely primarily on extensive cross-examination of the state's experts so as to negate their testimony and on the two main weapons in their arsenal: Mr. and Mrs. Hayden. Consequently, the experts produced by the defense were almost an afterthought.

The defense's medical experts focused on two points:

1. There wasn't enough blood where the body was found, so she must have been killed somewhere else. [The theory was that she was killed in her own home by her father and Ben Stevens, with Susan's knowledge, then carried to where she was found.]

2. The tumor on her ovary would not have caused her to experience symptoms of pregnancy.

But George Watrous was not the only experienced cross-examiner. Both Thomas Waller and Judge Harrison were stellar in their handling of the defense's experts (one of whom was the brother of the presiding judge). They were all forced to admit that under certain circumstances an ovarian tumor could cause symptoms of pregnancy and that a slow heartbeat (because of the arsenic) would result in very little blood from a cut throat.[17]

The doctor who said he found no blood on *any* of Hayden's clothes admitted he didn't use the guaiacum test—the most widely used and universally accepted—because he didn't know how!

The arsenic testimony presented on behalf of Hayden consisted entirely of a man who was currently in the legislature, had been involved with the grinding of arsenic thirty years previously, and for twenty years had been a supervisor in a barytes (barium sulfate) mill. He claimed that the grinding process could never produce uniformity, yet stated that *before* grinding he could tell which factory had produced the lot. The barytes from each manufacturer had its own distinctive look. What about after grinding if you were to look through a microscope? he was asked. The witness stated that he was not a microscopist.

So, in the end, the expert witnesses for each side bored and confused the jury and cancelled each other out. There was a feeling that if it took so much time to present all this evidence against Hayden, and there was *still* nothing you could hang your hat on, then they didn't have much of a case against him.

Perhaps the lay witnesses could shed some light on it.

Chapter 10

LAY TESTIMONY

"The horror of that moment," the King went on, "I shall never, never forget!" "You will, though," the Queen said, "if you don't make a memorandum of it."
—Lewis Carroll, *Through the Looking Glass*

During the presentation of expert testimony, which the public found boring and difficult to understand, there were seats to be had in the spectators' section. But when it was known that Rocklanders were to take the stand, crowds of men and women poked and pushed and shoved to take those seats. (During Susan Hawley's testimony, one wag suggested that the trial be moved to the Music Hall.[1]) The deputies who had to fight twice daily with these hordes must have welcomed those dull days of medical and chemical evidence.

But, while the lay witnesses were more interesting with their gossip and their quaint ways, their testimony had little probative value because it simply could not be trusted. Witnesses changed their stories from the first trial, or now claimed to "remember" things they had forgotten a year before. When confronted with inconsistencies, they would simply say, "I don't recall."

Luzerne Stevens across the road, for example, had originally said that he had seen Hayden at 2:00 P.M.; but when the time the defendant left for the woodlot became a critical factor, Stevens changed his story and said he had not seen him at all between 11:00 A.M. and 4:00 P.M.[2]

Some witnesses, for both prosecution and defense, would present incredibly detailed testimony regarding what Herbert Hayden had done or said or worn at the time, yet had no such recollection concerning others who were also on the scene—including themselves!

It became a monumental task for the jury to decide who was telling the truth. Even the judge, in his charge to the jury, admitted that between two sets of witnesses, one of whom was Mr. and Mrs. Hayden, there was no way to reconcile the testimony. But, he told them, you have to consider which ones had an incentive to lie.[3]

As it turned out, they all did.

A running motif throughout the prosecution's case was the presentation of "alibi witnesses": Rocklanders called simply to show that they were not in Rockland on the day of the murder or were nowhere near that area of town. This was to show that there was no one else but Hayden who could have been seen by Mrs. Ward and no one else who could have murdered Mary Stannard at that time and place.

The alibi witnesses testified to their whereabouts on that day, but most of them provided no proof of it. In fact, it seemed as if the entire town of Rockland was somewhere else except for Mary Stannard and Herbert Hayden. These witnesses raked in $2.50 a day from the state until they finally were able to testify and go home. One man waited six weeks to get on the stand and showed up in court every day.[4]

The alibi witnesses caused a great deal of amusement for the spectators because of the sarcasm they aroused in the defense during cross-examination and the sparring between the attorneys. After the defense had brought out the cost to Connecticut of the man who had waited six weeks to testify, the prosecution asked him on re-direct how long he would have waited "had the [defense's] cross-examinations been as brief as they had been brilliant." "I should say about a week," the witness answered.[5]

During another segment of alibi witnesses, all claiming to be elsewhere, Samuel Jones sarcastically addressed the crowd: "Well, if anybody did commit the murder let them speak out." The resultant uproar on the part of the spectators was so loud that the sheriff had to rap for order and one of the judges was horrified: "This laughter, gentlemen, is most unseemly—most unseemly."[6]

George Watrous asked another witness if he knew whether *anyone* had been in Rockland that day. "Not particularly," the witness answered. As he left the stand, Watrous gave him a bemused smile: "You have been here all the time just to tell your little story."[7]

Mary Stannard's handwriting and spelling were so bad that it was hard to decipher some of the words in her letter to Susan Hadley. The defense jumped on this and tried to make a case out of the possibility that the words "Mr. Hayden" in the letter were actually "Mr. Hazen." Then they claimed that the man known as Andrew Hazlett, a common laborer in Rockland, was really named Hazen.[8] This was a desperate stretch for many reasons, not the least of which was the fact that Mary would never have addressed someone in her same class as "Mr."

Hazlett testified that he had never been known by any other name and had documentation to prove it, including his discharge from the Civil War, where he had served with the Fifteenth Connecticut Infantry.[9] However, he caused much merriment in the courtroom with his answers and his delivery, and seemed to typify the Rockland resident to New Haven spectators. The sheriff had all he could do to control the outbursts of laughter during Hazlett's testimony.

Hazlett was emphatic in his answers, which he gave in a loud voice. He didn't know exactly how old he was, but thought he might be forty. When asked if he had two "e's" in his name (which he did not), he said he guessed so. And he couldn't tell if he was married or single.

"Why can't you tell?" Samuel Jones asked.

"Because the old woman left me rather sudden and I don't know where she went."[10]

Hazlett liked to drink, and one day in the court hallway during an intermission he almost got into a fist fight with a pro-Hayden witness who had testified that Hazlett was also known as "Hazen." Waller grabbed him before the two came to blows and, to the delight of the onlookers, reminded him that he might be "Hazen around" ("hazing around" was a slang term that would equate with our "horsing around") when he was drunk but Hazlett when sober.[11]

The women from the Rockland area were no less amusing to the spectators. Forthright, blunt, and with a quaint way of speaking, both prosecution and defense witnesses did their part to add to "the show."

As soon as Eliza Mills took the stand, she asked for a glass of water.[12] She stated that she had been in a nervous state for some time, but her testimony was couched in highly dramatic terms: "It came upon my ears"; "I was startled by a voice I could not account for"; "I stopped and listened and stopped again, and then again, and then again."

Amelia Ward, the woman who had a brief glimpse of a man darting across the road, was very deaf and used an ear trumpet.[13] In order for her to give her testimony, the lawyers had to sit next to her and yell into the trumpet, and even then she didn't always get what they were asking. For example, in asking her about the detective duo who had attempted to trap her into changing her story (Sherman Buell and "Pinkerton" Perry), Waller asked: "How did they come? Singly or in pairs?" Mrs. Ward answered: "They came in at the back door."

The defense tried to pin Mrs. Ward down as to what exactly she saw (and probably to show that she didn't see much of anything) and asked interminable questions on this. To Samuel Jones' question as to whether she had noticed if the man was wearing pants, Mrs. Ward briskly responded, "If he had *not* had pants on, I think I should have noticed it."

Next, Jones tried to get her to estimate the distance between her wagon and the man she saw in the road. She had trouble with this, so he took her over to the courtroom window and pointed to a nearby synagogue. Was that the approximate distance between her and what she saw? Mrs. Ward said she couldn't tell, since the church didn't look like what she saw.

Rachel Stevens, the mother of Luzerne, had been visiting her son across the road from the Haydens at the time of the murder.[14] Her daughter, Henrietta Young, was also visiting, and both spent a good deal of time looking out the windows, as did Louisa and Luzerne Stevens themselves. Rachel and her daughter had both testified at the 1878 trial, but neither had mentioned at that time the very important testimony they now divulged: they had seen Mary Stannard and Herbert Hayden go into his barn together the day before her murder. The Haydens both insisted that Herbert had gone into the barn alone to get the rake Mary came to borrow for her father. Now the two women across the way were claiming that they hadn't mentioned this earlier because they hadn't been asked about it.

The cross-examination focused on things that might have blocked their line of sight (a syringa bush and other foliage) and their possible bias against the defendant (the selection of Mary Davis over Louisa Stevens as Mrs. Hayden's confinement nurse). Watrous tried to get old Mrs. Stevens to swear to certain aspects of her testimony, to which she would reply, "I am not in the habit of swearing" or "I am not willing to swear about so little a thing as that."

Rachel Stevens' answers were so quick and so forceful that Watrous at one point said somewhat testily, "Don't come at me so. I am nervous." Mrs. Stevens shot back, "I won't get mad if you won't." When she said she had lain down to rest for a while that afternoon, Watrous asked how long her nap lasted. "Until I got ready to get up," she snapped. The audience thoroughly enjoyed seeing the usually confident attorney discomfited by the old country woman.

But did Mrs. Stevens and her daughter really see Hayden and Mary go into the barn together? Probably not in the way they testified. For one thing, it is unlikely that they ever mentioned it to the prosecution at the Madison trial or they would surely have been asked about it then. The two women deemed it significant enough to "tsk-tsk" over, according to their testimony, so why didn't they give this information to the State at that time?

Here's what probably happened: the whole Stevens household had been noting the comings and goings of Mary and the Haydens for two days. Henrietta Young and Rachel Stevens most likely did see the two going toward the barn together, but the door they entered was not within sight of the Stevens windows. What *was* in their sight was a large hole that had boards over it.

The two women would have heard from Louisa Stevens, who had spoken to Susan, that Mary said she and Hayden had gone into the barn together, so they were safe in asserting this. And they wanted to make sure that Hayden did not get acquitted again, as had happened at the Justice Court trial, so they simply did some creative adjusting of what they really saw. They were not alone in this approach to the "truth."

The Stevens women would have had a clear line of sight from Hayden's house to his barn, and they should have been able to see enough to know that the Haydens were not telling the truth in court: it was *Rosa* who stood on the porch holding her baby, not Mary. And people who enjoyed spying on their neighbors as much as the Stevenses would have kept view-blocking foliage regularly trimmed.

The Stannard-Hawley clan came in for the most mistreatment, as their nearly total lack of education and culture made them appear even simpler than the other Rocklanders. They were easy targets. The lack of respect shown to Mary's family by the defense and even, to a certain extent, by the State, must have had a profound effect on the jury. And, contrasted with the deference shown to the Haydens, it would have weighed more heavily in their deliberations than all the expert testimony combined.

A symbolic example of this lack of respect can be seen in the visit made by the jury, attorneys, judges, and reporters to Rockland in December 1879.[15] The State had wanted this visit to take place in the fall, when the foliage would more nearly represent what had been there at the time of the murder, but the defense never took them up on this offer until the winter.

The entourage reached the Stannard home and, when no one answered the knock at the door, the sheriff took an iron bar and pried off the lock. After the jury was finished looking around, the reporters were allowed to go in and view the sparse, shabby interior, which they then described in detail for all the world to know. (One wonders whether the same approach would have been used had the current occupants of the Hayden house been unavailable.)

At the neatly appointed Hayden house, on the other hand, where the residents had been forewarned of the visit, the jury was served a delicious lunch.

On the stand, Mary's half brother, Sylvester Hawley, was the victim of merciless sarcasm on the part of George Watrous, some of which the hapless young man was not even aware. Watrous's cross-examination was laced with phrases like "put on your thinking cap" when the befuddled witness was not sure of an answer.[16]

Sylvester was so confused that he could not remember what he had done the week prior to giving his testimony. And when Watrous asked whether he had been conscious of something, he answered that he had not been "conscience" of it. The cross-examiner then delighted the audience by maliciously substituting the word "conscience" for "conscious" in his next question.

Sylvester's brother, Charles, fared no better. He couldn't remember if he got married in 1878 or 1879, which did not bode well for the reliability of his testimony about the oyster supper in 1878. What time did he get there? he was asked. Well, he had looked at his watch and it was 5:00; or maybe it was 6:00; or it could have been 7:00. Watrous told him to choose one, so he chose 7:00, to the raucous amusement of the courtroom crowd.[17]

Charles couldn't remember whether he had bought the watch or had it given to him, and Watrous asked a great many questions about this, probably trying to insinuate that he had no watch at all and therefore was lying about noticing the time.

When did he leave? he was next asked. He had looked at his watch at that time, too, and it was 11:00. So, how long was he there? Charles could not say for sure, at one time admitting that he was there only an hour. But the real truth was that Charles Hawley could not subtract. He knew he had arrived around 7:00 and left around 11:00, but it was useless to try to get him to estimate the time spent there.

Finally, Waller intervened, admonishing Watrous not to take advantage of "a poor weak-minded feeble witness." This characterization by the State of its own witness, as well as the performance of the two Hawley brothers, did nothing to further Mary Stannard's cause in the minds of the jury.

Charlie Stannard, Mary's father, was cross-examined as to his living in the Hawley household, his marriage to Mary's mother, his wife's divorce from her first husband, and Mary's age. The insinuation was that Charlie and his clan did not bother with legalities when it came to marriage and divorce. Charlie's inexact remembrance of dates for important events, like that of his stepson Charles Hawley, reinforced this opinion.

When Charlie brought in his wife's certificate of divorce from Horace Hawley, Waller said to the defense: "There now, it is resolved to merely a matter of taste as to her marrying the witness." The crowd got a laugh out of Waller's making fun of his own witness.[18]

When Charlie was asked what year Mary was born, he told Watrous spiritedly that she had died on her twenty-second birthday and "you can count for yourself." But Charlie couldn't subtract and didn't remember the exact year.

When he got to describing how Mary lay on the ground when he discovered her that day, Charlie broke down and could not continue for several minutes. During this time, Hayden was seen laughing and the newspapers were shocked to think that he could be enjoying the old man's sorrow.[19] Hayden said the next day that he had been reacting to something his wife said and not to Charlie's grief, and that is probably true: Hayden was extremely careful of how he behaved in public and would not have laughed at Charlie even if he had wanted to.[20]

Charlie was deaf and the attorneys had to yell in order to be heard, which must have added to the impression of stupidity. When Harrison was questioning him on direct examination, both Watrous and Jones jumped up at once to object to a certain question. Harrison remarked that it sounded like two record players going off at once when they did that, and the audience got another laugh at Charlie's expense with Watrous's response: "It makes more noise for the witness."[21]

When Charlie's testimony was complete, he was told he could step down. Humbly he asked, "You got through with me?" and shuffled slowly back to his seat in the courtroom.

Susan Hawley, who was closer to the tragedy than anyone because of her relationship with her half sister, was on the stand for five days. But unlike her father and her brothers, Susan was smart enough to be aware of sarcasm, disrespect, and tricky questions. She had sat in the courtroom day after day and watched the defense make mincemeat of even the distinguished Yale professors. And she saw that oftentimes the most relevant questions about Hayden's motive were not allowed to be answered. Moreover, she had heard the insinuations that her own family was responsible for Mary's death and that Susan herself had fabricated her sister's statements. So by the time Susan took the stand in December, she was feeling angry and defensive.

On the first day of her testimony, Susan brightened up her usual black mourning clothes with a red bow at her throat and a turban hat with purple ostrich feathers.[22] Notwithstanding her attempt, a reporter for the New York *Sun* commented that "poor Susan's toilet was not always in the best of taste."[23]

Susan's direct testimony was peppered with so many objections on the part of the defense and so many questions preceded by, "Now, Susan, do not answer this" that she must have been both confused and frustrated.[24] And, once again, the statements that she would have considered the most pertinent to the case—Mary's implication of Hayden as the person responsible for her supposed pregnancy and the person who was going to give her "quick medicine"—were being shot down.

Therefore, by the time cross-examination began, Susan was a mass of raw nerves and anger. What she didn't know was that her attitude of defensiveness and hostility would work against the very thing she wanted most: justice for Mary.

Like so many other witnesses, Susan was caught in a lie. At first she stated that Mary had been counting out change to their father after coming back from the store, but then she admitted that it was really Ben Stevens who had given Mary the money for those items. Susan had told the lie because she knew the defense was trying to insinuate a sordid relationship between her and Ben or between Mary and Ben. And she also didn't want the whole world to think that her family relied on Ben's charity. Then when Watrous asked her where

Ben slept when he was at their house, she declined to answer, which was not the wisest of choices.

The defense was doing its best to minimize the effects of the letter Mary had written Susan in which she mentioned the letter, since destroyed by Mary herself, to be delivered to Hayden. They claimed that the letter actually referred to Andrew Hazlett or that Susan had written the letter herself to implicate Hayden. (In signing her name, Mary had spelled her last name "Stanar" and the defense thought that even an ignorant girl like Mary would not misspell her own name.)

As part of Susan's cross-examination, then, Watrous asked her to give a sample of her handwriting, starting with "My dear sister" and ending with anything she liked. Susan knew exactly what he was after, and refused. "I don't write very often, and my hand shakes," she claimed. The State helped her out here with an objection (Waller told Watrous not to pick on a "poor, feeble-minded girl") and the court stated that she could not be forced to give a handwriting sample.

Why did Susan refuse to write if she had not forged her sister's letter? Quite simply, because she did not want the courtroom to witness the spectacle of a nearly illiterate woman struggling with the physical strain of writing. Added to that was her nervousness of doing it in front of so many people, and who knows what George Watrous would have made of any hesitancy on her part?

It is entirely within the realm of possibility that an ignorant girl like Mary Stannard could misspell her name. After all, Andrew Hazlett thought maybe he had two "e's" in his name. Or, it is possible that Susan, not wanting anyone to think that a *different* Mary had written the letter, added the last name and botched it. However, the state had had the letter in its custody from the very first, and it is doubtful that at that early stage Susan could have figured out the machinations of defense tactics.

Today, it would be possible to lift fingerprints from the letter and the envelope to determine who did or did not touch these, or to analyze the handwriting. A DNA test of the saliva on the stamp would not be helpful because it was Edgar Studley's son who put the stamp on the envelope. But it would at least prove that the letter originated from the place where Mary was staying.

After the writing confrontation, Susan became even more intractable, refusing to answer some of the questions before they were even asked:

Watrous: Now, won't you recall—

Susan [cutting him off]: No, I won't.

Watrous: Let me finish . . .

Susan: I don't want to recall it.

Watrous: Won't you try and recall it?

Susan: No, I won't, because I don't know anything about it and can't remember any such thing.

But what the defense never questioned Susan about—because they didn't dare—were the statements Mary was supposed to have made to her. That they stayed completely away from these only highlighted the importance of the statements, and one newspaper commented on the fact that it looked as if the defense was afraid of what further damage might be done if they pursued the issue.

Twice during her five days on the stand Susan broke down so badly that the court had to take a recess. And one afternoon she sent word that she wouldn't be coming back because of a violent headache. All in all, Susan did not come off as a sympathetic figure to the jury.

Some of it was her own doing, of course, but by far the largest part in Susan's portrayal was played by the defense. Even a little thing such as her remembering the date of one of Hayden's visits because it was the day after the Wallingford tornado was put in a bad light:

Watrous: Was there no other event that fixes the date in your mind?

Susan: No, sir.

Watrous: Wasn't it the day after Mrs. Hayden's baby was born?

Susan: Oh, yes, sir.

Watrous: That's the event you should have mentioned, then. What's a tornado to that?

Yet, when Hayden was testifying later, he stated his own remembrance of that same date as fixed by the tornado rather than by the birth of his child. But there was no comment made by either side about this.[25]

The prosecution was also somewhat responsible for Susan's effect on the jury in their polite, deferential treatment of Mrs. Hayden during her cross-examination.[26] The message was clear: the State had little respect for its own witness, and a great deal of it for the wife of the accused.

The suggestion that Susan had any part in or knowledge of her sister's death was a terrible insult to the woman who had, for all practical purposes, put her own life on hold to help her sister raise Willie. Her shock and dismay over Mary's death cannot be doubted. Louisa Stevens said that while she was washing the body, Susan lay on the bed in the front room so prostrate with grief that Louisa could not even ask her where she might find a towel. In the end, she used the towel that Mary had taken with her for her "abortion."[27]

And when the body was first brought back to the house, Susan, in a bewildered attempt to understand what happened, tried on her sister's bloody sunbonnet so she could see where the wound marks lined up on it.[28] This is not the act of someone with guilty knowledge of a murder.

Ben Stevens really had little information to add to the trial, but he had been at the house on the day Mary died and he was close to the Stannards and Hawleys. And the defense had made a valiant attempt to swing the blame in his direction, claiming that Ben and Charlie, or Ben and Susan, or Ben alone had killed Mary at her home, then carried her to where she was found.

That the defense did not really believe this but was only blowing smoke is shown by a statement Samuel Jones made during his objection to part of Susan Hawley's direct testimony: "It is not in dispute that Mary went to the woods."[29]

But Ben hurt the State's case and his own by the lies he told at both trials, lies that were designed to make himself look better and to cover up another human failing: showing off.

Nobody in Rockland was used to anything close to a limelight, and Ben let it go to his head. Once it was known he was an integral part of the mystery because of his relationship to the Stannards and his presence in their home that day, he puffed up his own importance. He intimated a knowledge of secrets he did not have, and foolishly stated that he had the oak club that had been used to hit Mary.[30]

The oak club he referred to actually belonged to a Rocklander who went to the murder site and stuck it in the pool of blood to see how deep it went. It is doubtful that Ben Stevens even saw this club, let alone had it in his possession. But he liked the attention it brought him from his neighbors.

Ben had bragged to others that he knew things that others did not know, probably never dreaming that those statements would be turned against him. Then, on the stand, he lied so as not to seem a foolish, imprudent old man. And he lied about being drunk at the barn raising party on Monday so he wouldn't appear to be a drunkard on top of being a fool.[31]

The murder of Mary Stannard was not a spur-of-the-moment, heat-of-passion event that took place in a fit of rage. The arsenic denotes calm planning and premeditation. Ben Stevens did not even know that Mary was home until he went over there on Tuesday morning. To say that he then was so upset at her reappearance that he scurried back out, got an ounce of arsenic, and then either followed her to the woods or killed her in her own home belies all sense as well as the evidence that exists.

Ben Stevens on the stand, though, was more entertainment for the New Haven spectators and the New York newspaper reporters. His country ways and blunt talk delighted the audience, which had waited a long time to hear him testify.

Stevens had been ill with dysentery since the beginning of the trial and did not make an appearance until January. Because he was still an invalid, he was carried into the courtroom on a chair by his sons, who then arranged a quilt around him. He talked in a low tone of voice and held a red silk handkerchief in his hand while he testified, occasionally stopping to take a swig of medicine. As the questioning dragged on, Dr. Jewett handed him a palm leaf fan to use.

Ben said he had known Charlie Stannard since the latter was "a little shaver." Mary, he said, left "a spell" after dinner on the day of her murder, but he didn't remember whether she had done the dishes first because "I wasn't picking around to see what she was doing." Throughout his testimony he had a tendency to laugh nervously.

Stevens denied that he had talked freely about the murder, claiming a perfect circumspection in this regard: "Folks came up and said, 'Ben, how's this?' I couldn't talk to every man that came along. I thought there might be some afterclap about it and I might have to go on the stand."

When he was asked if he was worth several thousand dollars, Ben retorted, "Can't tell what a man is worth till after he's dead, and then you don't always know." And he admitted that he laid on the girls' bed on occasion when they weren't using it: "Well, the bed was there, spread up, and it was warm. I lopped down on it. A great many people in my section hain't got chairs enough and so folks sit down on the beds sometimes."

The spectators thoroughly enjoyed Ben Stevens with his "hain't got no" and expressions such as "that's all the quirkom there was about it."

No witnesses, expert or lay, did as much to help the cause of the defense as did Herbert Hayden himself and his wife, Rosa. Their articulate, cultured, confident demeanor was in stark contrast to the appearance of the Stannards and the Hawleys.

Mrs. Hayden was the darling of the news media and the darling of New Haven. There was a constant outpouring of sympathy for her, whereas there was almost none for Susan Hawley or Charlie Stannard. Every day she sat next to her husband, who needed her support desperately. For once she had his undivided attention, and she rose to the occasion.

Although the Haydens gave an impression of closeness, there were intimations in Rosa's testimony that they did not always share things with each other. For example, she knew her husband had a turnip patch somewhere on the property, but had never been there and did not know where it was.[32] When he left the house, as on Tuesday morning to go to Middletown, he did not always tell her where he was going, and she didn't usually ask.[33]

There were some contradictions in her testimony. In the Madison trial, she had said she didn't know about her husband's trip to Middletown and his purchase of arsenic until she read about it in the newspaper the Tuesday following his arrest. But in New Haven she claimed that Hayden told her on the Sunday after his arrest and that he *may* have mentioned it on Thursday before the funeral.[34] If he had told her on Thursday, then, why did he tell her again on Sunday? She may not have heard him on Thursday because of her distraught state, but how would he know that?

In order to justify her sitting in the window, conveniently situated to see her husband's carriage stop for just a short while at the spring, Rosa said she was watching for the children to return from Mary's. It was her custom to watch for them an hour after they had gone there, as either Susan or Mary would walk them nearly down to the forks when they returned home. In that case, then, she was sitting there much too early, as they had only been at the Stannards' for half an hour when Hayden came along.

Mrs. Hayden said that Mary was not particularly attractive, but the universal consensus was that she was strikingly good-looking.

On cross-examination, some discrepancies were brought out, but by and large Mrs. Hayden was handled with kid gloves by the prosecution. Questions were asked in a respectful, inquiring tone rather than one of confrontation as had been done with the Stannards and Hawleys. She was never pressed very hard. Since Mrs. Hayden was a sympathetic figure to everyone, it may be that the State did not want to alienate the jury by treating her harshly. But this very congenial approach only served to strengthen her position in their eyes.

Rosa Hayden modified her position with regard to the carriage somewhat by stating that she *thought* she saw the top of it and that it stopped "but a minute or two." Whether she really did see her husband's carriage top, or whether she was even sitting in the window at all, a minute or two would have been more than enough time for Hayden to tell Mary about the "quick medicine" and arrange for a meeting.

When Waller asked about the discussion the Haydens had about buying poison to kill the rats that infested their house, Rosa broke down and cried. Whenever she cried on the stand, many women in the audience cried as well. But there had been no tears of empathy for Susan Hawley when she sobbed on the stand. Instead, it was noted that one woman smiled at Susan's tears.[35]

Waller would later come in for a great deal of criticism for what was referred to as "the question."[36] First, he asked Rosa Hayden a series of questions regarding Hayden's being a good provider, a good husband, and a good father. Then he asked her if, since she thought him innocent, she would not consider it unfair for him to be punished. To all of these she answered "yes."

Finally, Waller was ready with what he was leading up to, but he knew it would be objected to, so advised her not to answer it: "Would you, madame, under such circumstances, and under oath, make a misstatement to save him, whom you love better than your life, from punishment?"

At this, Rosa Hayden burst into tears and several others in the courtroom did likewise. Defense counsel jumped to their feet and called the question "an insult to the witness." But Waller said he had never intended to insult "this poor woman" whose "devotion challenges the admiration and respect of all." He went on to say that it was only natural that a loving wife should lie to protect a husband she believed was innocent and that, if he were on trial, he would love his own wife less if she didn't help him out in this way.

That the press, which represented the feelings of the public and the jury, was completely behind Mrs. Hayden is evident in this melodramatic rendition of her reaction to Waller's question:

Mrs. Hayden gave way under the intense strain and burst into a shower of tears as though the pull on her heartstrings had been too great. The very fountains of her life seemed to have overflowed and welled out of her beautiful dark eyes. The snap of the heartstrings met with a responsive breaking with every other woman in the courtroom, and tears flowed copiously from hundreds of eyes, many of the sterner sex being unable to control themselves.[37]

Waller's question had mobilized the spectators so that they were now firmly behind the defense, which had wisely put Mrs. Hayden on before their experts and before Hayden himself. After that, it probably wouldn't have mattered what they did.

As his wife had been, Hayden was impressive on the stand. On the surface, he seemed cooperative, forthright, and unruffled. He was extremely polite, lacing his answers with "Mr. Waller" or "Mr. Jones" along with "sir."[38]

Yet, a closer examination reveals cracks in the armor. During his testimony, Hayden kept his right arm outstretched with the tips of his fingers nervously drumming on the railing of the witness stand in front of him. And there were inconsistencies in his story.

At the 1878 trial Hayden had positively denied having told anyone in the Stannard household that he had been to Middletown. But now he just as positively claimed he *had* told them.[39]

When asked who had gone up to help carry the body on Tuesday evening, he named "Andrew Hazen" as one of the pallbearers and thereafter continually referred to him as Hazen. "I never knew him by any other name," he said.[40] Yet, at the Madison trial, he called this man *nothing* but Hazlett, and the name "Hazen" never even came up. There was no issue back then about a letter being addressed to "Hazen." Now, however, he flatly denied having called him "Hazlett" at Madison.[41]

At the time of the murder, Hayden had spent all week away from his family, getting home late Monday afternoon. Yet, instead of buying feed in Madison before going back up to Rockland, he chose to go all the way to Middletown and Durham for supplies on Tuesday morning. He had reasons for this: He didn't have any money and couldn't get credit in Madison, even though there were people in that town who owed him money that he could have collected. He didn't like to buy feed in Madison because he had to climb fourteen hills on the way home. Yet, he had bought feed for cash on occasion, apparently not bothered by the hills at that time.

Hayden had an account at a store in Rockland, but never checked to see if their feed supply was in before going on his Middletown-Durham trip.

Hayden said he had made up his mind to buy arsenic the last week in August because his rat problem was so bad, yet he didn't get it in Madison when he was there at that time. Instead, he went all the way to Middletown for it.

When Hayden was leaving on Tuesday morning, Rosa asked him to get some fuller's earth for the baby. He didn't think fuller's earth could be purchased in Durham (one of his main reasons for going all the way to Middletown), yet he never said this to her and claimed he hadn't even thought about going to Middletown until he got to Durham.

George Davis wanted to hire him to do some carpentry work, but Hayden couldn't do it right away because he didn't have his potatoes in. Yet, he supposedly went to his woodlot on Tuesday afternoon instead of getting his potatoes in. He desperately needed the wood, he claimed. But, instead of taking care of that on Tuesday morning, he went all the way to Middletown on a wild goose chase for some tools that he had reason to believe would still not be ready for him.

There were vines around the wood in the lot, Hayden said. That's why it took him so long to stack it. Yet, he claimed he didn't take his knife along to help him cut those vines because his wife needed it for fruit.

Hayden had planned on using the arsenic he purchased that very night, yet went through elaborate steps to put it into the spice box, then stand on his carriage to put it on the beam in the barn. He didn't use it that night after all because of Mary's death, but the next morning, instead of taking care of the rats, he went to the woodlot.

Hayden considered his horse extremely gentle, so there was no problem in handing the reins to his young children when he got down to take a drink of water from Mary's pail at the spring. But the reason he couldn't take the horse to the woodlot on Tuesday afternoon was that the horse was skittish and had a tendency to "cut up."

Hayden claimed he never knew he was a suspect until Wednesday night. However, he didn't tell his wife about it until Thursday morning. Until then he acted perfectly normally so she wouldn't suspect that anything was amiss: he slept soundly and ate his breakfast the next morning. That he was able to do this indicates an ability to fool others by acting as if he hadn't a care in the world.

On cross-examination, Hayden was evasive and occasionally arrogant. When backed into a corner, he resorted to the mantra that O. J. Simpson would use over a hundred years later: "I don't remember."[42]

Waller confronted Hayden with his testimony from Madison where he had insisted he had never told anyone at the Stannards' about having been to Middletown. How did he explain the discrepancy between his testimony then and now? Hayden said that he didn't remember those questions from the Madison trial or what his answers were—hardly a responsive answer.

Hayden was shrewder than he appeared. On the surface, he seemed to answer in a straightforward way. Yet, he was actually cagey and evasive. Sometimes he split hairs with an exactness that Dr. White must have envied.

Waller asked Hayden if he had borrowed money from Susan Hawley in the summer of 1878. The response was that he had not. Waller had to ask several more questions to get to the right answer: the money had been borrowed in the summer of 1877.

When Waller asked him if one of his reasons for getting out of his carriage at the spring was so Mary wouldn't have to lift the pail (something he had testified to on direct examination) and asked him to answer with "yes" or "no," Hayden responded, "I don't think I ought to answer the question in that way."

Waller then went on to another area, but Hayden was still being evasive:

Waller: I understand you to say that when you talked to Mary Stannard at the spring you didn't know where Big Rock was?

Hayden: What do you mean by the spring? I have never said I talked with Mary Stannard at the spring. When I talked with her in the road I had never heard of Big Rock, Fox Ledge, or Whippoorwill Rock.

Waller: Isn't it a fact that Big Rock is as famous in Rockland as East Rock is in New Haven?

Hayden: It may be now.

At one point, when Hayden was being evasive, Waller said: "If you will answer my questions directly you will save time," to which Hayden smugly replied, "I am in no hurry. I now have plenty of time."

Another interchange was reminiscent of Susan Hawley's cross-examination:

Waller: Did you not say before the coroner's jury that when you first saw Stevens he was
   sitting in the front room of Stannard's house?

Hayden: I was not questioned on that subject.

Waller repeated the same question three times in three different ways and got
the same answer. With his back to the wall, Hayden finally responded: "I do
not remember that I said anything of the kind, because I don't remember being
questioned on that subject."

   But in the eyes of the public it all seemed to be a David vs. Goliath confrontation, and the defendant scored points just by holding his own. The bottom
line was that no one wanted to believe that a family man, a preacher of God's
holy word, could have done what he was accused of doing. And, in the absence
of concrete proof, proof they could see for themselves and understand, no one
would believe it.

Chapter 11

VERDICT

It is all very well, but for myself I know
I stirred certain vibrations in Spoon River
Which are my true epitaph, more lasting than stone.

—Edgar Lee Masters, "Percival Sharp,"
Spoon River Anthology

At last, on January 14, 1880, The Great Case had reached its final act. All the evidence was in and it only remained for the two sides to present their arguments to the jurors and for the judge to give them his charge.[1] The arguments would mark the fifteenth week of a trial that had often gone as late as 6:00 P.M. during the presentation of evidence and had even met on New Year's Day.

Interest in the case had reached a fever pitch of intensity in the last week, primarily because of the testimony of the Haydens, and that feeling spilled over to the closing arguments. Everyone wanted to be there for the grand finale, and it was estimated that one thousand people were turned away that first day.

The "Big Guns" for each side would be presenting the case to the jury: first, Harrison for the State, followed by Samuel Jones in rebuttal for the defense, and Waller with the sur-rebuttal. Fittingly, the last word would be reserved for George Watrous.

On a somewhat auspicious note, court proceedings were delayed ten minutes on that day because of the late arrival of juror David B. Hotchkiss, a young farmer from Prospect.

Judge Lynde Harrison began his closing argument shortly afterward, taking the jury through the evidence step by step as it related to the chronology of the murder. It was a very straightforward, easily understood outline of the State's case and an accounting for those parts of the defense that contradicted it. But in spite of its lack of frills and pomp, the speech did not end until three hours later.

Samuel Jones, on the other hand, took a different tack. He immediately began speaking to the jury of the loyalty of Hayden's wife, "that good woman" who had stood by him throughout his ordeal. Jones never referred to her thereafter without the adjective.

Then, he promoted the defense theory that it was Ben Stevens and Susan Hawley who wanted Mary out of the way. Susan told nothing but lies on the stand. How do we know? Well, just compare her demeanor with that of Mrs. Hayden: Susan was sneaky, malicious, and sullen; Mrs. Hayden was open and honest. Susan faked the letter that was supposed to be from Mary. Mrs. Hayden's testimony in support of her husband could not be doubted.

Jones closed with something of a slur against Rockland residents. Insinuating that there were so many witnesses in the case because of the fees paid by the State, rather than because they had actually witnessed anything, he said: "Two dollars and a half a day brings 'em out better than charcoal." Then, thinking that perhaps he had been tactless, he followed it quickly with the statement that he himself had come from charcoal country and that maybe he should have chosen that as his occupation instead of the law.

The next day it was the State's turn again, represented by Thomas Waller. Despite his reputation as the "silver-tongued orator," his address was rambling and disconnected. He began one thread of argument and then jumped to another in a way that must have been confusing to the jury.

However, Waller did focus on rebutting what the defense seemed to be highlighting: the testimony of "good" Mrs. Hayden as the conclusive proof of her husband's innocence. Referring to the question that caused so much furor when she was on the stand, Waller repeated his belief that she perjured herself in protecting him and that, provided she really believed in his innocence, it was all right for her to do this.

Waller cautioned the jury not to let their decision hang on what would happen to Hayden's wife and children, not to be swayed by a woman's tears. If they felt more comfortable with a verdict of second-degree murder rather than first-degree, they should come back with that decision.

At last it was George Watrous' turn. Picking up the theme begun by Samuel Jones, Watrous attacked Susan Hawley. Sarcastically referring to her as "this immaculate Susan" and "Mistress Susan," he told the jury that she was not the saint portrayed by the prosecution. It was she, he said, who wrote the letter purporting to come from Mary. It was she who made up the story Mary supposedly told about her involvement with Hayden. Then he asked the jury to compare Susan's deceitful face with the truthful face of Mrs. Hayden.

Watrous, however, did a strange thing in his closing argument: he outlined a situation whereby an innocent man might destroy arsenic he had bought when he thought he was suspected of murder, then realize his folly and purchase more to replace it. It was the only time in the entire proceedings that the defense made any concession to the State's theory of the two different arsenics. It indicated that they were more impressed with Professor Dana's testimony than they let on and felt a need to account for it. And it gives a hint as to what Hayden probably told them about why it was missing.

As Watrous reached his conclusion, he walked over to the jury and addressed each one by name as he made his final points. He asked them *not* to go with a verdict of second-degree murder; it must be first-degree or acquittal. (This was to make it more difficult for them to find Hayden guilty, as a first-degree conviction would mean a death sentence.)

As he ended, Watrous focused on Hayden's family in an attempt to distract the jury from the main issue of the defendant's guilt or innocence:

You are to settle whether that woman henceforth is to be a widow with the stinging disgrace that her husband was a murderer. You are to settle whether those bright little children shall have a father whose name they cannot mention but with a blush of shame. You, gentlemen, are to say whether that devoted father . . . shall be sent from this courthouse disgraced. . . . And that loving old mother . . . waits upon your lips for the decision which shall either make her happy . . . or make her remaining days ten-fold more wretched. . . . So do your duty with that group that their hearts shall not be broken.

Before the jury could start on its deliberations, Chief Justice Park needed to explain the legal aspects of what they were and were not to consider. Normally, the charge to the jury is an impartial outline of both sides of the case, as the judge is supposed to be a disinterested party in the proceedings. Judge Park, however, caused much astonishment with an address that was almost entirely weighted on the side of the State.

The judge emphasized the claims of the State and basically re-argued them. As far as the defense's evidence, he either ignored it completely, minimized it as of no importance, or explained it away. It must have been a very disheartening experience for Hayden and his defense team. Park obviously believed him guilty and was afraid the jury would acquit him.

The jury deliberated from noon on Friday until nearly 10:00 P.M. on Monday, with Sunday off. They stayed in the courtroom at night, sleeping on the tables, the benches, and mattresses brought in for them. The accommodations were uncomfortable, and some jurors kept the others awake with their loud snoring, or what one reporter jokingly referred to as "sonorous nasal sounds."[2]

Out in the courtroom during deliberations there was almost a party atmosphere among the spectators and even the lawyers. George Watrous took the judge's seat and banged the gavel to call the room "to order," much to the delight of the crowd. There was laughter and applause, which was quickly silenced by threats from the sheriff.

Mrs. Hayden was prostrate nearly the entire time, crying incessantly. She had obviously won the hearts of the people of New Haven, as they sent her notes of encouragement, flowers, and even dresses.

Enterprising citizens attempted to find out how the jury was voting by going to the boardinghouse next door and watching through binoculars. They tried to set up a series of hand signs until the state's attorney found them out and put a stop to it. The jurors were throwing their ballots out the window when they were finished, and these were picked up and deciphered: 10–2 for acquittal, the spies told the newspapers, and they had seen the jurors arguing with a "refractory member."

The possible outcome of the trial was the number one point of discussion on everyone's lips throughout New Haven. Strangers talked with each other on the street and on the trolley cars: "What do you think the verdict will be?" Newspapers from other states sent telegrams asking what the decision was. A man from Texas wrote in to ask whether the Hayden trial was real or only a mock trial, possibly some sort of melodrama. It seemed fake to him.[3]

Twice during this time the jurors came back to the courtroom to ask a question of the judge. Each time, it was thought a verdict had been reached, and there was much excitement and nervousness. The first question concerned Mary's sexual intimacy with Hayden: did the State have to prove by direct evidence that the opportunity existed? This is a crucial point, the judge told them, because if there was no intimacy, there was no motive on Hayden's part. You don't need *direct* evidence of it, though; circumstantial evidence will do. Back they went for further deliberations.

The second request was for an explanation of the parameters of finding second-degree murder. When Samuel Jones heard this question, his face fell. Most people thought the jury would then come back with that verdict.

On Monday afternoon the jury asked to come into the courtroom. "Have you reached a verdict?" the judge asked. "We have not," answered the foreman, William Brotherton. It seemed they could not agree on a verdict, despite efforts to reach unanimity. Judge Park told them to go back and try again.

But at 9:45 P.M. Brotherton reported that they were hopelessly deadlocked. The vote was stuck at 11–1 for acquittal and they could not convince the dissenter to side with the rest. That one juror was the young farmer who had held up the proceedings by arriving late on the first day of closing arguments: David B. Hotchkiss, who held out for murder in the second degree.

On the first three ballots taken, nine had voted for acquittal and three (Perry, Brotherton, and Hotchkiss) for first-degree murder. With the next three ballots, one of the holdouts had moved over to second-degree murder (probably Brotherton, the foreman). On the next nine ballots, only Hotchkiss remained on the side of conviction.

The other jurors were furious with him. They berated him to his face and to the press. Were it not for Hotchkiss, they declared, their verdict would have been returned very shortly, as most of their time was spent in trying to convince Hotchkiss. The newspapers termed him "stubborn" and "obstinate."

Hotchkiss' holdout vote meant that Hayden could be retried if the State wished to refile the charges. However, the chances of that were slim and everyone viewed the decision as an acquittal. Swarms of people crowded around Hayden and his wife, shaking their hands and congratulating them. The party atmosphere escalated in the courtroom as even the jurors (minus Hotchkiss) shook hands with the Haydens and gave them warm, cordial greetings.

No one wanted to leave the courtroom. The crowds stayed behind for a long time, even after Hayden and his party had gone back to the sheriff's office. After the many long months of the trial, a trial which had become a way of life for some, there was a reluctance to see it all come to an end.

Why had Juror David Hotchkiss held out? Because he believed that Hayden was guilty and that Rosa Hayden had lied to protect him.[4] As it happened, the remaining jurors voted because of their belief in Mrs. Hayden's testimony and their reluctance to condemn her to a life of sorrow and widowhood. In his later years, Juror Horace Perry would relate his thoughts at the time and probably spoke for the others as well: "How can we convict a man with a beautiful wife like that?"[5]

In the end, then, the case came down, not to sophisticated forensic evidence, but to two women: Susan Hawley as the representative of her dead sister, and Rosa Hayden as the representative of her accused husband. Susan was defensive and uncooperative on the stand, a member of a family of poor illiterates whose sister, the victim, had already proved herself to be immoral. Rosa Hayden, on the other hand, was beautiful, vulnerable, loyal, educated, articulate, and highly moral.

As would happen in the O. J. Simpson trial almost 120 years later, the prosecution fumbled a winnable case. The jurors had completely disregarded the expert testimony on arsenic and blood. They probably didn't even understand it.

Why was there no one to testify to times when Mary and Hayden had been seen together? The rumors as to their involvement were rampant even before the murder, yet not one person came forward to give substance to those rumors. Even Leverett Leach, a close friend of Hayden's and therefore with no axe to grind, admitted he had heard the rumors as well.[6]

Why was no one put on the stand to testify to what seemed to be common knowledge regarding the fights between Mr. and Mrs. Hayden over his involvement with Mary and other women? Did the prosecution lawyers think they stood a better chance with science than with gossip? If so, they misunderstood and overestimated the jury. The human element, an element they could relate to, was exactly what they were looking for. And Rosa Hayden gave it to them.

Justice was not done to Mary Stannard with the verdict, but something of a moral victory was won for her by an unlikely Galahad, a young Prospect farmer who refused to be bullied out of his convictions.

When all the expert and eyewitness testimony is eliminated, we are still left with one crucial body of evidence: the statements and actions of Mary Stannard herself. The actions speak for themselves, but what about the statements? There are three possibilities:

1. Mary Stannard never said what Susan Hawley claimed. Susan made it up to frame Hayden.
2. Mary herself lied about Hayden's involvement with her.
3. Mary told the truth about Hayden.

Let us examine each of these:

1. SUSAN HAWLEY MADE THE WHOLE THING UP.

What motive would Susan have to do this? She had no ill feelings toward Hayden before her sister's murder and had even loaned him a large sum of money, which she declared she was not worried about his repaying.

Proponents of the theory that Benjamin Stevens and Susan killed Mary so they could be together will say that she wanted to divert suspicion from them. But why choose Hayden instead of the drunken Andrew Hazlett, for example, who could not always account for his whereabouts? How could Susan have known that everything Hayden did that day would dovetail so neatly into their plans and mimic those plans so precisely?

Stevens had been a widower for twenty-seven years. He could have remarried at any time. The *real* obstacle to any possible alliance between Ben and Susan would have been Willie Stannard, for whom Susan was responsible when Mary was working. With Willie out of the way, Susan would have been free to move in with Ben Stevens.

And there is the incontrovertible fact that Mary herself had told both Jane Studley and her son, Edgar, that Hayden was responsible for her supposed pregnancy. Mrs. Studley was questioned by the inquest jury before she was told of Mary's death and thought they were there about a bastardy complaint against Hayden. She told the very same story Susan Hawley related.[7]

Not even Hayden's defense team believed that Susan had made it up: They carefully avoided cross-examining her on any of Mary's statements, for fear the result would be more harmful to their client. If they were truly convinced that Susan invented the statements, they would not have hesitated to expose her on the stand.

Therefore, if the story was invented, it wasn't invented by Susan.

2. MARY MADE UP THE STORY HERSELF.

If Mary thought herself pregnant, what could she possibly hope to gain by blaming Hayden if he was not the father? She would have known how poor he was (so poor he was forced to borrow money from her sister), so blackmail would not have been a motive. And to blame him without cause would be to ruin not only her close relationship with Rosa Hayden, but any chances of future employment with them.

Mary was known for her truthfulness and her kindness. She could not have made up a story that would hurt a man who had been her employer, a man who by all reports had been kind to her in that capacity.

Mary told Susan that Hayden had been to Middletown that very day, and Susan repeated this to the inquest jury *before* anyone knew Hayden had been there. He himself told the court that he had not mentioned Middletown to the Stannards when he stopped for water. So how could Susan have known he went there unless she heard it from Mary? And how could Mary have known unless she heard it from Hayden?

Therefore, Mary didn't make up the story.

3. MARY TOLD THE TRUTH.

The only conclusion possible is that Mary told the truth: Herbert Hayden was the father of the child she thought she was having. There can be no doubt that she did, indeed, think she was pregnant, whatever the defense's experts said about her having no grounds to think so. Her statements to Mrs. Studley and her son, her statements to Susan, the things she took with her to the meeting with Hayden, her state of alarm over the possibility: all of these support Mary's claim.

Herbert Hayden got away with murder, although he was also punished to a certain extent for his moment of weakness: He spent over a year in jail, incurred enormous debt, caused great suffering to his wife and children, and was never able to preach again. For the rest of his life, he must have had to endure the stares of the curious and the gossip of his neighbors. Perhaps his relationship with his wife was strained as well. And his children must have had to put up with taunts from schoolmates and the stigma of having a father who had once been on trial for murder.

Hayden probably thought the Mary Stannard incident had begun to die down at last when, in August of 1881, his newly adopted community of New Haven was rocked with another, similar crime: the mysterious death of Jennie Cramer.

Mary E. Stannard

from a photograph taken shortly before her death in 1878.
Reproduced from the autobiography of Herbert H. Hayden.

Reverend Herbert H. Hayden as he looked during his 1879 trial in
New Haven. Reproduced from the autobiography of Herbert H. Hayden.

Mrs. Hayden, from a photograph taken in December, 1879.
Reproduced from the autobiography of Herbert H. Hayden.

Charles S. Stannard outside the Stannard home, c. 1880.
From the collection of Tom Hopkins.

Attorneys in the 1879 Hayden trial; defense at top, prosecution at bottom.
Reproduced from the autobiography of Herbert H. Hayden.

Graduation picture of Professor Edward S. Dana, Yale class of 1870.
Yale Picture Collection, Manuscripts and Archives, Yale University Library.

Under the microscope: representations of the charts prepared by Professor Dana.
At left, arsenic from Hayden's barn; at right, the Colegrove arsenic.
From a contemporary newspaper account of the trial.

Jennie E. Cramer
from a photograph taken shortly before her death.
Reproduced from the "Beautiful Victim" pamphlet.
Courtesy New Haven Colony Historical Society.

Asa Curtiss, the fisherman, finding the body of Jennie E. Cramer on the beach at West Haven, August 6, 1881. Reproduced from the "Beautiful Victim" pamphlet. Courtesy New Haven Colony Historical Society.

The fatal foursome. Clockwise from left: Walter Malley, Anna Kearns (a.k.a. Blanche Douglass), James Malley, and Jennie Cramer. Reproduced from the "Beautiful Victim" pamphlet. Courtesy New Haven Colony Historical Society.

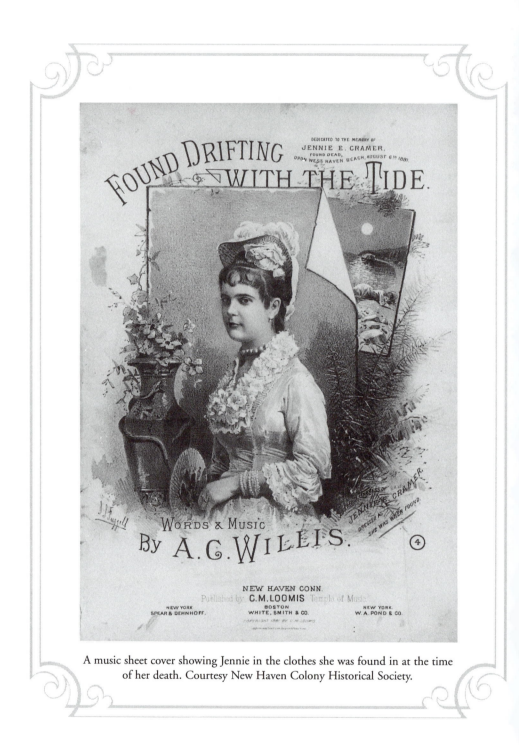

A music sheet cover showing Jennie in the clothes she was found in at the time of her death. Courtesy New Haven Colony Historical Society.

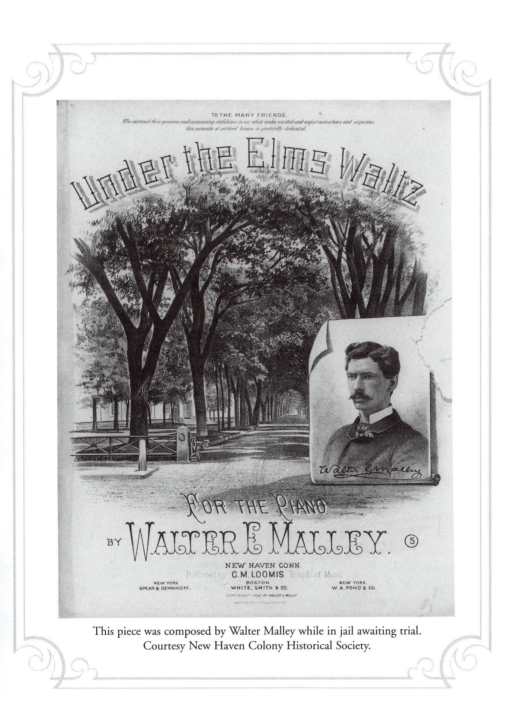

This piece was composed by Walter Malley while in jail awaiting trial.
Courtesy New Haven Colony Historical Society.

Part II

The Belle of New Haven: The Tragedy of Jennie Cramer

Chapter 12

"Drifting with the Tide"

Hark! to the wind's gentle whisper,
In the gray, misty light of the dawn;
And the waves, that, re-echoing, murmur,
"She has gone, darling Jennie has gone."
Like a bark adrift on the ocean,
Without anchor, or compass, or guide;
She heeded not the storm fast approaching,
But gaily drifted on with the tide.

—A. C. Willis, "Found Drifting with the Tide" (1881)

Friday, August 5, 1881, had been a hot, steamy day in New Haven, and it hadn't cooled off much by nightfall. Dr. Cortlandt Van Rensselaer Creed couldn't sleep. He got up quietly so as not to disturb his wife, Mary, and went into his study to work on the problem he had been pondering earlier: how to locate the bullet lodged somewhere in the president's spine.[1]

James A. Garfield had been sworn in as the twentieth president of the United States in January 1881, and after only seven months in office was shot by a disgruntled office-seeker, Charles J. Guiteau, on July 2. The bullet had to be removed, but in those days before the x-ray, it was uncertain where it was located. Surgeons were reluctant to operate without knowing exactly where the bullet was, and so the White House had engaged the minds of several prominent physicians to help solve the problem.[2]

That the forty-six-year-old Dr. Creed had been among those selected was something of an anomaly for 1881: he was African-American, the first such to graduate from Yale's medical school. His 1857 graduation thesis was entitled "Dissertation on the Blood" and is still on file in the library there.[3]

Dr. Creed's father had been employed for many years as the medical school's janitor, and young Cortlandt often tagged along behind him. As the boy grew older he began to be noticed by the professors and students. "He's a smart one," they told his father. "You should send him to the medical school." Later, some of these same students and professors helped the young man financially with his education.

When the Civil War came along a few years after Dr. Creed's graduation, he was appointed assistant surgeon with the Thirteenth Connecticut Infantry. His practice in New Haven in 1881 consisted of both blacks and whites, and he was a highly esteemed physician.[4]

Now, at 2:00 A.M., as he sat by an open window in his study to read through the White House dispatches, Creed's attention was distracted by loud voices coming from a carriage stopped in the street. The two young couples seemed to be fairly intoxicated and it was hard to make out anything they were saying. But the doctor did hear one thing loud and clear: a young woman cried out, "Oh, dear! I want to go home." The carriage then disappeared quickly up the street and Dr. Creed thought no more of it that night.

Over in West Haven, three hours later, a grizzled, middle-aged oysterman named Asahel Curtiss was bailing out his boat before going out for his day's catch on Long Island Sound. His eye was caught by a white object on a nearby sandbar, swaying back and forth with the incoming tide. Curtiss waded in a little ways to investigate and was shocked to discover the body of a young girl face down in the shallow water.[5]

Quickly, he turned her over to carry her to shore. Curtiss had pulled many bodies out of the water over his years as a clam digger, fisherman, and oysterman, and he noticed something strange about this one: her eyes were closed, her hands were not clenched, and no water came from her mouth when she was turned over. That, plus the fact that she had been face down, made Curtiss think that maybe she hadn't drowned.

As the oysterman laid the girl's body gently on the sand, he noticed that her dress had been wadded up around her hips and bound her hands loosely across her chest. Soon Curtiss was joined by S. L. Marsden, who had witnessed the scene from the porch of his cottage on the hill overlooking the shore.[6] The two men examined the victim more closely while awaiting the arrival of a town official.

In spite of the dark coloring of her face, caused by the blood settling in places of lower elevation, they could see that she was remarkably pretty. She was dressed all in white except for the blue belt and purse around her waist; a white muslin dress with a white overskirt and a white lace top cut low in a V; white "mitts" (sheer gloves extending from the elbow to the knuckles); new white leather shoes with brass heels; a white straw hat smashed in at the crown, but still pinned to the back of her head; two pairs of stockings, one white and one flesh-colored; and three strands of white glass "pearls." The beads of a fourth strand had shattered and sprinkled her dark brown hair like pixie dust.[7]

In the belt around her waist they found fourteen cents: a dime, a two-cent piece, and two pennies. She wore four rings on two fingers, all of imitation stones. The most unusual ring was a square-ish band from which hung a gold chain with an imitation gold dollar as a charm. On the dollar was a monogram: "J.E.C."

The girl's forehead and right shoulder were bruised slightly, probably from being scraped on the sand. Her left ear and lower lip had been cut, and Curtiss thought the fish had been nibbling on the lip.[8]

That a young girl should be at a beach area all dressed up like this was not unusual, for close by was the Savin Rock Amusement Park, visited by thousands each day during the summer. The park boasted a merry-go-round (or "flying horses"), swings, and carnival games such as pitching baseballs for prizes. People came from all over New England to visit Savin Rock, and in October 1879, during the Hayden trial, the New Haven horse cars decided to extend their West Haven route to go all the way to the Rock in an attempt to entice visitors to "park and ride."[9]

In fact, said Deputy Sheriff James Peck as he joined the group at the body, he had seen that same girl on his rounds at Savin Rock the previous night. She had been in the Railroad Grove area around 8:00 P.M. sitting on a bench near the swings. She seemed distant, pensive even, or maybe just bored as she put her elbow on the rail of the bench and her face in her hand. Near her on the bench lay a young man with a black mustache, his head in the lap of another, larger woman. The girl had not been looking at them, but Sheriff Peck thought they were together.[10]

At the seaside on that early Saturday morning was a local retired physician, Dr. Henry Painter, who came to look at the body. And now a crowd had begun to gather as well. As people gazed at the tragic scene, several of them seemed to recognize the dead girl as Jennie Cramer, the daughter of the New Haven cigar-maker, Jacob Cramer.[11]

The body was covered with a flannel blanket and carried to a nearby boathouse for privacy. Then a telegram was sent to Chief of Police Webster in New Haven, who responded that the Cramer girl had been missing from her home for two days. Webster would send the girl's father down to identify the victim.

While they were waiting for Jacob Cramer to arrive, an inquest jury of six was formed by Justice George Metcalf, four of whom were already witnesses in some way: Asahel "Asa" Curtiss, who had found the body; S. L. Marsden, who had arrived soon after; Deputy Sheriff James Peck; Dr. Durell Shepard; Dr. Henry Painter; and George Kelsey, from whose nearby wharf they thought the girl might have fallen.[12]

Jacob Cramer, fifty-three, a German immigrant, was no stranger to tragedy. As a young man in Prussia he had joined in his country's revolution against

Denmark, and when the victorious Danes sought to punish the rebels by confiscating their property and impressing them into military service, Cramer fled to the United States. He had to leave without saying goodbye to his parents or his friends, whom he never saw again.

In Syracuse, New York, home to a large German community even today, Cramer met his future wife, Christina, who had come from the same little town in Prussia. They were married in 1855. Their first child, a son, died in infancy, and after that the Cramers moved to New Haven where Jacob set up a cigar manufactory and retail tobacco shop.

Their second child, Edward, was born in 1858, and Jennie followed in 1860. Lydia, nicknamed "Minnie," came along in 1867, and then another son a few years later. But that boy did not live long and now the Cramers were suffering the loss of yet another child.[13]

Jacob Cramer entered the dusty boathouse accompanied by his friend William Stahl, an undertaker. His stooped shoulders and listless appearance denoted not only his sadness but the consumption he had been suffering from for many years. Someone pulled the flannel blanket off the face of the dead girl, and Cramer's face contorted in grief: yes, that was his daughter, Jennie, who had just turned twenty-one a few months before.[14]

Jennie had been sickly, her father explained, and so he and his wife had somewhat pampered her and allowed her to do as she pleased. They wanted her to have good times. Lately, she had been going out for rides and dinners with James Malley, accompanied by his cousin Walter and a young woman from Long Island named Blanche Douglass. They had been keeping Jennie out later and later, it seemed, and on Wednesday night the girl never came home at all.

On Thursday morning, according to what his wife had told him, Jennie arrived back home in the company of Blanche Douglass.[15] As soon as Mrs. Cramer saw Miss Douglass, she knew she was no lady, and she feared for her daughter. She scolded Jennie and asked where she had been and why she had stayed out all night.

"I couldn't come," Jennie told her mother. "They wouldn't let me." She seemed embarrassed.

"I'm sure you could have come if you had really wanted to," Mrs. Cramer said.

"No, Mama, I couldn't."

"You will disgrace us with the neighbors by staying out all night." Mrs. Cramer was getting more and more upset, especially as she looked at the broad Irish face and cheap, tawdry outfit of the so-called proper "lady" from Flushing, Blanche Douglass.

"The neighbors won't know anything about it," Jennie said. "Here it is almost noon, so it looks as if we had been out shopping or walking."

Jennie's nonchalance about this was making her mother's blood pressure rise.

"I think they do know it already, Jennie," she said. "And if they don't, they are sure to find it out." She was shouting quite loudly by now.

The Douglass woman said something about Jennie staying with her at her hotel because of an illness, but Mrs. Cramer did not quite believe her. She got the impression that Blanche had come along just to defend Jennie or as moral support, since Jennie had earlier told her mother she intended to change her clothes and stay home.

She turned to Blanche now. "You had no right to keep her out all night. James Malley will hear from Mr. Cramer about this, you may be sure of that."

"It was perfectly all right," Blanche tried to assure her. "No gentlemen are allowed in the hotel at night."

But Mrs. Cramer knew better. "Don't tell me that," she said. "There isn't a hotel in the country that could keep a gentleman out if he wanted to stay."

Addressing herself to her daughter again, she said, "Jennie, if you are going to keep yourself away at night, it is best for you to look for another home. When your sister comes home from New Britain tomorrow, we will look for another place for you."

At that, Christina Cramer stalked out of the room in anger and went to find her husband downstairs in the cigar store. She told him of what had transpired.

"She is lost to us, then," he said sadly.

When Mrs. Cramer came back to the parlor to talk further with Jennie, both girls had gone. She was already regretting her awful words spoken in anger and only hoped that Jennie would know she didn't mean them. She could never bring herself to kick her daughter out of the house.

When Jennie had still not returned later that afternoon, Mrs. Cramer sent Jacob to the Elliott House hotel to look for her. Blanche Douglass, however, refused to see him, instead sending down a message that Jennie had gone to New York City to see her brother, who was working as a telegraph operator there.

But Jacob Cramer did not think Jennie would have gone to see Eddie without notifying the young man in advance. Besides, she only had forty-two cents with her, hardly enough for the fare to New York. He went back home to tell his wife, and she agreed with him: Jennie was probably in the hotel that very minute and not on her way to New York at all.

Later that afternoon, the worried mother went to the Edward Malley Department Store to confront James Malley, the nephew of the owner. She demanded to know where her daughter was, as she had disappeared with Miss Douglass. James told her he had assumed Jennie was at home. Maybe his cousin, Walter, knew, and he would ask him when he came in.

But Mrs. Cramer was not to be put off. She told him she thought he *did* know where Jennie was, and she scolded him for keeping her out as late as he had the past couple of weeks. Jennie herself had complained about it, she said, and she didn't want it happening any more. At this, James Malley turned pale.

"And," Mrs. Cramer continued, "Miss Douglass is not the person you recommended to Jennie. I don't like the looks of her."

But James assured her that Blanche was a perfectly upstanding lady: "She's all right," he said.

"She's *not* all right," the mother insisted. "And please be kind enough to see Jennie home at a decent hour tonight."

"I don't know as I can," Malley said. "I have an engagement to go to the shore tonight. Anyway, Jennie might not want to come home. I can't make her if she doesn't want to."[16]

From there, Mrs. Cramer went to the Elliott House and asked for Blanche Douglass. The young bellboy, Patrick Early, took her upstairs with him and knocked on her door. But there was no answer.

When his wife arrived home around 6:30 that night, discouraged and brokenhearted, and told him this story, Jacob Cramer decided to go to the police. Surely, *they* would be able to force Blanche Douglass and the Malleys to produce his daughter. But the detective he wanted to see had gone home for the night, and Cramer didn't feel comfortable telling anyone else about the situation.

Jennie didn't come home on Thursday night, either, so early Friday morning he went back to the police station to talk to his friend, Detective James Brewer. Unfortunately, Brewer told him, he couldn't do anything about it: the law stated that this kind of thing had to go through the chief of police. Brewer ushered Jacob Cramer into the office of chief Webster and Cramer told his story once again.

"How old is your daughter?" Chief Webster asked.

"She's twenty-one," Jacob Cramer told him.

"Well, she's old enough to be away from her parents' home, then," Webster said. "I'm sure she's fine and will turn up soon."

Discouraged, Jacob Cramer went back home, his last hope shattered.

This was the story he now related to the men in the boathouse. And he had brought with him two letters that his wife had received from James Malley and Blanche Douglass concerning Jennie's disappearance.[17] He handed them over to Deputy Sheriff Peck, who read them to the group:

New Haven, Conn., 1881

Mrs. Cramer:
  Dear Madam:
As promised, I called on Miss Douglass to learn if she knew anything about your daughter, Jennie. She informed me that she did not know where she was or where she had gone to, and feels very much hurt that you should blame her for any of Jennie's do-

ings. As you say she had no means to leave town with, it is my belief that she is stopping with some of her friends, and trust she is home by this time.

Yours, etc.

J. Malley, jr.

New Haven, Aug. 3, 1881

Mrs. Cramer:

Dear Madam—

It has pained me exceedingly to learn from Mr. James Malley that you were under the impression that your daughter Jennie was with me. I thought when I requested her to remain over night with me that I was doing her a favor and a kindness, but it has turned out otherwise. This morning when you left the room she started up immediately and wished me to follow her. I refused to go till you returned, feeling you would blame me further. After Jennie had left the room some ten minutes, not seeing you, I left. Since that time I have not seen her, except that I think I saw her in a horse-car going toward Savin Rock. She mentioned yesterday that she thought of going to her brother, who lived in New York, soon. When you called at hotel today I was at dressmaker's, and was unable to tell you this much in person. If I should by any chance see her I shall deem it my duty to acquaint you immediately.

Very truly yours,

Blanche Douglass

After Peck finished reading, the men were silent. Then Justice Metcalf asked Jacob Cramer if his daughter had been in good health on Thursday. When the father answered that she had been, Metcalf asked him what he thought might have caused her death.

"I am sure I don't know," Cramer said with great agitation. "I suppose that when Mrs. Cramer scolded her for remaining away overnight she thought she couldn't return without being blamed again, and so took it to heart and drowned herself."[18]

It was what they had thought themselves, and so they put on the death certificate "death by drowning." They were about to conclude the whole matter right there and let Undertaker Stahl take the body back to the mortuary, when Dr. Painter made the suggestion that they should take a closer look before sending the body away. It wouldn't hurt, he said, and there were enough indications that the girl hadn't really drowned at all.[19]

Dr. Shepard performed an examination of the body there in the boathouse, with Dr. Painter assisting. What they found shocked them: Jennie Cramer had lost her virginity within 24–48 hours of her death. Not only had the hymen been only recently perforated, showing ragged sections, but the fourchette was torn. The fourchette, the tough tendon closest to the vaginal entrance, is never torn except under great force and with great pain to the woman. It is not even torn during childbirth, and therefore it must have been done against her will. Jennie Cramer had been raped. [20]

An inquest hearing was set for Monday. It was time to talk to the Malley boys and Blanche Douglass.

Chapter 13

JENNIE, JIMMY, WALL, AND BLANCHE

Well now, let me ask you:
If all of the children, born here in Spoon River
Had been reared by the County, somewhere on a farm;
And the fathers and mothers had been given their freedom
To live and enjoy, change mates if they wished,
Do you think that Spoon River
Had been any the worse?

—Edgar Lee Masters, "Mrs. Williams,"
Spoon River Anthology

Jennie Cramer's beauty was so pronounced and so universally acclaimed that she was known as "the Belle of New Haven," a title that rankled young women of the social classes above her.[1] She was petite, with luxuriant dark brown hair and dark blue eyes that snapped with a love of life and fun. But her most noticeable, her most recognizable characteristic was her complexion, so pale and so soft as to seem to consist of alabaster.[2]

Mrs. Cramer was very much aware that her daughter's beauty might well be her ticket to a higher class, and so she took great pains to highlight it and show it off.[3] Unfortunately, Mrs. Cramer's eagerness sometimes got in the way of her good sense.

Jennie was taken out of school when she was about fifteen, and from that time until her death at age twenty-one did absolutely nothing but attend to her appearance and her social life. She did no housework and did not help out in the cigar store, as her brother Eddie had had to do from the time he was nine.[4] Her parents indulged her love of fine clothes, and Jennie probably had more in this line than most other girls of her class.

Part of Jennie's indolence, at least in the beginning, was due to an unspecified illness, which may have been primary amenorrhea (failure to begin her menstrual period) caused by anemia. She was weak and tired much of the time, and her parents encouraged her to take it easy.

Mrs. Cramer made sure that Jennie was seen at New Haven's German balls and picnics, and encouraged her to talk with the young men there. The girl would go out for walks around New Haven, in the company of her mother or her sister, in order to be noticed by those outside the German enclave.

And notice they did. Yale students, clerks, butchers, and merchants—all flocked around Jennie and eagerly sought her attention. She loved it, and her mother did nothing to discourage it. However, she kept a watchful eye on the *kinds* of suitors her daughter had, putting an end to a relationship Jennie had with a barber because his occupation wasn't good enough.[5]

As Jennie got older, the indulgence and pampering of her parents combined with the flattering accolades of the young men of New Haven made her more daring. She didn't always wait for a formal introduction to a young man before talking to him, sometimes putting herself in what was at that time considered a compromising situation. And she developed a taste for wine.[6]

Jennie loved having a good time and often exceeded the bounds of decorous behavior for young ladies of the Victorian era. After her death, the papers noted that she was a "hoodlum," a "rowdy," and had been noticed by the police for this. Put in today's terms, this probably meant that she hung out with other young people and engaged in loud, boisterous activities, fueled by the wine she loved so much. She was also criticized for socializing with people "of questionable character."[7]

Yet, for all her imprudence, for all her flirting and accepting of gifts and not waiting for proper introductions, Jennie seemed to draw the line at sexual freedom. Although she often gave the *appearance* of being loose and "easy," and possibly attracted many young men in this way as well as through her beauty, she never compromised her virginity. Possibly, she was holding out for the right kind of marriage and did not want to jeopardize it by an act of indiscretion.

During the last year of Jennie's life, she was able to go out without her mother or her sister, and she found this freedom heady indeed. Now the inhibitions of home began to rankle: constant questions about where she was going and with whom and how long she would be there. She was tired of it, she told one suitor, and was secretly saving money to go to New York City to live. She even showed him where she was hiding it: in the recess of a table whose top slid off.[8] That Jennie got this money from her parents and her brother, and that she had never held a job in her life does not seem to have entered into her calculations as to how she would support herself in New York.

When young men called on Jennie at her home, she answered the door herself. Sometimes her mother was not even aware that company was in the house. Mrs. Cramer would later claim that she and her husband stayed awake until Jennie's company left, but it seemed that often they fell asleep as the suitors routinely stayed past 10:00 P.M.[9] Although nothing untoward ever happened, it gave evidence of a laxness and a carelessness on the part of the Cramers as well as the *appearance* of impropriety.

Jennie's lack of education and her neglect of any kind of intellectual activity after leaving school made her a poor conversationalist.[10] For many young men smitten with her beauty, this would not matter, but it was probably a hindrance to her retaining the attentions of the Yale students who sought her company. Her interests were narrow, vapid, and shallow. The beauty could only go so far.

But for all her faults, Jennie Cramer was the light of her family's life. Always cheerful and sunny, she frequently sang around the house. She spent time with her little sister Minnie. Her brother Eddie adored her and gave her money for clothes and social outings. They all seemed to enjoy pampering her and seeing her dressed well.[11]

Eddie kept an eye out for his sister, knowing her somewhat free and trusting disposition and also knowing the ways of young men. When he was getting ready to move to New York in May of 1881, he took her aside and gave her a brotherly lecture. If anyone ever took advantage of her, he told her, she was to notify him immediately, and he would take care of the young man responsible. He made her promise she would do this and she assured him she would.[12]

James Malley, Jr., was very much like Jennie in some ways: he liked to party and he liked to dress well. Born in 1859, the year after Eddie Cramer, Jimmy was the fifth child and fourth son, and in 1881 the only boy still living at home. His father, James, Sr., was the older but poorer brother of New Haven's largest taxpayer, Edward Malley, whose department store was incredibly successful.[13]

Although he was considered handsome with his Irish good looks, long eyelashes, freckles, and sandy mustache, Jimmy Malley was exceptionally short and tended to be stocky. He was also cursed with a stuttering problem.[14]

Jimmy was a sales clerk in his uncle's store, working behind the gentleman's clothing counter. Like Jennie, he had left school at an early age, but unlike her, he had done so to go to work. Although he still lived at home with his father (his mother had been dead for about sixteen years) and his three sisters, he was able to come and go as he pleased, sometimes not coming home at all.[15]

An energetic, lively, quick-witted young man, Jimmy was popular with almost everyone. But his most frequent companion in 1881 was his cousin, Walter, only child of Edward Malley. They were definitely an "odd couple": Walter (or "Wall" as he was called by those close to him) was college-educated, wealthy, and Jim's supervisor at the Malley Department Store. In personality, he was stiff, reserved, and humorless.[16]

For both boys, the alliance was advantageous: Walter supplied the money and Jimmy supplied the fun; and Walter became more social under his cousin's tutelage. Because of their family relationship and their companionship, most people assumed that Jimmy was as rich as Walter. However, although Jim dressed well, his family had no horse or carriage and they lived in no mansion as Edward and Walter did.[17]

Jimmy was not ambitious like his brother Andrew, a successful physician in Wilkes-Barre, Pennsylvania, or his brother Edward, a medical student, nor even like his cousin Walter, who was being groomed to take over the Malley empire. Instead, he lived for fun and pleasure. As the only boy at home, he was spoiled by his sisters, who waited on him hand and foot, and was allowed great leniency by his father, James, Sr., a somewhat passive and ineffective individual.

Jim's cousin, Walter Edward Malley, was quite different. Born in 1856, Walter was slightly older than his cousin, and the only child of Edward and Mary Ward Malley. His slight, almost effeminate build and his predilection for art and music, coupled with a disdain of sports and male camaraderie, frequently incurred his father's ridicule. As a result, Walter became a "mama's boy."[18]

Edward Malley could not believe that the only son of his loins should be such a pantywaist. Walter would sit around the house reading, or playing the piano, or drawing, and this would make Edward's blood boil. "Go play ball or ride a horse or *something!*" he would bellow in frustration. "Get out of the house and get moving!"[19]

To add fuel to the fire, Walter seemed totally disinterested in girls as he moved through his early manhood, almost never going out on what could be called a real date.

Walter must have suffered a great deal from his failure to earn his father's approval, and as a result he did his best to try to please him. He enrolled in Seton Hall College in New Jersey in 1873, where his cousin Andrew had gone to school, but spent all his time in the music room or in painting and drawing instead of at his studies.[20]

Walter's aesthetic bent is also shown in his formation of a secret society at Seton Hall called the M.F.S., or Merry Few Society. It was made up of other young men who enjoyed fine music and reading and cultural pursuits. They put together music and literary programs, which they then performed for other students. Several of these young men went on to become Catholic priests, and the reclusive Walter had probably given the monastic life more than a passing thought himself.

A student who was at Seton Hall at the same time said Walter was so shy and retiring that he had almost no friends. He had a lot of spending money from home, but was very careful how he spent it.

Walter left Seton Hall in 1874, having received no degree and no distinction other than the Silver Medal for Proficiency in Drawing.[21] Edward must have been furious.

A few years after this, Walter once more tried his hand at education, this time at Yale's Sheffield Scientific School in a curriculum that was far afield of his natural inclinations. He was there during the time of the Hayden trial and went to the courtroom on a school "field trip" during some of the arsenic testimony.[22] But he left Yale in 1880, still without a diploma.[23]

If Walter was a failure as a man's man in his father's eyes, however, he more than lived up to Edward's expectations as a businessman. He was conscientious, responsible, and had an eye for improvement and expansion, as well as for saving money. Edward had no qualms about placing him in charge of the store when he was away on business, and even gave him the duty of writing checks. At the age of twenty-five, Walter's position at the Edward Malley Company was equal to that of his fifty-year-old uncle, James Malley, Sr.[24]

In May 1880, Walter received a terrible blow from the sudden and somewhat mysterious death of his mother at the relatively young age of fifty. She had been his lifeline, his buffer zone between him and his father, and he felt her loss deeply. She left him $25,000 in her will so that he would not have to be completely dependent on Edward Malley.[25]

It was shortly after this that Walter began hanging out with his fun-loving cousin, Jimmy, and also began making frequent trips to New York City. It was there that he met Blanche Douglass.

Blanche Douglass was not her real name. It was Anna ("Annie") Kearns, and she had been born around 1860 of immigrant Irish parents in New York City. Annie spent her formative years in the Bowery and in what is today the upscale, trendy SoHo district. Her father, Frank, was a peddler and her mother, Ellen, made wax flowers. Annie had almost no education, as she had to work at a very early age, and by 1881 she was only barely literate.[26]

Frank Kearns died of unspecified causes in an insane asylum when Annie was about four, and her mother then married a man named Matthew Hines, of various occupational pursuits. Hines had been blinded by a chiseling accident, and his little stepdaughter guided him around the streets of the Bowery. But Hines was not a good provider and, according to Annie, was abusive.

Ellen Hines died of cirrhosis of the liver on March 22, 1877, and that December Annie married John Zimmermann (who may have been related to her, as their mothers were both Kerrigans). Their daughter, Kate, was born ten months later, but she died of pneumonia just two months shy of her second birthday.[27]

Annie's married life was no better than it had been with her stepfather: John beat her so badly on several occasions that she had to escape him if she wanted to live. With nowhere to go, she ended up in a house of prostitution, a place called Lizzie Bundy's in New York City. Two weeks after she arrived there, she met Walter Malley.[28]

Walter, who had always had his problems with women and was not even sure he liked them all that much, had been introduced to Lizzie Bundy's by a Seton Hall chum, John Duff, son of a New York theatrical agent. Duff took Walter under his wing to loosen him up and cure his virginity problem, and they frequently visited Lizzie Bundy's house.

Walter had plenty of money to spend and he felt freer with women he could control, women he could feel superior to. Women in his own class were intimidating, especially those who were well-educated, but the girls at Lizzie Bundy's suited him just fine. He never told them his real name, though: he always introduced himself as Walter Haviland of New Haven.[29]

But when he met Anna Kearns, or Annie Blanche Clements, or Blanche Douglass, as she was variously calling herself, Walter fell in love for the first time in his life. Annie seemed to possess the qualities of two extremes—the madonna and the whore—and Walter found both very appealing. She had a worldly, survivor aura about her, yet she had not been on the street long enough to have lost her natural vulnerability.

Annie had a round Irish face and lively eyes. She was short and tended to be chunky, but Walter liked that. And she was a project, someone he could play Pygmalion with. He intended to make her over completely and turn her into a real lady. He wanted to introduce her to reading, writing, and culture. He wanted to slip her into his own society back in New Haven in such a way that she would be accepted. He wanted to marry her if he could get away with it.

Once Walter met Annie, she became his focus. He spent two or three nights a week with her, and the rest of the time wrote letters and telegrams. ("It was all the time telegrams and telegrams and letters," said Lizzie Bundy in an interview.[30]) He got a box at the New Haven post office so his father wouldn't find out about his serious relationship with a prostitute from New York. And he told her his real name.

Blanche, as she preferred to be called in her new life, resisted most of Walter's pleas to visit him in New Haven, feeling instinctively that she would be out of place in his world. ("We'll get into some kind of scrape," she told him vaguely.[31]) But once when Edward Malley was out of town, she gave in and went up on the boat with him. Walter bribed the Malley housekeeper for the key to areas of the house normally kept locked, and proudly showed Blanche the whole mansion. She had known he was rich before, but when she actually saw the evidence of it, she was overwhelmed.[32]

Jimmy Malley was also a frequenter of Lizzie Bundy's, going down with John Duff and Walter on occasion. He, too, became friendly with Blanche Douglass, although it is not known if he ever paid for her services.

It was around this time that Jim became infatuated with the Belle of New Haven, Jennie Cramer. He had, of course, noticed her around town—as who had not?—and had even been introduced to her in the spring of 1880. But at that time she was being courted (although not too seriously) by a fellow employee at Malley's, George Higgins, and Jim did not pursue it.[33]

Jennie had flirted with him even then, and once they had walked across the New Haven Green and sat talking for a half-hour on one of the benches there. He asked if he might call on her, and she coyly told him she had so many callers that it would be best to send advance notice before coming over. After that, she came to his counter at Malley's a couple of times, pretending to have lost George Higgins' new address in Forestville. And once she pointed him out to her mother on a trip to the Malley store.

But when Jimmy asked Jennie to go riding with him in July 1881, she turned him down. She must have known that he was not to be trusted because she told him she would only go if another lady were present. According to Mrs. Cramer, Jennie thought that Jim would try to "get the best of her" and felt she needed a chaperone if she were to go with him.[34] On Jim's part, he felt sure that Jennie could be easily conquered in the long run. He just had to find the right formula.

That Jennie was right in her instincts was demonstrated by the events that followed. Together, Jim and Wall concocted a plan that would help them both out: they would get Blanche to pose as their rich cousin and Walter's fiancée and they could then double-date. This would serve the two-fold purpose of getting Blanche to New Haven, which is what Walter wanted, and lulling Jennie into a false sense of security, which is what Jim wanted.

At first, Jimmy approached Jennie and asked if she would be willing to "receive and entertain" his and Walter's rich cousin from Flushing, Long Island, who was also Walter's fiancée. This meant that Jennie would be responsible for hosting parties and suppers for Blanche, to which other young people would be invited to meet her. But when Jennie asked her mother about it, Mrs. Cramer told her to tell James Malley that she had neither the money nor the time to do this.

On Saturday, July 23, Jennie received a note from Jim, brought by one of Malley's cash girls and on Malley Company stationery. After apologizing for the short notice, he invited her to go with him and Walter and Walter's friend to Coney Island and stay over until Monday. It was a bold invitation for a first date! Jennie refused because of the short notice, but mostly because she didn't have any clothes ready. She doesn't seem to have had any qualms about an overnight stay with a boy she hardly knew.

Shortly after this, while Edward Malley was away in Maine, Jim showed up at Jennie's in a carriage with John Duff and a divorcée named Lotte Brown. They were on their way to Branford Point Hotel for a shore supper and would be joining Walter and Blanche. Could she join them? Mrs. Cramer at first said "no," but Jennie begged and pleaded and she finally gave in.[35]

This was the first time Jennie met Blanche Douglass, and she was not impressed. She told her mother the next day that she seemed "haughty and diffident," which was probably the result of Blanche's discomfort in her new role as debutante. (After seeing her a few more times, Jennie amended her impression: Blanche was much too bold to be considered completely ladylike.) And she complained that James Malley had made improper advances.[36]

There were other invitations, some of which Jennie accepted. For others she was either genuinely busy or she lied to avoid them. But it wasn't easy to lie to Jim, as Jennie once told her mother: "I won't deceive him, Mother, for he cross-examines me until he finds out the truth."[37]

The next outing was on Thursday, July 28, when Jim called at the house to take Jennie to Buell's, another popular shore resort, once again to meet Walter and Blanche. This time Jennie didn't get home until 4:00 A.M., and Christina Cramer was beside herself.

"Where have you been until this hour?" she asked her daughter.

"I'm tired and I don't want to talk about it right now," Jennie answered, and went up to bed.

The next day Jennie told her mother that they had gone back to the Malley mansion and talked until Jennie got up to leave. Then the other three tried to pressure her to stay all night (Edward being away again).

As Jennie told the story, she resisted their importunities and headed for the door. "If you don't take me home," she told Jimmy, "I'll go myself. When I meet a policeman, I'll ask him to escort me."

"Why do you want to leave?" Jim asked her.

"Because I don't feel I can trust my body with you," Jennie told him.

Jimmy laughed at her. "You're nothing but an innocent child," he told her. But he relented and walked her home.[38] As it turned out, there would be more than one version of this event.

After this incident, Jennie heard nothing from the other three until Wednesday, August 3. She got dressed up in her finest white outfit and new kid boots and told her mother she was going to the Elliott House to see Blanche. Blanche had lost a handkerchief the last time she was with her, and had subtly insinuated that Jennie had stolen it. Jennie resented the implication, she told her mother, and wanted to see if the handkerchief had ever turned up. It seemed a flimsy excuse to go see someone she had reason never to want to see again.

Jennie didn't know it, but Blanche had written her a letter inviting her to spend the evening with her and the boys at the Malley mansion. The letter arrived after Jennie was on her way to the Elliott Hotel, and had been—of course—written at the behest of Jim. (Edward Malley was away once more, this time in Saratoga until Saturday.)

When Jennie arrived at Blanche's room, Jimmy was already there. He repeated the invitation to the Malley house, and Jennie said she didn't mind going. If she were as bothered by his advances as she had told her mother she was, it was a strange choice for her to make. But possibly she had trust in her ability to fend him off, and possibly she still had trust in Blanche Douglass.

It was a trust that was grossly misplaced in both.

Chapter 14

BOYS WILL BE BOYS

Very well, you liberals,
And navigators into realms intellectual,
You sailors through heights imaginative . . .
You found with all your boasted wisdom
How hard at the last it is
To keep the soul from splitting into cellular atoms.
While we, seekers of earth's treasures,
Getters and hoarders of gold,
Are self-contained, compact, harmonized,
Even to the end.

—Edgar Lee Masters, "Thomas Rhodes,"
Spoon River Anthology

Not again! the newspapers cried. Not another Mary Stannard case! With the third mysterious death of a young woman in as many years (including the Abby Riddle poisoning of 1879), what would people think of Connecticut?[1] But the new case would occupy center stage in the minds and talk of New Havenites and rival the presidential health bulletins for space on the front page.

Even before Jennie Cramer's body had arrived at the funeral home of Stahl and Hegel and placed in a refrigerated room to await an autopsy, eager newspaper reporters and detectives, both self-styled and legitimate, were busy unearthing the mystery of her death. It was part of the duty of inquest jurors in Connecticut to investigate, and several of the six newly appointed Orange citizens did just that. (West Haven was a section of the Town of Orange until 1921, when it became a separate municipality.) So by Saturday evening, there was a great flurry of investigative activity in the New Haven area. Even a distraught Mrs. Cramer was sought out by at least two rival newspapers, whom she graciously obliged by granting interviews after much pressing on their parts.[2]

An enterprising reporter from the New Haven *Union*, William Countryman, hastened to the Malley Company to talk to James Malley, Jr., who had been named as Jennie's Wednesday night date.

"Have you heard that Jennie Cramer drowned?" the reporter asked him.

"Yes," James replied. "Where was she found? Off President Hinman's?"

"No," said Countryman, somewhat startled. He hadn't heard any controversy about where the body was found. "It was in front of Hill's. You knew the girl, didn't you?"

"No, I didn't," Jimmy told him.

"Are you sure about that?" Countryman persisted.

"Well," Jimmy hesitated. "I knew her to look at. I've seen her around."

"Did you ever visit her or write her letters?"

"No, definitely not."

"But letters have been found in her belongings with your name on them."

"I can't help that," young Malley said. "I didn't write any. And don't you go mentioning my name in your paper in any connection with this affair."[3]

Jimmy's decision to deny facts that could most certainly be proved against him did nothing to help his case. And when Sheriff Peck later came to question him about the last time he saw Jennie, he said he really couldn't remember.

But Walter, overhearing him, prompted him out of his paralysis: "Why, yes, you saw her Thursday morning at the Elliott House."

"Oh, so I did," Jim assented.[4]

It was obvious from this that the Malley party line would be that the girls had not been in the Malley house on Wednesday night. Walter wanted to keep this from his father if at all possible.

In the meantime, reporters converged on Blanche Douglass, who was supposed to have been the last person to see Jennie alive as far as anyone knew for sure. She repeated what she had told Mrs. Cramer: the last she saw of Jennie was at noon on Thursday as the dead girl was getting on a Savin Rock horse-car. Sheriff Peck had no luck with Blanche, either. "I am unable to explain to you," he told reporters later, "the way in which she backed and filled."[5]

Walter, James, and Blanche all insisted that they had not seen Jennie after Thursday noon, and swore they had not been at Savin Rock on Friday night. But little by little, as the story spread around town and in the newspapers, people were coming forward who knew either Jim or Jennie or both and claimed to have seen them together on Thursday and Friday in New Haven, and on Friday evening at Savin Rock. And there were several reliable witnesses who had seen Jennie and Blanche together *after* noon on Thursday, into that night, and at Savin Rock on Friday. The girls had also been seen leaving the Malley mansion on Thursday morning in what was to be one of the very few undisputed sightings.[6]

Edward Malley arrived home that Saturday to be faced with the fact that his son and his nephew, both employees of his store, were being mentioned in conjunction with the tragic death of Jennie Cramer. One can only imagine his interview with Walter.

But Edward Malley lost no time in shoring up a bulwark to protect the family name and the family business. Although no arrests had been made, he immediately hired two highly esteemed lawyers, ex-Judge Levi N. Blydenburgh and former prosecutor Timothy J. Fox, to represent the Malley boys and Blanche Douglass. Then he hired two private detectives to hunt down all available witnesses and clues.[7]

Edward Malley had a reputation in New Haven for shrewd dealings and "always having a sharp eye out for business." He had arrived there in 1855 from New York City with only $240 in his pocket, having come from Ireland in 1847 (where he was born "O'Malley" but later changed it to the more W.A.S.P.-ish "Malley"). From such modest beginnings he had built a clothing empire throughout New England around the flagship store in New Haven.[8]

Edward Malley was always dapper and debonaire, with his white top hat, a flower in his lapel, and an Oscar Wilde hairstyle. Every year he gave large, catered parties for his buyers and sent gifts of game and produce to the newspaper editors.[9] And he was very loyal to his family and his native country: almost all of his employees were either family members or Irishmen.

But there was a limit to loyalty and that limit was profit. The year before the Jennie Cramer tragedy, Malley had had his own brother arrested, and William Malley was still languishing in the same jail where his two nephews would soon reside.[10]

William Malley was in charge of the Malley store in Ansonia. Edward claimed his brother was embezzling from him, so he had him thrown in jail for fraud in a sort of debtor's prison arrangement. To complicate matters, William could not plead poverty and be released without bail because in 1879 Edward had borrowed $20,000 from him! William's holding of Edward's note, even though none of it had been paid, prevented William from being declared a legal pauper.

Around the same time, and probably connected with that incident, Edward Malley was having financial difficulties and needed to hide some of his assets from his creditors. He transferred $25,000 to his wife, Mary, but when the financial crisis was over, she refused to give it back to him. Legally it was hers because he had put it in her name, so there was nothing he could do about it.

But Mary Malley had long been unhappy in her marriage, and this was not only a way of getting back at her husband, but a way to ensure that her son, Walter, would not have to be dependent on his father. She knew how vindictive Edward could be and how displeased he often was with the boy.[11]

Suddenly, Mary Malley found herself stricken with severe stomach cramps and vomiting. She began wasting away until she was sent to the south to recuperate, probably on her doctor's orders. She was gone for a few months and, when she got better, returned to New Haven in February 1880. But soon she began to get sick again, and died on May 9 of that year. The cause of death is listed as chronic gastritis, an illness which shares its symptoms with arsenical poisoning.[12]

Did Edward Malley poison his wife for her disobedience, for her defiance of his authority? No autopsy was ever done, so it can never be known for sure. However, it is known that the Malleys were constantly buying arsenic for rat control in the several stores they owned. Walter himself was sent to the drugstore to buy four ounces of it five months after his mother's death.[13]

When he was interviewed about the Jennie Cramer matter, Edward Malley was outwardly congenial with reporters and scoffing of the evidence against Walter and James. He denied that he had hired any detectives; there was no case, so why hire detectives? A lot of the talk, he claimed, came from his competitors who wanted to put him out of business. On the contrary, the tragedy had been terrific for business, with people coming from all over to shop in his store. In fact, business had never been so good.[14]

As for the alleged events in his house Wednesday night or Walter's trips to New York City, he was certain none of these had occurred. Walter with a girl? Why, it was such a rare occasion that even the milkman said he had never seen Walter with a girl before he saw him riding out to Branford Point with Blanche on Friday. But, then again, Malley said with a sly wink at the reporter, "Boys will be boys. And you'll find that's all there is to the matter."[15]

That Saturday night people flocked in droves to the murder site, walking up and down the beach looking for clues and speculating on what might have happened. Conspicuous among these were Eddie Cramer, who carried a photograph of his sister and was trying to find someone who might have seen her on Thursday or Friday, and Blanche Douglass, who (according to a horse-car conductor) was seen walking on the beach with a man.[16]

After the Cramer story appeared in the newspaper, the Elliott House, whose name had been besmirched in connection with the sordid affair, asked Blanche to leave.[17] On Sunday, in her new hotel, the Austin House, there was a meeting of Blanche, Walter, Jimmy, John Duff, and ex-Judge Blydenburgh, who would be acting as Blanche's attorney at the next day's hearing. Their main goal was to coach Blanche as to the story about her background, where she lived, and how she had met Walter. Walter did *not* want her real occupation or residence to come out.[18]

They tried out a couple of stories, but Blydenburgh didn't think they rang true. (As in the Hayden case, the attitude of attorneys toward perjury seemed to be that it was all right if it wasn't material to the issues.) Finally, they agreed on one version and set out to make Blanche memorize it. She had such a hard time remembering her "new" address, 231 East 34th Street, that Walter finally wrote it on the corner of a handkerchief for her to hold on the witness stand. Other prompts were written there as well.[19]

Unfortunately, when she was first approached by reporters on Saturday, Blanche had already given a different address, and when it was printed in the New Haven paper, a New York *Tribune* reporter went to 175 Spring Street to get an interview with someone who knew Blanche. A very surprised Andrew Roth, a gentleman above reproach who had lived there since 1865, declared he had never even heard of Blanche Douglass. No young woman had *ever* stayed there.[20]

On Monday, at Stahl and Hegel's Funeral Home, Jennie's body was removed from the refrigeration unit and the physicians who would be performing and assisting at the autopsy gathered: Dr. T. Mitchell Prudden of the College of Physicians and Surgeons in New York City; Dr. William Hotchkiss, who had testified for the State in the Hayden trial; Drs. Shepard and Painter of the coroner's jury; Dr. Cortlandt Van Rensselaer Creed; and Dr. Frederick Bellosa, a local physician. (Another doctor, when approached to be on the team, said he didn't have time because he thought the case would last as long as the Hayden trial.[21] He was right.)

The autopsy took nearly seven hours. After the examination was complete, various organs were put in glass jars for further examination (as had been done with Mary Stannard): pancreas, spleen, liver, heart, lungs, stomach, windpipe, intestines, ovaries, vagina, uterus, tongue, brain, and esophagus. Dr. Prudden also removed the lip and placed it in a separate jar, hoping he could discover what had caused the cut on it.[22]

The autopsy took so long that Jennie's funeral had to be delayed. Finally, the few segments of the body that had not been put in jars were placed in a plain rosewood coffin with silver handles and a silver plate across the top: "Jennie E. Cramer, Age 21 years and 3 months." The coffin was then carried to the Cramer home for the simple service and after that to Evergreen Cemetery.[23]

The results of the autopsy shed little light on the cause of death:

- No marks of violence over general surface of body.

- Numerous small abrasions and scratches over face.

- Two irregular wounds on lower lip. (This and the preceding wounds were thought to have been inflicted post-mortem.)

- Considerable congestion of the membranes of the brain; brain otherwise normal.

- Heart healthy and contained very little blood.

- Lungs healthy and contained no water; fairly well filled with air.

- Small quantity of reddish fluid in both pleural cavities.

- Stomach healthy and contained no water. Small quantity of partially-digested food taken within 8 hours of death: huckleberries, lean and fat meat, and mushrooms.

- Intestines healthy.

- Uterus bent forward and to one side.

- Small cystic tumor on right ovary. (This was something else Jennie Cramer shared with Mary Stannard.)

- Could not draw conclusions about violence re: generative organs because of advanced state of decomposition.

- Conclusion: cause of death not determined by post-mortem examination.[24]

Because of the absence of water in the lungs and stomach, the physicians tended to rule out death by drowning. And because it was known that Dr. Prudden had placed the internal organs in glass jars, word quickly spread that they would be looking for poison and drugs.

At this point the most popular theory was that Jennie had been drugged in order to be seduced and that the laudanum or chloroform had killed her. After her seducer discovered she was dead, he put her in the water and hoped everyone would assume she had drowned.[25]

On Monday morning a large crowd gathered outside Thompson's Hall in the town of Orange where the inquest hearing was to take place. The jury had decided to accommodate as many people as possible, and so had arranged for the large hall to be used. Newspapers likened the excitement to that of the Hayden case. They also cheerfully reported the record sale of papers.[26]

James and Walter drove to the hearing together, accompanied by their cousin Michael (son of the incarcerated William, and an executive at the Malley Company) and a host of friends and relatives. Judge Blydenburgh had driven "the fair Blanche" (as she was sarcastically referred to by reporters even before her true occupation was revealed) in a carriage owned by Edward Malley. Timothy Fox arrived on his own.[27]

After great discussion and argument, it was finally decided to let the attorneys sit in and listen to the proceedings, but they were not to ask questions or make any statements. It was considered an ex parte rather than an adversarial proceeding and nobody had been arrested at that time. In order to ensure that the questioning was done correctly, Justice Metcalf had hired a lawyer, Charles Bollman. The inquest jurors themselves would also be asking questions, some of them suggested by the State and defense attorneys. Then, somewhat anticlimactically, the hearing was postponed until the following day.

On, Tuesday August, 9 the three principals in the investigation answered questions before the inquest jury but were excluded from hearing each other testify. It probably didn't matter, though, since they had had ample opportunity to rehearse before this.

Blanche took the stand first and gave her name as Annie Blanche Douglass, then recited the story Walter had made up for her: She lived at 231 E. 34th Street in New York City. She had met Walter only a few weeks before, through John Duff, Jr., the theatrical agent, who was a friend of her brother. Blanche said that her parents were dead and she and her brother were well-to-do. Her brother, John, a patent engineer who traveled about the United States for the railroad, wanted her to stay in New Haven and had asked Walter Malley to find her a place to stay while there. Her brother John could not be contacted because he was currently traveling out West and staying in various, unknown hotels.[28]

Blanche talked in such a low voice that it was nearly impossible for her to be heard. Still, the reporters were able to detect a slight Irish brogue. As streetwise as she probably was, Blanche must have felt that she was over her head in this high-stakes game for which she had few skills. When asked when she had met Jennie Cramer and when she had seen her last, Blanche burst into tears. "Oh, I wish my mother was here!" she exclaimed.

She told of meeting Jennie at Buell's for the first time, and how after that Jennie sent her notes wanting to get together. Unfortunately, she had not kept these notes; and, in fact, no one believed in them, as the evidence did not show any great eagerness on Jennie's part to become intimate with Blanche.

Regarding the night Jennie got in at 4:00 A.M., Blanche said they had gone for a ride to Buell's Restaurant, but they didn't stay there. Jennie wanted to go to another restaurant, which they did; they then got back to the Elliott House around midnight to drink claret. Then she contradicted herself and said they reached Malley's house between 1:00 and 2:00 A.M. and walked down to Redcliffe's.

At Redcliffe's, considered the Delmonico's of New Haven, they took a private sitting room over the restaurant and ordered soda water because Jennie had said she was thirsty. After that, Walter walked Blanche back to the Tontine Hotel where she was staying, and Jimmy walked Jennie to her home.

At the Wednesday night party at the Malleys', Blanche said they sang songs while Walter played the piano. They also had a supper of white wine, bananas, and ice cream (a strange combination!). Around 11:30 P.M. Blanche began to feel quite ill. Jennie got up from where she was sitting next to James and put her arm around her friend in sympathy. Blanche asked Walter if she could stay in one of the Malley guest rooms that night, as she felt too ill to go home, and Walter agreed.

At that point, Jennie felt she should be going home, but Blanche begged her to stay with her: "If you go, I will have to also, and I don't feel well enough to leave." Jennie asked Walter to send for a doctor, but Blanche said it was too late in the evening for that. Finally, reluctantly, Jennie agreed to stay. Jennie and Blanche occupied one room, and Walter and James another.

In the morning, the two girls went to Redcliffe's for breakfast: double Porterhouse steaks, mushrooms, potatoes, and milk. (Someone noted that it was hearty fare for someone who had been so sick the night before.[29]) While they were eating, Jennie begged Blanche to accompany her home and tell her mother that they had spent the night at the Elliott House because of Blanche's illness. Blanche claimed that she was reluctant to tell Mrs. Cramer a lie, but Jennie insisted: if her father found out the truth, she said, he would kill her. He once dragged her around the house by her hair when he was upset with her, and this was a far more serious incident. (When Blanche testified to this violence on the part of Jacob Cramer, one reporter said the audience moved around in their chairs as if they didn't believe it.[30])

The girls reached the Cramer home about 11:00 that morning. When Mrs. Cramer came into the room where Blanche was sitting, she began yelling at Jennie about being out all night. She called Jennie a bad girl and said she had been out that way three or four times before. Mrs. Cramer said Jennie would have to leave the house, then went out in a rage to find her husband.

At this point, Blanche claimed, Jennie got up and said, "Let's go. My father will kill me when he gets back." But the ever-honorable Blanche wanted to stay behind to make sure that Mrs. Cramer was clear on what had happened Wednesday night: Jennie had stayed with *her* at the Elliott House, not with James Malley. Jennie left first, and Blanche followed ten minutes later when Mrs. Cramer did not return to the parlor.

From the Cramer home, Blanche said, she took a horse-car to her dressmaker's. Around noon she saw Jennie on a horse-car headed for Savin Rock, but Blanche hid her face so Jennie wouldn't see her and want to come with her. Blanche felt she was in enough trouble with the Cramers and didn't want to be blamed for anything more.

After leaving the dressmaker that Thursday, Blanche said she met Walter Malley on the street at 12:30 and told him of the trouble at the Cramers'. They went to her hotel together. When asked how she could have seen Jennie on a streetcar at noon, gone to her dressmaker's, and been back at her hotel by 12:30, Blanche amended her story and said maybe it was 1:00 when she had seen Walter.

Blanche also told about a man in a flannel shirt who had come to her hotel room on Thursday to get some information for the coroner. He told her of Jennie's death. How could that have happened on Thursday, when Jennie wasn't found until Saturday? she was asked. But Blanche insisted several times that she was positive it was Thursday; then she said, no, it was Friday; then that it was Saturday because she got her dress that day. (The man turned out to be a reporter who had come by on Saturday and used the coroner ruse to get information.[31])

All in all, Blanche's testimony did not come off well because there were so many contradictions and inconsistencies in her statement. She was on the stand for four hours, and during that time was asked many things that could not have fit on the little handkerchief she was holding, even if they could have been anticipated.

James Malley was the next to take the stand.[32] His attorney, Timothy Fox, told the jury that his client had a speech impediment and that they would be better off if they didn't hurry him. Jimmy told basically the same story about Wednesday night as Blanche had, and swore that the last time he saw Jennie was on Thursday morning about 8:00 as the girls walked across the lawn to the street. One of the girls waved her hand, but Jim couldn't tell which one.

Why couldn't Jim or Walter have taken Blanche to her hotel in a carriage? they asked him. First he said there were no carriages, then said it was a long way to get one. Miss Douglass was getting too sick to go for one. Why weren't the girls invited for breakfast the next day? Why did they have to go to Redcliffe's? Jim didn't know: it wasn't his house and therefore not up to him to ask them to stay.

Jimmy first heard of the death of Jennie Cramer around noon on Saturday from a fellow employee, Patrick "Patsy" Carroll. He told him he didn't believe it, and went to find Walter.[33] He and Walter got in a carriage and drove past the Cramer house on Grand Street to see if there was mourning crepe on the door. There was none. When they came back into town, they happened to see Blanche near the Green. All three took a long walk to discuss the news.

Jimmy stated that on the Friday night when it was thought Jennie died, he was at home. When asked whether all the members of his family had seen him there, he made a curious misstatement: "Yes, sir. My father came to me after the newspaper reports were concluded and asked me where I was Friday night. No, he came to me and said, 'It's a lucky thing for you that you were home Friday night.' " Jimmy claimed to have retired at the unusually early (for him) hour of 9:00 that night.

Interestingly enough, however, when Dr. Painter asked Jimmy how he thought Jennie had died, he said he didn't know, but that he was certain it wasn't suicide: it wasn't in her nature.

Walter's testimony was basically the same, but he did add a few details.[34] He told of meeting Blanche Douglass through his old Seton Hall buddy, John Duff, but had to admit that he had never introduced her to his family or friends. Why not? he was asked. Didn't he think she was respectable? No, he assured them, he felt she was perfectly respectable.

On Friday night, August 5, he and Blanche had driven out to Branford Point Hotel for dinner and had gotten back to New Haven at about 11:00 P.M. He took Miss Douglass back to her hotel and then went to his home.

On Thursday, he heard that Jennie and Blanche had gone to New York, and feared that Jennie was going to alarm her brother about the difficulty over staying all night at the Malleys'. He got on the train to intercept them, but got a telegram from Jim saying that Blanche was OK and had been located at her dressmaker's. At this he turned back. Prior to this, however, he had sent a telegram to Jim asking for "Cramer's brother's address in New York."

The reason Walter gave for going after the girls was that "I was afraid that Miss Cramer's mother had driven her out of the house and that we would be exposed for taking them to my father's house." But hadn't he heard from Blanche that Jennie had been seen on the Savin Rock car? Oh, well, he had forgotten about that at the time (which can't have been more than an hour or two before he left for New York).

Walter claimed that he had sent a note to the Cramer house Friday morning and had received a note from Jennie's father saying that the girl was "all right." Needless to say, no note had ever been received by the Cramers nor could Walter produce the one sent in response.

The same day she testified, Blanche Douglass left New Haven and went back to New York City, fully intending to return to the inquest proceedings on the following Tuesday. There was some panic that she had left the state, but there was nothing that could be done: no arrest warrant had been issued.

However, over the next days of testimony, as people began talking about having seen the group of four together or in pairs after Thursday noon, it was realized that perjury had been committed if those witnesses were to be believed. Moreover, a check of the second residence address given by Blanche turned out to be false as well, and some detective work turned up her true abode at Lizzie Bundy's house of ill fame.[35]

The inquest jurors and their attorney, Charles Bollman, probably realized that Blanche Douglass was the weak link in the chain. If they could isolate her from her rich friends, the Malleys, and take her from their influence, they felt they could break her story. Maybe the threat of jail would scare her enough so that she would talk. It was worth a try.

Accordingly, Detective James Brewer of the New Haven police was sent down to New York with an arrest warrant for Blanche on Saturday, August 13. The charge was perjury. When she was arraigned in New York and asked how she would plead to the charges, Blanche burst into tears as she had in New Haven.[36] She had tried to do a favor for Walter and James and maybe make some extra money for herself, and ever since then her life had gotten complicated way beyond her control.

At first, her lawyer, Blydenburgh, wanted to fight extradition, but it was pointed out to him by the New York authorities that it would be granted without trouble.

On top of that, Blanche was eager to return to New Haven. Why? Because Dr. Painter, one of the inquest jurors, had also gone to New York and explained to her that it would be advantageous for her to do so. Edward Malley had offered a $1,000 reward for information leading to conclusive proof as to what or who had caused the death of Jennie Cramer. And the Town of Orange had matched that amount. If Blanche could tell what she knew, she might be eligible for that award. And, Painter hinted, she would probably be immune from prosecution if she cooperated.[37]

But there was something else she would have to do: break off all contact with the Malleys, including the attorney they had hired for her. He worked for the Malleys, not for her, and if she thought for one minute that he would protect her if it came to a conflict between them and her, she was sadly mistaken. She would be the sacrificial lamb, Painter told her. The rich boys would not hesitate to use her to save themselves.

For Blanche's part, she was willing to do this, but most emphatically did *not* want to go to jail. Well, that could be arranged, too, Painter assured her. They would put her up with Sheriff Peck and his family in their home on the shore. Blanche agreed.

Back in New Haven, two very important witnesses testified before the inquest jury: Charles Rawlings, the maître d' of the Redcliffe Restaurant, and John Henry, a waiter. Both remembered Blanche and Jennie's being there for breakfast on Thursday morning and what they ate. Blanche, they said, paid the check, and they still had that check.[38]

Later that night, at about 10:30, Blanche had come in again, with Walter and another lady they were certain was the same one as with Blanche in the morning. They could not be mistaken about Walter, as he was in there often and his father was their landlord. The girl they remembered from the morning was dressed the same way: all in white. The party wanted chicken salad and, when it was discovered there was none left, ordered lamb chops instead.[39]

John Henry had the checks from that night and the one for Walter's party of three was written by Walter himself. After the testimony, Walter and his attorney went to Redcliffe's and demanded that Henry turn over the check. He refused; besides, he had already given it to the sheriff. Next, they pressured him to "remember" that it was a different night he had seen them, or that it was not Walter and two ladies, but Walter and *James* and a lady. Henry wouldn't budge. He knew what he saw. "My God!" cried Walter. "That point has got to be sustained or I am a ruined man!"

James later came in, also with the attorney Fox, and demanded that Henry remember his being there in the party. "Don't you recall my hat was in the way and you stepped on it?" The waiter said he stepped on lots of gentlemen's hats and didn't remember this one in particular. Fox stated calmly that Henry was mistaken as to the night, and that's all there was to it. For Henry's part, he felt he was being bullied to change his testimony.[40]

To counteract this very damaging evidence of Jennie's presence with the other three *after* they claimed to have last seen her, Blydenburgh put an ad in the newspaper asking the party of one man and two ladies who had had supper at Redcliffe's on that Thursday night to come forward. The Hartford *Times* sarcastically commented that Blydenburgh's ad "smells of 'barn arsenic.' "[41]

When Blanche came back to New Haven, she said she would now tell what she knew. She dismissed her attorney, Levi Blydenburgh, and a new one was appointed for her: Edwin C. Dow, a somewhat incompetent man who hadn't become a lawyer until later in life and whose sole achievement so far was getting a law passed for the licensing of dogs. By doing so, he had incurred the wrath of most of the dog owners in New Haven.[42]

The architect of this turnaround on Blanche's part was a New York bartender named James Reilly, who claimed to be merely a friend but who was variously reported to be either her lover or her pimp. Reilly got Blanche's best friend and roommate at the Lizzie Bundy house, Sadie Monroe, to write her a letter begging her to cast off the Malleys and save herself.[43]

But Blanche, though young and decidedly outmatched in this entire proceeding, even with Reilly's intervention, was not without some weapons of her own. It suited her just fine to stay with the kind Sheriff and Mrs. Peck at their lovely seaside home and eat good meals, rather than linger in the county jail. In order to keep this state of affairs, Blanche dribbled out her information over a period of time. She also undertook an appearance of reform with modest behavior, prayer and meditation, and tearful claims of repentance for her past life.[44]

West Haven citizens were irate. Why was a prostitute being treated in this privileged way to the tune of $6 a day of taxpayers' money? If she were shut up in a real jail, she'd come to her senses. And why were the Malley boys allowed to run free while their cohort—whose connection with Jennie's death, if such connection there was, was undoubtedly lesser than theirs—had been arrested? Wasn't there just as much evidence of perjury against the boys as against Blanche?[45]

Over the next few weeks, bits and pieces of Blanche's confession to the inquest jury, which was taken in private (including one marathon session of seven hours), were leaked out to the press. Sometimes these leaks were the result of indiscretions on the parts of jurors, and sometimes they were reporters' guesses based on jurors' responses (or lack thereof) to pointed questions.

Blanche's confession was never made public and was never produced in its entirety. And there were two major problems with it: it was fluid, changing frequently; and it gave no insight into how Jennie Cramer might have died. But it did validate what everyone suspected: that Blanche had been induced to lie to protect Walter Malley, and that Jennie had lost her virginity against her will in the Malley mansion, probably that Wednesday night.

Blanche revealed that her role in the seduction scheme over the weeks preceding Jennie's death had been to keep the girl calm and unsuspecting.[46] The night that Jennie had not arrived home until 4:00 A.M., they were all in the private room over the Redcliffe, as Blanche had originally testified. But then she and Walter retired to one room, leaving Jimmy and Jennie in another. Soon, Blanche heard Jennie protesting loudly, "Don't! Don't!" After that the party broke up.

On that Wednesday night at the Malley mansion, August 3, Walter played the piano while they all sang. They were drinking wine and getting drunker and drunker (Blanche's other versions of this were that the girls had ten glasses each and the boys only one, and that Jennie's drinks were being drugged). Eventually, they began throwing banana and orange peels at each other, laughing hysterically.

Jennie was acting really crazy, running around, sitting on Jimmy's lap, and even once collapsed giggling on a couch and had to be propped up. Jim had his arms around Jennie around 11:30 when, according to the prearranged plan, Blanche doubled over and pretended to be sick. Jennie immediately left Jimmy and came over to Blanche to comfort her (a gesture that made Blanche feel guilty for her charade). Then followed the discussion as to the girls' staying at the mansion that night because of Blanche's illness.

While the discussion was going on, with Jennie trying to find a way to leave, Jimmy picked Jennie up and carried her upstairs to where the bedrooms were. She protested all the way up, kicking and demanding to be put down. Then he threw her on the bed. Blanche said she looked into the room and Jennie begged her to stay there with her. But Blanche told her she couldn't, that she was going to stay across the hall with Walter.

Blanche related to the inquest jury that Jennie's screams that night were so loud and so frightening that she got up to see if she was all right. However, this act of charity probably took place only in Blanche's own mind, as she later said that it was Walter who got up to tell them to keep quiet for fear the neighbors would hear.

The next day Walter gave her money to take Jennie to the Redcliffe for breakfast and to think up a story to tell Mrs. Cramer. They made Jennie swear that she would not tell what had happened to her.

Another revelation was that, two weeks prior to Blanche's arrival in New Haven, she and Walter had exchanged a series of letters in which the entire seduction scheme was laid out. Blanche still had those letters and turned them over to the jury.[47] Although the letters were never read in court (because Walter admitted writing them, and begged the jury not to do so), a few snippets got out that showed his deep infatuation with Blanche. One postcard pictured a little boy presenting a bouquet of flowers to a little girl. On the back, Walter had written: "Somebody loves Blanche."[48]

Blanche could read and write at only the most basic level, and had great difficulty even with this. The smooth, polished letters sent to Jennie and, after her disappearance, to Mrs. Cramer, had been written entirely by Walter, who signed Blanche's name.[49]

And, Blanche said further, while she was in New York before coming back to New Haven to confess, two men came to see her and asked her how much money would convince her to take the next ocean liner to Europe and stay there for a year. One of the men was Michael W. Malley, the son of Edward's brother, William, and an executive at the New Haven store. The other man she didn't know.[50]

But Blanche still insisted ("If you was to hang a rope around my neck I couldn't say different") that she had not seen Jennie after 12:00 noon on Thursday, as she watched her ride by on a horse-car bound for Savin Rock.[51] And she claimed that neither Walter nor James had ever told her anything they might know about Jennie's death, either.

The inquest was put on hold while jurors looked for corroborations of Blanche's story. Again, citizens and newspapermen complained about the state of affairs: come up with a verdict, they said, and let's get on with it.

As rumors of the Wednesday-night seduction trickled out, there was an outcry that seemed to see the violation as an even worse crime than the murder. Did the girl not have a father? a brother? Let them take care of this themselves! Fathers and brothers everywhere were urged to take matters into their own hands should such a thing ever happen to their daughters and sisters. Jacob and Eddie Cramer, and even Sheriff Peck, received anonymous hate mail calling them worse than cowards for not going after the Malleys.[52]

A physician connected with the Hayden case, who wanted to remain anonymous (but who sounds suspiciously like Dr. Moses White) said that the inquest jury should have ordered the autopsy on the Saturday the body was found instead of waiting until Monday. Some drugs that might have been found right away would have evaporated by then. The girl's organs should then have been sent to Dr. Samuel Johnson at Yale for an immediate analysis.[53]

Speculation as to the cause of Jennie's death was the favorite pastime of New Havenites. Many favored the theory that the marks on her face were the result of her being suffocated by being pressed against the sand. Dr. Creed, who had assisted at the autopsy, was one of these. Yet another suggestion was that the expert who had come up with the "boot heel" theory in the Hayden trial should be hired to see what could be made of the marks on Jennie's face.[54]

Blanche's statement as to the attempted bribery on the part of the Malley family coincided very closely with the prevailing feeling among inquest jurors and reporters that the Malleys were getting to witnesses who had previously made statements that were harmful to the defense. Suddenly, witnesses who had been previously cooperative were hard pressed to remember what it was they saw or heard, and some changed their stories altogether. This stonewalling, it was claimed, was because of Malley money being spread around, and because some of the witnesses were Malley employees.[55]

One of the latter was the coachman, James Bohan. On Saturday morning, before news of the discovery of Jennie's body had spread, Bohan was in a saloon complaining to a drinking buddy that he had been kept up late the night before, until 3:00 or 4:00 in the morning, waiting for Walter to come in with the horse and carriage. Later, Bohan claimed he never made such a remark and that, if he had, he must have been referring to another night entirely.[56]

Katie Mains, a floor manager at the Malley store, had told a fellow employee that at 8:00 on Saturday morning, Jimmy Malley had come over to her desk and just sat on the edge of it, silent for several minutes. "You've got something on your mind, Jim," she said. "What is it?" She told him he looked terrible and asked him what was going on. For a few minutes, Jimmy had looked as if he might say something to her, then shook his head and walked back to his counter. But when Mrs. Mains was questioned about what she had told the employee, she denied she had ever said it.[57]

Blanche had been put under arrest for perjury on August 13 in a strategic move to force her to reveal what she knew. After she divulged some of her confession to the inquest jurors, they finally issued warrants for the arrest of Jimmy and Walter.

On the morning of August 15, officers showed up at the James Malley, Sr., home to arrest Jimmy. Some reports said that Jim was calm, and others, that he was nervous. Still, whatever his actual demeanor, he asked if he could eat his breakfast before he went and was given permission for this. Jim also had plates prepared for the deputies, who then sat down and ate with their prisoner.[58]

Walter took his arrest with aplomb, even ordering a hack (a large hired carriage, like today's taxi service) so that one of the deputies wouldn't have to walk back to town. He arranged his white straw hat with the blue polka-dot band at a jaunty angle on his head, picked up two novels by Edward Bulwer-Lytton, and got into the carriage with his captors.[59]

At the New Haven County Jail, the boys were issued cells 13 and 15, with an empty one in between so they couldn't communicate. Walter gave one of the Bulwer-Lytton books to Jim, who had brought nothing with him to read.

In spite of public misconception to the contrary, the Malley boys were not given any special treatment. They had demanded better quarters and eventually asked for more freedom to wander around, as Herbert Hayden had been given, but the only concession they were granted—which they had to pay for themselves—was for meals to be brought from Redcliffe's. They simply could not tolerate jail fare.[60]

And on court hearing days, Walter hired a special carriage and driver to take them over to West Haven. Sometimes they would leave early and drive along the shore before going to Thompson's Hall.[61]

Neither of the boys received visits from any friends they might have had. Jimmy's sisters came daily, frequently with a bouquet of flowers that they put on their brother's and their cousin's cell bars. And Edward Malley usually showed up once or twice a day, as did the defense attorneys and the many reporters who tried to get the boys to give interviews.[62]

To the latter, Walter was much more communicative than Jim. Newspapermen commented on how carefree Walter looked, compared with Jimmy's pallor. Of course, that could have been their own prejudice, as it was universally assumed that, if a murder had been committed, it was Jim who had the motive. And it was Jim who eventually came down sick with what his brother, Andrew, said was a combination of neuralgia and malaria. ("Nonsense!" scoffed one paper. "Everyone knows you can't have them both together."[63])

Dr. Andrew P. O'Malley, who had been born with the O'Malley name in Ireland and insisted on keeping it, had temporarily abandoned his successful general practice in Wilkes-Barre, Pennsylvania, to come to the aid of his family in New Haven.[64]

Resentment and jealousy seem to have been the watchwords throughout the Jennie Cramer proceedings. The inquest jurors, who had to do much of their own investigation, at their own expense, didn't want to share their findings with each other. Moreover, they criticized each other in the press for what they thought were indiscreet statements made by their colleagues.[65]

The West Haven authorities, who had never had a murder in the history of the town, did not want the New Haven authorities to interfere with any offers of "help," while the New Haven authorities, who knew that this matter would eventually end up in their laps, resented not being able to protect their own interests.[66] They were still smarting over the Hayden fiasco and now the Malley affair had all the earmarks of an acquittal or a hung jury. To add to the spirit of noncooperation, the many reporters and detectives were all trying to outscoop each other and refused to pool their information. And there were rumors of a rift between the elder Malley brothers, Edward and James, Sr.[67]

In the meantime, Professor Russell Chittenden of Yale was quietly going about his analysis of Jennie Cramer's organs, the results of which would put an entirely new perspective on the theories of how and when the "beautiful victim of the Elm City" had met her death.

Chapter 15

AN END AND A BEGINNING:
INQUEST VERDICT

Darling Jennie, home's brightest treasure!
Found drifting, drifting with the tide,
Found floating alone, in the morning,
For death had claimed her as his bride.

—A. C. Willis, "Found Drifting with the Tide" (1881)

Out on the streets, vendors hawked pictures of each of the principals for a quarter. The photographer who had taken the last portraits of Jennie Cramer advertised in the newspaper that he had copies for sale.[1]

Asa Curtiss, the oysterman who had found Jennie floating in Long Island Sound, placed a white memorial flag in the sand to mark the site.[2]

Daily reports of the case were placed side by side on the front page with daily reports of President Garfield's up-and-down condition. Many headlines never even mentioned Garfield's name or title (as in "He is better today"), since everyone in America was aware of the health crisis. As time went on, Washington officials worried about whether to declare Garfield unable to carry out the duties of the office, or to wait for an ultimate resolution: death or recovery.[3]

In New Haven, Edward Malley offered an immense sum of money to George Watrous, the lawyer made famous by the Hayden case, to join the defense team. Watrous refused.[4]

Edward Malley was having problems of his own. On the same day his son and nephew were being arrested, the *Hartford Times* announced that the elder Malley had also been arrested on a charge of seduction made by a former servant. She was suing him for $2,000 damages and claimed that Edward Malley had already paid her $800 to keep quiet about it.[5]

Citizens of West Haven voiced their concerns, heightened by Jennie Cramer's death, that Savin Rock was being taken over by "toughs" and "libertines" and was becoming a place where it was no longer safe to bring children. They complained that it was badly undermanned by the West Haven police.[6]

Rumors abounded concerning the case and its main players: Blanche had died of a heart attack; Blanche had escaped; Jimmy had shot himself in his cell; Jennie was found living in a house of prostitution in Philadelphia; cantharides (Spanish fly) had been found in the body.[7]

Spanish fly, or cantharides, was considered to be an aphrodisiac because of its property of engorging the blood vessels around the genitalia (much as Viagra works today). Young men were supposed to have slipped it, in powdered form, into their dates' drinks to make them more compliant, and this was why the rumor had surfaced regarding Jennie Cramer. In fact, however, cantharides would never work as an aphrodisiac because the amounts necessary to cause sexual arousal would be so high that the person taking it would die first.[8]

Cantharides was used as an abortifacient, and it was also an ingredient in a prescription for amenorrhea, a condition Jennie Cramer may very well have had.[9] So it would be entirely possible that cantharides could be found in her system from the medication she was taking. However, as it turned out, no cantharides was found by Professor Chittenden.

From "Hotel Stevens," as the Malley boys jokingly referred to the jail run by Sheriff Stevens, Walter Malley sent a note to Blanche Douglass in her hermitage at Sheriff Peck's.[10] It was delivered by a Malley employee all decked out in a blue blazer with brass buttons and read by the sheriff before it was delivered to Blanche. Although the contents were never revealed to the public, it was assumed to be a plea "to remember old friends"—in other words, not to betray them.[11]

The prosecutor, Charles Bush, who would be representing the state at the next two levels (Justice and Superior Courts) asked for a delay until after Professor Chittenden's chemical analysis was completed. The inquest jury was waiting for the same in order to render a verdict, as there was no definite evidence indicating murder at that point. Fox and Blydenburgh, for the Malleys, argued that it was not fair to keep the boys in jail without a decision. If this is all the evidence you have, they insisted, well, render your verdict and let's get on with the next phase.

Calling to mind the Hayden case where Justice Wilcox refused to grant a continuance and dismissed the accused, Bush said that if they had waited a few more days, they would have had the evidence of arsenic. As it was, they had to go re-arrest Hayden, and what if he had skipped town during that week he was free? Fox retorted that ultimately eleven jurors had agreed with Justice Wilcox.[12]

Eventually, Justice Steven Booth, who would be trying the case after the inquest, granted a postponement of the Justice Court hearing until after Chittenden's analysis was submitted and denied the Malley boys bail.

Around this time, it was decided that Blanche Douglass was to be taken from Sheriff Peck's home and placed in jail. Public opinion had always been against her favorable treatment, but there was a method in the madness of the West Haven authorities. They knew that Blanche did *not* want to go to a regular jail, and they were hoping to use that threat as a means of getting usable testimony from her. At the same time, the relaxed atmosphere of the Peck home caused Blanche to let down her guard on occasion and confide things to the sheriff and his wife.[13]

The perjury charge was dangled over Blanche's head like the sword of Damocles. Every once in a while they would run her into court to set a date for a hearing or a trial. Then it would be postponed and back she would go to the Pecks'.[14] It was obvious to everyone that there was never any intention of proceeding with the perjury charge, and it must have been obvious at some point to Blanche as well. The charge was made only to keep her under their control and to blackmail her into giving testimony against the Malleys.

Why had Blanche not been arrested for murder? Alternatively, why had the Malleys not been charged with perjury instead of murder, since there was definite proof of the former? Once again, there was a strategy at work. If Blanche had been charged with murder, she would have felt more threatened than she did with the perjury arrest. But her bail on the perjury charge was set at $1,000, an entirely feasible amount for the Malleys to post if they wanted some control over Blanche Douglass. So the West Haven authorities had a warrant made out for Blanche's arrest for murder, and if bail were ever posted for her, the warrant would be served immediately, since murder is a nonbailable offense.[15] As for the Malleys, the lesser charge of perjury would have entitled them to post bail, and nobody wanted that to happen.

But now West Haven officials felt that Blanche's usefulness had come to an end. Not only was she steadfastly sticking to her story of not seeing Jennie after noon on Thursday, but she could not—or would not—provide any clues as to how she might have met her death. And Blanche had changed parts of her story so often that her value as a witness was compromised. She was simply not believable, and her credibility could further be destroyed by her occupation as a prostitute. The prosecution could only hope that the defense would make her their own witness so the State could get her on the stand that way; but they did not dare put her on themselves.

Blanche was calm at first as they took her to the New Haven jail, where they at first placed her in Cell 29, far away from the Malleys, but later she cried bitterly. Soon, however, she was removed to the section of the jail where Sheriff Stevens and his family lived so that she would not be subjected to the rude stares of the curious who came to look at the Malleys.[16]

Thus, even though Blanche was not, strictly speaking, living in someone's home, she was still reaping some of the same benefits: privacy, removal from the visible stigma of being in jail, and meals provided by the sheriff's family. Occasionally, she was invited to join them.

In the meantime, the inquest jury continued to take testimony from those claiming to have seen any or all of the four principals after 12:00 noon on Thursday, August 4.

It seemed that every day a new person surfaced who claimed to have seen Jennie or Jimmy or Blanche or Walter somewhere, and many of those sightings had taken place at Savin Rock on Friday evening. Some of the Jennie sightings hooked her up with Jim, a few with Blanche, and only one with Walter. Most people seemed less sure about having seen the Malleys, although it also may be that there were many young men who resembled James.

One of these Savin Rock witnesses (one of what the *New York Times* called "a wagon-load of queer-looking witnesses") was Benjamin F. Brady, a liquor-loving Irishman who ran the baseball tent in the Grove.[17] Visitors paid a nickel to pitch three baseballs at a row of dolls to win prizes. One of the objects to be thrown at was a "coon's head" on a chimney. ("Coon" was a pejorative term for African Americans.)[18]

Brady liked to look at pretty girls, and Friday evening one stopped at his tent to ask about the game. She was with another girl not as attractive, so Brady didn't pay much attention to that one. The pretty young girl, who he testified was Jennie Cramer, was dressed in white, had mitts on her hands and rings on her fingers. She seemed to be having a good time and was acting somewhat silly. She and the other girl left without playing the game.

Right after the girls left, a young man approached the booth, leaned on his walking stick, and then went away in the direction of the girls without saying anything to Ben Brady. The man wore a white straw hat with a blue polka-dot band, and Brady claimed that, although he didn't know him at the time, he later recognized James Malley as the man he had seen.[19]

Jennie Cramer must have gone out nearly every day of her life and to all sections of New and West Haven in order to have been recognized by so many people. Some of those who said they had known Jennie for years had never even spoken to her! But she had a distinctive look, with her usually white clothing, almost black hair, and exceptionally white face, and it is possible that she really was that well known.

John "Happy Jack" Gilchrist said he had seen Jennie Cramer on the night of August 5 in the company of another woman and three men. The women walked ahead of the men, chatting and laughing. The men were not in so good a mood, and Gilchrist heard one of them, a man in a black mustache, say, "I'll have it or someone will die." The other two men were James and Walter Malley.[20]

The man with the black mustache became an even more intriguing figure when several other witnesses claimed to have seen Jennie riding on the "flying horses" next to such a man. Her companions, two men and a woman, rode more sedately in a box with seats, but Jennie had climbed onto a horse after falling off on her first attempt. As the carousel went around, she leaned dizzily over on the man riding next to her and asked the proprietor to stop the machine so she could get off.

These witnesses said that when the merry-go-round finally stopped, the woman they claimed was Jennie walked off with the three from the box and said, "My God! I'm paralyzed!" The man with the black mustache, who was drunk and had an Irish brogue, went off in a separate direction and did not seem to be part of Jennie's group.[21]

Many of the people who hovered around Jennie's body on Saturday morning were sure they had seen her in the Grove the night before, either alone or in company with others. It seemed that everyone at Savin Rock that night had noticed Jennie Cramer.

From that time on, the mystery of "the man with the black mustache" would be a leitmotif that would run throughout the case, and the hunt was on to find him. In time, some such men were found by both sides, but the elusive figure continued to remain a part of the mythology of the Jennie Cramer tragedy.

Some observers of the case thought that the man with the black mustache and the many sightings of Jennie at Savin Rock were "a Malley job" and paid for with Malley money. The inhabitants of one bar, who were supposed to have known something about the whereabouts of Jennie and the Malleys, were suddenly quiet when reporters went to talk to them, and this was suspected to be the result of Malley interference also.[23]

In fact, the rumor of Malley money was so strong that one witness, who realized the state would not pay him for his testimony, tried to approach the Malleys to pay him *not* to testify.[24]

A Foote Building chambermaid named Bertha Williamson came forward with an interesting story.[25] The Foote Hotel was over the Redcliffe Restaurant and the entire building was owned by Edward Malley. Walter had a key to Room 26, which he used on occasion. On the morning of Thursday, August 4, Walter went to Bertha Williamson and asked her to make up Room 29 (adjoining 26) as well. He took the key with him.

The next morning, Friday, at about 8:00 A.M., Miss Williamson was making her cleaning rounds and found the door to No. 29 locked. She peeked in at the keyhole and saw two people in the bed: one was a man with dark hair, who she thought was James Malley, and the other person—she could not tell whether it was male or female—could not be discerned under the covers. (It should be noted that men back then did not have the same feeling about sharing a bed as they do today.)

Later, Miss Williamson saw both James and Walter exit Room 26 together. The sheets of that room were not overly wrinkled or soiled, but those in Room 29 were extremely so. (Although it was not stated, the insinuation was that there was semen on the sheets, as the chambermaid was greatly embarrassed during this portion of the testimony.) She had told her employer, Rudolph Neuman (who answered to Edward Malley), about it, and both he and his wife insisted that she not say a word about it to anyone.

After Bertha Williamson's testimony, Neuman published a notice in the newspaper saying that it was "a lie of the first water" and that she had the incident mixed up from the week *before* the death of Jennie Cramer. Neuman also took his employee aside and impressed upon her the fact that she was confused. Later, Bertha Williamson changed her testimony.[26]

And Robert Taylor, who worked with Jimmy in the gentlemen's clothing section at Malley's, testified that he was originally not sure whether Jim had been at the store all day on Friday, so he went to the jail to ask him! Jim had then refreshed Taylor's memory, and the witness was now sure that Malley had not left the store.[27]

It can readily be seen, then, that the lay testimony in this case was almost useless, as it was hard to know whom to believe. Had they been bribed? Did they misremember? Did they really recognize the person they claimed to have seen beyond all doubt? Did the incident take place when they said it did? Were they prone to suggestion by defense or prosecution? There were so many possibilities for false testimony, whether intentional or unintentional, that the multiplicity of witnesses for both sides just tended to confuse things further.

Take, for example, the testimony of the James Malley family. There were in the household at that time (besides Jimmy) his father, his three sisters, and a young servant girl. All of them claimed to have seen or heard Jim throughout the entire night of Friday, August 5. And two other employees of the Malley Company came by that evening as well: Mrs. Catherine Malloy, the milliner, with her two daughters; and Theresa Healy, the seamstress.

Although Jimmy usually was out partying late every night, sometimes not coming home at all, on this particular night—a Friday to boot—he was home by 7:00 and retired by 9:00. From his arrival at 7:00 to his rising at 6:30 the next morning, there were so many notable incidents, unlike any other night that week, that the entire testimony has an air of being trumped up, even if it was not: Jimmy was scolded by his father for not helping his sister with watering the flowers; he had supper, fixed by his sisters and the little servant girl,

Minnie Quinn; he couldn't turn the gas lights on because he had taken his shoes off; he reminded Mrs. Malloy that she had seen him driving fast the night before; he took a bath; yelled for a towel; sang a song while shaving in his sister's room (something from the 1880 Gilbert-and-Sullivanesque comic opera, *Billee Taylor*, by Edward Solomon); yelled for a pen for his father, who was writing to Andrew; asked his sister to test his bath water and get him clean underwear; yelled at the girls for making noise at 10:00; gave up one of his pillows for the girls at 11:00; yelled for a mosquito net around midnight; yelled at a barking dog at 2:00 A.M.; and walked to the store with his father the next morning.[28]

All that yelling to call attention to his presence was possibly done intentionally if Jimmy were trying to establish an alibi. But it could also have been a simple matter of "let's help Jimmy out because we know he didn't do this terrible thing" on the part of his family, just as Rosa Hayden had done for her husband. (In a reference to a song from the popular *H.M.S. Pinafore*, the *Hartford Times* sarcastically referred to the alibi provided for James Malley by "his sisters and his cousins and his aunts."[29])

Most likely, the incidents testified to *did* occur at some time or other, but possibly not on the same night. In a telling lapse of memory, neither the family members nor the employees could remember the incidents of any other night that week in the Malley household.

One thing that rings false is James Malley, Sr.'s, statement that he scolded his son for not helping his sister water the flowers. This was a young man who seems to have done *nothing* for himself, but expected his sisters to wait on him. For example, when James Malley asked for a pen so he could write to his son Andrew, he and Jimmy were both in the house and the girls were outside in the yard. Yet, Jimmy called out to one of them to come inside to get a pen for their father. And when he went to take a bath, he apparently didn't think far enough ahead to bring a towel in with him, nor was he capable of testing the temperature of his own bath water.

If these incidents really did occur, then Jimmy was either exceptionally lazy or was making sure that everyone knew he was around for the entire night.

In the meantime, Dr. Painter, the inquest juror, made a startling discovery: undertaker Stahl had given Mrs. Cramer a pin that had either stuck on or been purposely attached to Jennie's hat. Mrs. Cramer did not recognize it as belonging to her daughter, and was positive she had seen that same pin in James Malley's tie when she confronted him at the store on Thursday. She turned the pin over to Dr. Painter, who swore her to secrecy about it.

But Mrs. Cramer could not keep still. She described the pin to a reporter, not seeing any harm in doing so, and as a result, the details of the horseshoe-shaped tie pin were given to Jimmy, who then had a chance to prepare himself and not be caught off guard. He said he had only one tie pin, the one he wore every day in the courtroom.[30]

Dr. Cortlandt Creed told a reporter about the scene he had witnessed that Friday night as he pored over the president's medical bulletins, and thought it possibly had nothing to do with the case. He was reluctant to mention it at all because of his position as autopsy assistant. But he did express his opinion that the facial wounds should be examined more closely. Dr. Creed's impression was that one of them had been caused by the impact of a ring worn on the attacker's finger.[31]

Toward the end of the inquest hearing, three witnesses came forward whose testimony was the most believable of all: Mrs. Klippstein, Mrs. Crofut, and Henry Allen.

Mrs. Minnie Klippstein, wife of a New Haven barber, lived with her family directly across from Room 7 of the Elliott House. Room 7 had been the room occupied by Blanche Douglass the week of Jennie Cramer's death.

Like the members of the Luzerne Stevens household in Rockland, Minnie thoroughly enjoyed watching the doings of the inhabitants across the way. It wasn't spying, really, just a sort of nineteenth-century television show. Minnie would finish her chores for the morning, then sit down to do her mending and look out the window.

Minnie Klippstein had known Jennie Cramer practically all her life, but for some reason she had never actually spoken to her. What is most likely is that Jennie and her family worked and traveled in the same socioeconomic circles as the Klippsteins, but without ever being formally introduced.[32] At any rate, that Thursday afternoon, Minnie noticed Jennie and another woman (later identified to her as Blanche Douglass) entering the door of the Elliott House at about 1:30.

Later in the afternoon, Mrs. Klippstein saw Jennie standing by the hotel room window adjusting her dress and looking out at the men coming home from work. Once she jumped back from the window as if she did not want to be recognized by someone. (Possibly her father, who was out looking for her about that time.)

That same evening, Mrs. Klippstein saw Blanche, Jennie, and a man she later identified as James Malley, walking together. She remarked to her friend, Mrs. Charles Crofut, who was also looking out the window with her, that Jennie seemed to be in a good mood, but that Blanche and James looked very sad. Mrs. Crofut thought so, too.

Minnie recognized Blanche as the woman who had been in that same hotel room with Jennie the previous day (Wednesday) at about 10:00 P.M. Jennie appeared to be getting ready to leave, and Mrs. Klippstein was mentally urging her to go home where she belonged. "I feared for her safety," she said, although she couldn't say why and her feeling could have been a hindsight one. There was a man in the room at that time whom she recognized as Walter Malley.

On Friday evening Minnie saw a buggy parked in front of the Elliott. James Malley held the horse's head as Walter escorted Blanche from the hotel to the carriage. Once again, Minnie noticed how sad the three of them looked. She thought that neither of the Malleys was much of a gentleman because they both allowed the lady to get in the buggy by herself. And she said as much to her friend, Mrs. Crofut, who was once again enjoying the view from Minnie's window.[33]

Minnie Klippstein's testimony is valuable because she had known Jennie for such a long time, had a good vantage point to view the hotel room even by gas-light (as tested by a reporter), and had been extremely reluctant to come forward with what she had seen. It was only after a reporter ferreted her out and impressed upon her the importance of her story that she consented to do so.[34]

However, it doesn't exactly conform to the undisputed facts admitted to by the Malleys and Blanche: that it was James who was in the hotel room with the two girls on Wednesday, and that by 10:00 P.M. that night the four of them were well into their party at the Malley mansion.

Henry Allen, a former Northford resident, said that Jennie Cramer had been pointed out to him on one of her visits there. He seems to have been struck by her beauty, and thereafter paid special attention to her whenever he saw her around Northford. He had moved to New Haven that May, and on Friday, August 5, was riding on a horse-car past the Redcliffe Restaurant around 7:00 P.M. when he noticed Jennie in a slow-moving buggy with red running gear.

Allen turned to watch Jennie as long as he could, since it was the first time he had seen her since moving to New Haven. With her was a young man he had bought a tie from at the gentlemen's counter at Malley's the day before. The man was wearing a white straw hat, and Jennie was dressed in white or light clothing.

When Allen was taken on a tour of the jail to look at all the prisoners in a procedure resembling a lineup, he didn't see the man he saw with Jennie. But on his way out he passed the prison barber shop and there in the chair he recognized James Malley.

When Allen got outside, he told the authorities that he was sorry to have to say that the man in the barber chair was the one he had seen that Friday evening. Then he burst into tears.[35]

Finally, Professor Chittenden's long-awaited chemical analysis was released: he had found eight-tenths of a grain of arsenic distributed throughout the stomach, esophagus, liver, kidneys, heart, lungs, intestines, and brain. Such distribution indicated that between two and four grains (considered to be a fatal amount) had been ingested prior to death.[36]

The inquest jury met one final time to render its verdict, and there were rumors of wrangling and dissension as to that verdict.[37] That this was probably true is substantiated by the fact that it took three and a half hours of deliberation to come up with the decision:

That said Jennie E. Cramer came to her death by poison and violence and that James Malley, Jr., of New Haven, Conn., is criminally responsible for her death. We also find that Walter E. Malley, of New Haven, Conn., and Blanche Douglass, of New York City, are morally responsible for the same.

The verdict was dated Saturday, September 3, 1881, which by coincidence was the third anniversary of the death of Mary Stannard. The inquest jury had been convened since August 6 and had examined fifty witnesses. Yet, it had only held court sessions for ten of those days.

The torch had at last been passed to the Justice Court, which would begin its adversarial proceedings that Monday and attempt to unravel the still-unsolved mystery of the death of Jennie Cramer.

Chapter 16

JUSTICE COURT TRIAL IN WEST HAVEN

What is it in the human make-up which invariably leads men to take sides when they come into court? In the first place, witnesses usually feel more or less complimented by the confidence that is placed in them by the party calling them to prove a certain set of facts, and it is human nature to try to prove worthy of this confidence. This feeling is unconscious on the part of the witness and usually is not a strong enough motive to lead to actual perjury . . . but it serves as a sufficient reason why the witness will almost unconsciously dilute or color the evidence to suit a particular purpose and perhaps add only a bit here, or suppress one there, but this bit will make all the difference in the meaning.

—Francis L. Wellman, *The Art of Cross-Examination* (1903)

The tragic death of Jennie Cramer soon became a cautionary tale for all parents and their daughters. Editorials, letters to the newspapers, and similar occurrences all underscored the moral of this story. "Girls, take warning," wrote one reader. "Remember the fate of 'the silly lamb' that chose to roam without the fold."[1]

An editorial, in a not so gentle vein, had this to say:

There are thousands of foolish girls that think they know more than whole families ought to know, who would be greatly benefitted if they were taken across somebody's knee and compelled to listen to the reading of the life of Jennie Cramer. . . . And when a girl will not listen kindly to advice from her mother, she should have the conceit taken out of her with a pressboard.[2]

Even Blanche Douglass served as a role model, albeit a reverse one: two young girls were arrested for "lascivious talk" in public and brought to trial. "This is the way Blanche Douglasses are made" was the prosecutor's argument. In an incredibly harsh sentence, the girls, who seem to have been sisters, were sent to the state industrial school until they should turn eighteen.[3]

But it was Mr. and Mrs. Cramer themselves who came in for the most public criticism and were held ultimately responsible for the death of their daughter. This excerpt was typical and must have caused them a great deal of pain:

[T]he responsibility for her dreadful end comes back upon the criminal recklessness and blindness of her parents, who permitted her to fall into the trap of which they had due warning. In her giddy vanity and love of admiration the girl herself went blindfolded to her doom; but those who should have guarded and saved her appear to have interposed no obstacle in her way. There are too many parents like the Cramers in America, and that is why there are so many Jennie Cramer mysteries.[4]

That other parent, Edward Malley, was once again in trouble of his own. The "chickens" of the incident between himself and his brother William in 1880 had come home to roost in the form of a writ of attachment served on his store.

The suit was for $60,000: $30,000 by William's sons Michael W. and Edward J. Malley, whose store in Ansonia was attached in 1879; and $30,000 by William for false imprisonment and for Edward's trying to steal goods from the Ansonia store. However, Edward retaliated by having the servers of the papers—Michael Malley, his own employee, and Edward Carroll, William's son-in-law—arrested for malicious proceedings.[5]

The inquest trial of the Malleys had ended on Saturday, September 3, and the Justice Court, whose officials had been "champing at the bit" to get going on it, began its proceedings that Monday. As with the Hayden Justice Court trial, this was merely in the nature of a preliminary hearing to see whether there was probable cause to bind the defendants over to the New Haven County Superior Court. Accordingly, there would be no jury.

The trial in West Haven before Justice Steven Booth would last until the end of October and examine a total of two hundred witnesses, the majority of them people claiming to have seen one or more of the principals at various locations.[6]

During the trial, President Garfield, who had been lingering since being shot on July 2, would succumb to blood poisoning on September 19, and Vice President Chester A. Arthur sworn in.[7]

Five counts of murder were listed in the indictment against the Malleys: arsenic, drowning, suffocation/asphyxiation (pressing and holding Jennie's face down into the sand), chloroform, and the use of liquor and drugs.[8] The defense asked Justice Booth to limit the prosecution to one, but, citing the Hayden case and its multiple counts, the State was allowed to keep them all.

At the arraignment, Walter stood straight and tall to answer "not guilty" to the charges. Jimmy, however, leaned on the table in front of him with one hand, with the other on his hip and his legs crossed. This could have been insolence on Jimmy's part, but was probably indicative of sickness: he had been being tended by his brother Andrew for either malaria or neuralgia (which was more likely sciatica) or both and was in such pain on the morning of the hearing that the jailer had to help him out of bed.[9]

Dr. Andrew O'Malley knew his uncle's nature and he suspected that what everyone else was saying was true: that Edward Malley wouldn't knock himself out to help Jimmy. So Andrew had gone to Philadelphia and hired the most successful criminal defense attorney in Pennsylvania to represent his brother: Lewis Cassidy.[10]

Lewis Cassidy was a large man: large in size, large in reputation, and large in presence. With his balding head, gray hair, and deep, booming voice, Cassidy was the bane of prosecutors throughout Pennsylvania. The great man's capacity in the Malley affair was simply to watch out for Jimmy's interests, in case it looked as if Walter and Edward would be setting Jim up to be the "fall guy." As a result, Cassidy did very little except sit there, and this incurred the ire of the other defense attorneys because he did almost no cross-examination. The others felt they were doing all the work, and they resented it.[11]

With the discovery of arsenic in Jennie Cramer's body, both the prosecution and the defense became more limited in their approach. The prosecution would find it difficult to claim that Jennie had been drugged with opium or laudanum (since no organic poisons were found); and the theory that James Malley had, in a sudden fit of desperation, knocked her down on the sand and smothered her—an easier case to establish than arsenic poisoning—was not as tenable as before. The defense, for its part, had to rethink the position that Jennie had fallen or jumped into the water and drowned. Each side now had to account for the arsenic.

Death by poisoning connotes deliberation and forethought. While someone might strike out or grab a gun in the heat of anger, poisoning must be planned. And the condition of Jennie Cramer's body did not indicate that her death was the result of any sudden rage on the part of her attacker.

Consequently, the defense would try to prove that Jennie had been an "arsenic eater," a girl who followed the Victorian female fad of taking small amounts of arsenic in order to keep a pale complexion, and that her death was not due to arsenic but to some other cause.[12] Or, in the alternative, that she had committed suicide by overdosing on the arsenic she normally ingested for beauty purposes.

A pale complexion was considered a sign of beauty in that era because it signified not only delicacy, but sophistication and a higher social class: farmers had tans, while people of leisure stayed indoors.[13]

Young women reportedly achieved and maintained a pale complexion by the use of Fowler's Solution, a lavender-colored mixture of arsenic (four grains per ounce), carbonate of potash, water, and compound tincture of lavender. Fowler's was also used for medical ailments, notably heartburn, malaria, and neuralgia (which, coincidentally, were maladies afflicting James Malley). Druggists dispensed Fowler's Solution, but only through a medical prescription.[14]

After the Hayden trial, two important laws were passed which had only been in effect two months when Jennie Cramer was found dead. Although these laws were already in the works at the time of that trial, The Great Case probably did much to hasten their passage. One law forbade the dispensing or selling of drugs or poisons by anyone who had not passed an examination. The second required a record of sale to be made whenever arsenic, prussic acid, or strychnine were sold. This record had to contain the buyer's name, residence, nationality, race, purpose of purchase, and amount bought. But, since Fowler's was only dispensed through prescription, no record was required of its sale.[15]

There was no doubt that Jennie Cramer did have an unusually pale complexion, and her use of arsenic to acquire this was a natural supposition. However, those who had known her as a child said she had that same delicate face back then, too. Her family and her physician strongly denied her use of arsenic, and no druggist could ever be found who remembered selling any Fowler's Solution to her.[16]

Jennie was reputed to have been ill or sickly. It was the reason given by her parents as to why they indulged her. And she had been under a doctor's care for two years, from the ages of about fourteen to sixteen. It is possible that Jennie was severely anemic, which would cause the weakness and fainting spells alluded to and account for her pale complexion, and that this anemia also prevented her from getting her period on time (primary amenorrhea).

A gynecological cause of Jennie's illness is inferred from the fact that, in spite of all the references to her being "sickly," the nature of this was never specifically stated. Only once is there any hint of what it was about: "extreme female irregularities," which apparently was thought to have been explained by the ovarian cyst.[17]

Jennie's own physician, Dr. Charles Lindsley, in defending her virtue against allegations of loose, flirtatious behavior, made a curious statement to a reporter: that she was "not even ordinarily passionate." And the writer of the article said that, although Jennie was a "lively girl," she was virtuous because "for reasons explainable in the laws of nature, [she was] not tainted with sinful proclivities."[18] To the Victorian mind, for whom sex was equated solely with reproduction, this might have meant that she could not feel passion because she had not yet begun her menstrual cycle.[19]

On the first day of the trial, Asa Curtiss once again testified to his belief that Jennie had been dead before she was in the water. This was corroborated by Dr. Prudden, who could find no indication that there had been any struggle for breath.[20] On cross-examination, he said that she could have drowned if she had been unconscious when she fell or was put in the water (and therefore would not have breathed), but today's medical examiners know that the human body continues its breathing functions even when unconscious.[21]

Another relatively modern discovery is the fact that in approximately 15 percent of drowning cases, a closing of the throat (laryngospasm) will prevent water from entering the lungs.[22] However, Asa Curtiss said there was no foam around the nose or mouth, and that "in drowned cases there is always foam." Modern pathologists support him in this: Dr. Mary Case, the chief medical examiner for St. Louis, has testified that "there are few certainties in medicine, but that's one that is a certainty."[23] Therefore, Jennie did not drown.

Professor Chittenden's arsenic analysis indicated that there was .025 of a grain in Jennie's brain, which was more than was found in the brains of Mary Stannard and Abby Riddle combined.[24] It takes a while for arsenic to reach the brain, and yet the large amount found in the intestines and the kidneys indicated that it had been taken not long before her death. This led Professor Chittenden to the conclusion that, to reach the brain that fast, the arsenic must have been administered in soluble form: namely, Fowler's Solution.

Chittenden testified that the liver absorbs arsenic very quickly and is saturated in fourteen to fifteen hours. Yet, Jennie's liver contained very little of the poison, another indication of recent ingestion. (The professor sickened not a few people with his detailing of how he had first cut Jennie's organs with a pair of scissors, put them in a mortar and ground them into a thick paste to test for poison.)

Dr. Durell Shepard thought the body had been in the water only three to six hours because it wasn't bloated or water soaked. The insides of her hands were whitened and soaked, which would indicate she had been in seawater for at least three hours. There was no decomposition when the body was brought to the morgue, but three hours after the discovery, there was a slight stiffening.[25]

Dr. Painter said that Jennie's limbs were flexible when first taken to the morgue. And when Asa Curtiss took the body from the water and turned it over, the mouth fell open easily. Since the first signs of rigor mortis occur in the mouth and jaw, and had obviously not progressed that far by 5:30 A.M., it may be possible to come close to establishing the time of death.[26]

Rigor begins in the eyelids and facial area two hours after death, and between four and six hours there should be some stiffness in the neck and jaw.[27] This was probably what Dr. Shepard was noticing in the morgue three hours after Jennie was brought there.

Lividity (settling of the blood at the point of lowest gravity) also begins two hours after death, becoming inflexible in six to eight hours. Jennie's face was darkened because it was face down, and apparently the blood did not leave her face when she was turned over (witnesses on the beach said the face was "dark" or "black," and her father had to use her clothing to help him make a definite identification).[28]

What all these factors indicate is that Jennie was most probably dead three hours before she was found, or at approximately 2:30 A.M., and that she was put in the water close to the time of death. This would make her last meal at around 6:30 Friday night to fit the eight-hour time span for the last meal. The theory that she died or was killed prior to Friday night, then, cannot be sustained in view of the fact that, in very hot weather, which New Haven was undergoing at that time, decomposition occurs very rapidly.

Both doctors, Shepard and Painter, agreed that rape had occurred not more than three days before her death and had been accomplished with great violence, as the fourchette was never torn, not even in childbirth.[29]

Mrs. Cramer came to court dressed in deep mourning. As she testified, she kept herself cool with a palm-leaf fan. She told her sad story once again, but even so there was just a hint of bragging about her daughter's many gentlemen callers. She refused to name one suitor, as he was "a man of means" and probably would not appreciate it. Finally, however, she divulged his name: Mr. Plant of Plantsville.[30]

Her cross-examination by Blydenburgh was so vicious that Justice Booth had to remonstrate with him, and he was later criticized in the newspapers as being insensitive.[31] The defense ploy here was obvious: to show that Jennie was already corrupt before she was seduced by James Malley, and that the Cramers had not sought to monitor her activities as decent parents would have. Blydenburgh tried to get Mrs. Cramer to say that she had often gone to sleep before Jennie got home at night, that Jennie had stayed out all night prior to that Wednesday night, and that Jennie did not always tell her mother where she was going.

When Blydenburgh asked Mrs. Cramer why she didn't take Jennie into another room to scold her on Thursday instead of doing so in front of Blanche Douglass, the beleaguered woman got up from her seat and wailed, "Oh, if I had only known I might have acted differently." Then she pointed at the Malleys, and with her voice rising ever higher, cried: "If I had got out a warrant for them for keeping Jennie away overnight she would be alive today and they wouldn't have forced poison down her as they did."

"Control yourself," Blydenburgh told her harshly.

"I can't," she said, her face getting redder and her voice getting shriller. "You are asking me so many questions and my heart is breaking, and you seem to want to annoy me."

People in the back of the courtroom stood up to get a better look at Mrs. Cramer's tirade. Walter gave a scornful laugh and Jimmy sneered. Edward Malley threw back his head and laughed out loud.

Outside the courtroom, Blanche's ex-husband, John Zimmermann, paraded around trying to cut himself a piece of the media action and also cash in on the sale of Blanche's pictures.[32] He carried their marriage certificate with him and showed it to one and all: they had been married December 16, 1877, in New York City when Blanche was only sixteen.

Zimmermann claimed that he had been very good to Blanche, trying his best to make her happy, but that she was "incorrigible." She had left him for Reilly, the New York bartender, he said, and so he gave up on her.

The more people Zimmermann spoke to, the more he changed his story: first claiming that their daughter had died because Blanche wasn't watching her and she fell out of bed, then saying that she had died of pneumonia. He had had his name tattooed on his right arm as proof of who he was, in case anyone should doubt him, and all in all he came off as a swaggering bully.

Sheriff Peck had gotten to know Blanche well while she had stayed with him and his wife, and became fondly protective of her. Photographers and artists were trying to get a likeness of the famous procuress so they could sell it on the streets, but Peck helped Blanche fill out the papers to register a copyright on her likeness, whether photo or drawing. There was some debate as to whether a likeness (a *drawing* made from a photograph) was copyrightable, but Peck got one anyway. This meant that Blanche could make some money off the sale of her photos, too.[33]

Henry Allen repeated his testimony about having seen Jennie and Jim from the streetcar, then going down to the jail to identify Jim in the barber's chair. Defense attorney Fox cross-examined him so minutely on every aspect of his life that Bollman finally objected. If this kind of thing were permitted, he said, rich defendants could prolong a trial until they died of old age. The courtroom erupted in applause at this.[34]

Minnie Klippstein, the barber's wife who liked to look out the window, told Fox on cross-examination that she could fix the date when she saw Blanche and Jennie together by the fact that she had bought her husband a pair of slippers for his birthday. She had volunteered too much, apparently, because Fox said, "Hold on, I didn't ask you that." Dr. Painter, the inquest juror and now a spectator, was so involved with the case that he inadvertently answered for the witness, blurting out, "I know you didn't, you fool, you!"

Everyone turned to look at Painter, who immediately recognized his gaffe. Embarrassed, he muttered, "I shall get mixed up in this myself if I don't look out."[35]

But Fox was so effective in confusing Mrs. Klippstein that she broke down and wept on the stand. She said her memory was poor because of a fever and for that reason she had been reluctant to testify.

Samuel Mattoon, a clerk at Sperry's Drugstore, testified that he saw Jennie and Blanche come into the drugstore at about 7:00 P.M. on Thursday. They asked if they could wait there, then got sodas and sat down. Mattoon, who had gone to school with Jennie, noticed a small mole on her neck, which he could see because of the low cut of her dress. (The relatively low cut of the neckline, which went in a V toward the cleavage area, was one of the things that drew the attention of many men who claimed to have seen Jennie on the Thursday and Friday before she died.)

The girls stayed in the drugstore for ten minutes, where they were also seen by Mr. Sperry, the druggist. Then they went out and looked up Chapel Street, according to Mattoon, and in this he was corroborated by John Hubbell from across the street.[36]

Each day in court, Walter and Jim showed up with flowers in their lapels, which was a trademark of Edward Malley and probably his idea. Their attorneys did the same, and the purpose seems to have been the projection of an image of both nonchalance and wealth. The *Hartford Times* noted that both boys wore mocking expressions, and whether it was from "guilty bravado or because of mere shallowness of intellect, their behavior is distasteful."[37]

The chambermaid Bertha Williamson repeated her testimony about the rooms in the Foote Building, and this time gave more information concerning the stains on the sheet in No. 29: they were in the middle of the sheet and some of them were red. But after her employers finished "helping her" fix the date, Miss Williamson was hopelessly confused about exactly *when* this incident had taken place.

At the inquest testimony, the chambermaid had said that Friday morning, August 5, was when she had seen James, Walter, and the stranger under the covers in Room 29. Later, after talking with the Neumans, she "remembered" that it was July 26, which date she fixed by the burning of the Foote Hotel barn. But, as it turned out, the barn had burned on July 19. All in all, then, she was worthless to both sides because her testimony could not be trusted.[38]

However, some information did emerge that might give some insight into why the Neumans were so quick to disparage what she said ("a lie of the first water") and also supports the theory that Walter wanted to keep his father from knowing about his relationship with Blanche.

Mrs. Neuman had told someone around the first of August (when Blanche was in town) that she didn't like Walter bringing girls to the Foote House. If he did it again, she told her friend, she was going to report it to Edward. At the same time, her husband, Rudolph, mentioned it to the night watchman at Malley's, and told him he would tell Walter's father if the incident were repeated.[39]

On August 1, the watchman told Walter what had been said to him by Neuman. Walter immediately confronted Neuman, essentially telling him to mind his own business. "If I hear anything more about it," he warned the janitor, "you will lose your position."

Toward the end of the State's case, the prosecution managed to stun the defense so much that there was a noticeable reaction. John Manning, an employee of Malley's, was put on the stand to testify to Walter's handwriting. Then he identified the letters supposedly written by Blanche as having been written by Walter. The defense reacted "like a thunderbolt," according to the *Register* reporter, and huddled together with the defendants.[40]

The conference completed, the defense said they would stipulate that Walter wrote the notes for Blanche because her writing was so poor. Well, that's not all, the State said: we have some other letters from Walter to Blanche that were written before August 5, and we want to enter those as well. These letters indicated that he had known her longer than he testified to at the inquest. Another defensive huddle took place.

It was obvious that Walter did *not* want his letters to Blanche admitted to evidence and read to the court. As a result, the defense had to make the following concessions: that Walter had known Blanche since April 6 (actually, he had known her since February), that James had known her since June, and that both were aware of her status as a prostitute.

When the court recessed for the day, Walter went over to the prosecutor, Charles Bollman, and begged him not to read or publish the letters. Nevertheless, at least one reporter got some hints about what they contained: nothing about how Jennie Cramer met her death, but lots of sexual innuendo.[41]

Bertha Williamson had testified as to the soiled sheet at the Foote Hotel on Friday morning, and now Nellie Sullivan, the Malley chambermaid, testified that *none* of the sheets were soiled in the two rooms used by the quartet on Wednesday night at the mansion.[42] If both were telling the truth, then possibly Jennie's seduction or rape did not take place that Wednesday night, but on Thursday night instead—which would explain her cheerfulness on Thursday morning.

Joseph Brunt, a first cousin of Walter Malley's and an employee at the store, testified that Jimmy had come to him around 5:30 on Friday and practically begged him to accompany him to Buell's that night after work. Brunt had already made plans for the evening, but Jimmy asked him to change them and go with him instead.[43]

After Brunt's refusal, Jim went home and made himself conspicuous there. As Buell's is in a separate location from both Savin Rock and Branford Point (where Walter and Blanche went), it looks very much as if the three conspirators wanted to provide separate alibis for that night.

The State put on the witnesses it had used for the shore-sighting testimony, with the comic Ben Brady pointing in dramatic fashion at James Malley with a trembling finger. The entire courtroom was silent as he uttered the words, "That man there." Several visitors to Savin Rock that night testified to the incident on the flying horses and the man with the black mustache.[44]

One of the men who claimed to have seen Jennie Cramer at the shore on Friday was cross-examined by Timothy Fox so extensively as to where he went and what he drank *after* he had seen her that Bush objected to it as immaterial and a means of harassing the State's witnesses. Fox said that it *was* material, because drink could affect what he thought he saw. Bush said that would not happen *after* he had already seen it, to which Fox retorted that intoxication made people think they saw things they hadn't, but perhaps Mr. Bush had no brains to be affected by drink. Yes, it was true, Bush admitted, he had no experience in drink; however, he had been to law school with Fox, so had a lot of opportunity to observe it.[45]

As the defense began its case, the main question on everyone's lips was: will the Malleys testify? Their attorney Fox said they had no reason not to take the stand, and did not fear even the most severe cross-examination.[46] In fact, however, they had *much* to fear from cross-examination, as at the very least they had perjured themselves in the lower court. And James would have been questioned about the seduction or rape of Jennie. Anything the boys could have said for themselves would have been severely offset by the damage from cross-examination.

In the end, the Malley boys would never take the stand again after their perjured testimony at the inquest trial. It was a calculated risk on the part of their defense counsel.

The police officer, Richard Waite, told of seeing the girls leaving the Malley mansion on Thursday morning. One of the girls turned and waved, and he thought this was Jennie, but wasn't sure. (Jimmy had said at the inquest that he was not sure of this, either.) At any rate, no matter who did the waving, both girls were laughing and joking.[47]

A clerk at Blackman's Drugstore came forward with an opium mixture prepared for Jennie a few days before her death. But it turned out that this was a favorite cough remedy in her family, and Eddie had asked his mother to send him some. It had to be boiled with water and then bottled up, and the Cramers were later able to prove that the entire amount had been sent to Eddie. Besides, no opium or opium derivative had showed up in Chittenden's chemical analysis.[48]

Probably the most intriguing witness for the defense was a woman named Maggie Kane.[49] She had been reading the accounts in the newspapers about the incident on the flying horses and came forward to say that it was *she* on the horses that night, not Jennie Cramer. Maggie had gone down to the shore with some friends, and these were the people who rode in the carousel box. Next to her on the horses was another acquaintance, Tom Degnan, who was there by himself that night. Degnan had a black mustache and an Irish brogue.

They were joking around, and Degnan, who had had quite a bit to drink by that time, was getting insulting in his language. This is why she wanted the horses stopped.

When the merry-go-round stopped, Maggie felt dizzy and made the statement about being paralyzed. She and her friends then went down toward the swings, and Degnan went off by himself. Later, after Jennie was discovered and the witnesses were coming forward, Maggie had gone to Degnan and said that maybe they should tell someone that they were the ones on the horses.

Maggie Kane was very pretty, with a very white complexion and black hair in the current "bangs" fashion (as was Jennie's). That night she was wearing light colors, but not white, except for a white straw hat. Maggie did not look like the portrait of Jennie being passed around the courtroom, but the witnesses who thought they had seen Jennie on the merry-go-round were not personally acquainted with the dead girl.

After Maggie testified, Tom Degnan took the stand and corroborated her story, as did Maggie's male companion for that Friday night.[50] It seemed that the mystery of the man with the black mustache had been solved.

The defense produced another Jennie look-alike in the form of Mary (Mamie) Harland, who had come down from Wallingford for a piano lesson and visited Jimmy at the store that Friday. Like Jennie, she was a pretty girl, but did not look enough like her to be taken for her by someone who knew Jennie well. Moreover, on cross-examination, Miss Harland said that she had definitely not walked with Jimmy on the Green that day.[51] Since he was seen there with a woman who was said to be Jennie, the defense would obviously have produced that woman if it were *not* Jennie. That they did not must have meant that they *could* not.

And there was another problem with Mamie Harland's testimony: She had said that when she visited Malley's store that Friday to see Jimmy, she had also seen the company timekeeper, Theresa Kennedy. However, Miss Kennedy was ill that day and did not go to work at all.[52]

But if Maggie Kane was the most intriguing, little Minnie Quinn was "the most interesting" defense witness.[53] Just twelve years old, little Mary Ann

(Minnie) had had to be taken out of school so she could go to work and help support her family. Her father had gone blind and could no longer work, and Minnie was hired by the James Malley, Sr., family to run errands and do odd jobs. She lived in and took her meals there.

What was so remarkable about Minnie was her intelligence and her incredible memory. For her age, she was also extremely articulate and self-possessed on the stand. Other than depending on the Malleys for her family's income, Minnie had no stake in the outcome of the trial and so came off as a very believable witness.

Minnie was able to track Jimmy Malley's whereabouts on Friday evening from about 6:30 until 11:00 P.M. She was in the kitchen when he asked for supper, heard him singing upstairs, and saw him shaving in Katie's room. Since she slept in a room with two of the girls, she walked through Jimmy's bedroom to get there and saw him asleep in bed. She preferred going that way, she said, because the alternative was to go through a dark room at the head of a set of stairs. (Jim's sister turned his gaslight off later.)

She knew this had taken place Friday because of what was served for supper (hot cakes cooked by Lizzie), because the night before Jimmy had taken Miss Lulu for a ride in Walter's carriage, and because the next night she went to the Malley store. The store was only open two nights: Monday and Saturday.

The cross-examination of Minnie Quinn by Charles Bollman took one complete morning, during which the little witness sat with her hands and feet crossed and seemed to be at ease. Bollman's object was to show that her story had been memorized and rehearsed, so he was asking her questions about other events and other meals in the Malley household. Because she had had such poor fare in her own home, Minnie was able to remember the delicious meals at the Malleys' with great precision and for approximately a month prior to the death of Jennie Cramer. (Prominent on the dessert menu was huckleberries, which had been part of Jennie's last meal.)

When he finished, Bollman said that Minnie had "the most remarkable memory of any witness I ever saw." The newspapers referred to her as "the little prodigy."

Bollman later recalled Minnie Quinn to the stand to read from a newspaper. She had testified that she knew of the facts of the case from reading the newspapers, and Bollman wanted to make sure this was the source of her knowledge and not extensive prepping on the part of the Malley household. He handed her the paper and asked her to read anything at all. In an eerie coincidence, she began to read about the mysterious death of a young girl in Albion, New York, an incident that was very similar to the Jennie Cramer case.[54]

Another poignant incident occurred when the defense recalled Mrs. Cramer, whom they had asked to bring in the hat and dress Jennie was wearing when she died. As she placed the items on the table in front of Blydenburgh, her misery was obvious.

"These are the hat and dress of your late daughter?" he asked.

"Yes, sir, they are." Mrs. Cramer's voice was so low it was hard for others to hear her. She took the hat, removed the covering from it with shaking hands, and threw it on the table. As it landed, some of the sand it had accumulated fell out.

Blydenburgh had obviously taken to heart the scolding he had received from the judge and the press about his treatment of Mrs. Cramer on cross-examination. In a kind and apologetic tone, he said to her, "That is all, madam. We did not mean to annoy you, madam, but this is the only way we could get at those things."

Mrs. Cramer continued to sit in the witness chair, blankly unresponsive. Justice Booth told her she could step down, and she finally walked slowly to the back of the room. But before taking her seat, she said bitterly, "There were Scotch pearl beads that she wore. They were taken off at the undertaker's and never came back to me."

Although Walter and the defense counsel examined the hat, Jimmy couldn't bring himself to touch it.[55]

Jimmy's three sisters—Elizabeth (Lizzie), Louisa (Lulu), and Katie—also came to testify to his ubiquitous presence at home that Friday night. That day in court, as they awaited their turn, they sat in back of their brother and proceeded to whisper and laugh so much that Justice Booth got annoyed. He sent Sheriff Peck down to tell them to keep quiet.[56]

At the inquest hearing, only Lulu, the middle sister, had taken the stand to give Jimmy an alibi. Now Lizzie, the eldest, and Katie, the youngest, would shore up the defense with details of the Malley family at home on that crucial Friday, August 5.

Lizzie Malley, 26, had spent the previous summer in Wilkes-Barre visiting her brother Andrew, and through him had been introduced to Nathaniel Wolfe, owner of a large drugstore there.[57] Over the following year, Nat made trips to New Haven to see Lizzie, and by the time of the Justice Court trial, they were engaged. In July of that year, Nat had given her a watch and some earrings as a gift.

On the stand, Lizzie went through the litany of the Malley household doings, and at one point stated what time it was. As in the Hayden trial, the prosecutor focused on what it was that made her check the time. She had received a new watch, she said, and had gone to get it to show Mrs. Malloy. On her way downstairs, she glanced at it and noticed it was 9:00 P.M.

Not to be put off, however, Bush asked her when and where she had received the watch. He was trying to show that perhaps she had had the watch for some time, and was only making up the story about having an excuse to look at it. But Lizzie turned obstinate once she realized that he didn't trust her story. She wouldn't divulge where she had gotten the watch, she said. It was personal and nobody else's business.

Bush's persistence only served to make Lizzie truculent and haughty. The two went back and forth, to the delight of the spectators, until the judge finally intervened and effected a compromise: if Lizzie would write the name of the gift-giver on a piece of paper, the prosecutor would not read it out loud.[58]

After the Malley sisters had all testified, the attorneys, judge, and defendants made visits to two places at the request of the State: the Foote Building and the James Malley house. At the Foote Building, the prosecutors wished to see whether someone could keep out of sight by going out the window in Room 29, walking along the roof of the building attached to the restaurant, and then re-entering the hotel by way of another window. Both prosecutors accomplished this with ease.[59]

At the Malley house, Justice Booth and the attorneys walked through the various rooms and locations where the Friday night sightings of Jimmy were to have taken place. Bollman and Bush sat where the dressmaker, Theresa Healy, said she had seen Jimmy coming through the gate. They could not see the gate from where she sat at the sewing machine, they said. Defense attorney Timothy Fox tried the same experiment and claimed he could see the gate perfectly.[60]

This little incident serves to underline the problem of the eyewitness testimony for both sides. As in the Hayden case, one side simply cancelled out the other and was not helpful in getting at the truth of what had happened to Jennie Cramer.

Back in the courtroom, Sheriff Peck, now a witness for the defense, probably because of his sympathies for Blanche Douglass, said he had *not* seen Jennie Cramer on his rounds that night, although when her body was first discovered he thought he had.[61]

The only expert witness for the defense was Dr. Pliny Jewett, who had assisted at the autopsy of Mary Stannard and testified for the State at Hayden's trial. Jewett said a normal death from arsenical poisoning would include inflammation of the mucus membranes of the stomach. That Jennie's stomach had not been so inflamed would indicate that she had been used to taking small doses of arsenic over a period of time.[62]

Dr. Jewett also introduced a new possibility into the evidence: that the mushrooms found in Jennie's stomach could have been poisonous toadstools.

A death by suffocation was as likely as a death by arsenic, Jewett said, and Jennie could also have drowned. The doctor's scenario as to what happened to her included all three: she possibly took a fatal dose of arsenic (on purpose), jumped off the dock, and died of suffocation because the water was too low. If it weren't for the suffocation, he said, she would probably have recovered from the arsenic since it was in such a relatively small dose. The discoloration on her forehead could have been a pre-mortem wound from where she struck her head on the sand after jumping.

Dr. Jewett claimed that the autopsy examination of Jennie's genital region was not done right, and should not have yielded a conclusion of rape.

On cross-examination, Jewett admitted that in some instances inflammation of the stomach does not accompany arsenical poisoning.

The State's rebuttal testimony included the assistant time clerk at Malley's, who stated that Jimmy could pretty much come and go as he pleased and the time book wouldn't show it. (This was probably true, as there were at least two instances where the boys showed up late for work by their own admission, and the time book said they were there before 8:00.[63])

A bartender had overheard the Saturday morning conversation between James Bohan, the Malley coachman, and Charles Wilson (who had since gone to England and was not available for trial). Wilson had asked Bohan why he looked so sleepy and stupid, and Bohan told him he had been up until 3:00 or 4:00 that morning waiting for the horses to come in.[64]

Constable John Lovejoy had known both Jennie and Jimmy for some time, and testified to having seen them walking together on the Green between noon and 1:00 on that Friday. The defense cross-examined this witness for a full three hours in the belief that his testimony had been manufactured by a State detective who had formerly been working for the Malleys. (That detective, also a constable, had quit over a wage dispute with Edward Malley.[65])

But, after all the evidence had been heard and final arguments made, Justice Steven Booth found probable cause to bind the Malleys over to the Superior Court. It was too late for the current term, however, and so the boys, as Hayden had done before them, would have to sit in jail until their jury trial would commence in April, six months after the Justice Court hearing had ended.

The perjury charge against Blanche Douglass was nolled, which was no surprise to anyone, and a charge of murder entered instead. For Blanche, there was only one count: causing Jennie Cramer to ingest a fatal dose of arsenic. For the Malleys, there were the same five counts. But by the time the matter came to trial the following April, those five counts would be reduced to one: arsenic poisoning.

It was a decision that was to prove to be a drastic mistake.

Chapter 17

SUPERIOR COURT TRIAL IN NEW HAVEN

Sad are the tear drops,
Hearts laden with sadness
Mourn we the death of this beautiful one,
Stricken in Spring time,
When life was all gladness—
By the death messenger called to her tomb.

Ah, visit we pray from the home in the skies,
The gloomy dark cell where the guilty one lies,
Enter his heart and give him no peace,
Bid him beware and from sin bid him cease.

—Excerpt from poem by Mary Fowler,
sent to Mrs. Cramer, May 1882

Shortly after the Justice Court trial ended, Lizzie Malley married the druggist Nat Wolfe and moved to Wilkes-Barre, taking her sister Lulu with her. The rest of the James Malley family likewise moved out of their Whalley Avenue home, where it stood vacant throughout the Superior Court trial.[1]

After his daughter's death, Jacob Cramer attended to his cigar store business only halfheartedly, sometimes not even remembering to put the Indian statue out on the front walk to let people know the store was open. Although only 53, Mr. Cramer looked like an old man with his stooped posture and depressed attitude.[2] Then, in December, only five days before Christmas, his wife found him dead in his bed. Although the physician, Dr. Lindsley, recorded the cause of death as phthisis (another word for consumption or tuberculosis), there were strong indications that Jacob Cramer had committed suicide.[3]

Jennie's father had suffered from his pulmonary difficulties for the past seven years and took an opium mixture to control it. He often had to sleep in a separate bedroom so that his labored breathing would not disturb his wife. In the weeks before his death, he had told friends that he thought he would die soon, and two days before he died had even told his young daughter, Minnie, that he would only live a few days longer. The night before he died, he told his wife, "I shall die some time when you don't expect it."

On the morning of his death, Mrs. Cramer found a note written in German on a table in the cigar store:

Dear Wife—To-morrow morning if you find me dead, don't you be discouraged. It is the best for me. Give my love to Eddie and Minnie. Pray let me be buried by Mr. Stahl. Don't let my funeral expenses exceed $50. Send to Dr. Lindsley to have him make out the certificate of death. I hope I shall soon be relieved of all suffering.

Your loving husband in death,
Jacob Cramer
P.S.—I shall rest in peace by my children.
Tell Eddie to be a man and take care
of his mother.

When reporters questioned Dr. Lindsley about the possibility of suicide, he scoffed and said that Mr. Cramer had suffered for many years from consumption. However, it is likely that, even if he suspected suicide, Dr. Lindsley wished to save the Cramer family any more grief, and hurriedly filled out the certificate. As a secondary cause of death, though, he listed "exhaustion," which probably indicated a mental as well as a physical state.

Mrs. Cramer herself was of the opinion that Jennie's death hastened her husband's: "Jennie was his idol, and her murder broke his heart. . . . Since Jennie's death I believe that the thought of her was hardly out of his mind," she said.[4]

Jacob Cramer was buried in Evergreen Cemetery next to his daughter, Jennie, and the young son who had died a few years previously.

Edward Malley continued to have more legal and financial difficulties. Before the Jennie Cramer murder, he had announced that he would sell his business; however, when he thought his competitors were gloating over his misfortunes in the Cramer affair, he immediately announced he would "show them" and stay in business. But if Edward Malley had lost money before the events of August 1881 (as evidenced by the intrafamilial lawsuits), the legal difficulties of his son and his nephew presented an even greater drain on his wallet.[5]

Then, in the early hours of a morning in February 1882, a fire raged through the Malley building and destroyed most of the goods. Because the night watchman also doubled as a janitor (Edward Malley always wanted the most for his money and was reputed to be something of a cheapskate), he was busy doing his cleaning chores when the fire started. The fire was out of control by the time he noticed it and he was lucky to escape with his life.[6]

The Malley Company was heavily insured, but the insurance companies must have suspected arson, something also suggested by at least one newspaper.[7] Relying on a technicality, they claimed that Malley's taking on of a partner (William Neely) a few days before the fire had nullified the agreement. Moreover, they believed Malley's estimates of damage to be overinflated.[8] Thus would begin a series of lawsuits on Malley's part to force the insurance companies to pay up. (Another newspaper theory was that the store was destroyed to prevent anyone from checking out the stories of the clerks in the gentlemen's clothing section as to whether they could see Jimmy Malley behind his counter.[9])

To add insult to injury, the *New Haven Register*, stung by accusations of partiality to the Malleys because of the heavy amount of advertising done by the Malley Company in its newspaper, refused to carry those ads in 1882.[10]

Still, although Edward Malley had not been able to lure George Watrous to the cause of the defense, he did spend money to secure the services of Watrous' affiliate in the Hayden case: Samuel Jones.[11] Jones' fee was not given, but it must have been high.

The grand jury indictment against the Malleys and Blanche Douglass adopted more of a moral than a legal tone, alleging that the defendants "not having the fear of God before their eyes, but being moved and seduced by the devil, wickedly contriv[ed] and intend[ed]" to poison Jennie Cramer.[12]

Both the defense and the prosecution wanted further examination of Jennie's body, and so an exhumation order was issued in January. The defense wanted the bones analyzed, as the presence of arsenic there would indicate usage over a long period of time; the prosecution wanted the entire body examined for arsenic so they could tell the jury exactly how much Jennie had ingested.

When the coffin was opened, the physicians in attendance noticed only a normal degree of decomposition. This would seem to indicate that Jennie had *not* been an arsenic eater, since arsenic acts as a preservative. The remaining organs were taken away, as well as the left shoulder, right leg, a piece from the back, a segment of the transverse section down to the pelvic bone, and a chunk from the right breast.[13]

Back in the New Haven jail, the Malleys passed their time reading Walter Scott and Edward Bulwer-Lytton, among others. Walter exercised his artistic talents in composing a waltz, "Under the Elms," and in drawing on the walls of his cell. Under one bucolic scene he wrote "Sketched in twelve minutes" and proudly showed it to a reporter.[14]

But Walter was not always so eager to see the public, which was allowed to come in just to look at the inmates. Once he hung a pink curtain in front of his cell for privacy, and the jailer tore it down. Walter was furious, demanded the return of the curtain, and a heated argument followed between him and the jailer. "You do not at this time run the New Haven jail or make its rules," he was told. For his insubordination, Walter had some of his privileges taken away.[15]

When this incident was reported, newspapers took sides. The *Register* noted that both Malleys had often spread themselves out in the jail corridor with their feet up on the radiator while visitors were around, and that several times they had to be asked to move so people could get around them. Why so picky about visitors now?[16] The *Hartford Times*, on the other hand, took Walter's side and said that he was not a convict but only awaiting trial. He had a right to his privacy.[17]

At last April came around and it was time for the proceedings to begin. Sharing space in the news with the Malley case were the shooting of Jesse James out in Missouri, the trial of Charles Guiteau for the assassination of President Garfield, and the death of Ralph Waldo Emerson.[18]

On April 4, Jimmy, Walter, and Blanche were brought to the Superior Court to enter their pleas. Their trial would take place in the same courtroom as the Hayden trial. Walter wore his glasses and looked serious. Jimmy had gained weight in jail (a result of all those special suppers ordered from the Redcliffe and from home). The boys gave only a quick glance at Blanche, who fixed her eyes on Walter as she entered with Sheriff Byxbee. Blanche's attire was more tasteful than in the past and was probably picked out by her attorneys or their wives to present a conventional appearance: a black wool dress, a long fur-trimmed coat, and a black hat with black ostrich feathers.[19]

However, even though the boys pretended indifference to Blanche, they had been communicating with her silently at the jail with looks and hand signals: Blanche's room overlooked the exercise yard and she would often stand in the window when the Malleys were down there.[20]

The chemical analysis of Jennie's body and bones came in shortly after the Malleys and Blanche entered pleas of "not guilty": There were more than three grains of arsenic throughout the body, and none to speak of had been found in the bones. The latter finding would serve to destroy the defense theory of Jennie's arsenic eating, although they would not abandon it entirely. After this analysis came out, however, it was rumored that they would focus on another theory: that Jennie had committed suicide on Thursday, with the body not floating to the surface until Saturday morning; the witnesses who thought they saw her Friday were mistaken.[21]

Heading up the prosecution would be the State's attorney, Tilton E. Doolittle, who had been part of Herbert Hayden's defense team at the Justice Court trial in Madison. With him was Charles Bush, the prosecutor at the Malley trial in West Haven. The two prosecutors would face a plethora of defense attorneys: Timothy J. Fox, Levi N. Blydenburgh, William C. Case, and Samuel F. Jones for the Malleys; Edwin C. Dow and ex-judge William B. Stoddard for Blanche; and Lewis C. Cassidy for James Malley. It was reported that Cassidy had been paid $10,000 for his minuscule part in the trial.[22]

On the first day of jury selection, Walter and Jimmy were dressed in new suits. Blanche wore another black outfit and presented a "cheerful innocent appearance." Her good mood was probably due to getting out of the jail cell for a while. To a reporter, she insisted that she was "through with the Malleys and her old life forever."[23]

Several jurors in the pool had served on the Hayden jury, and these were all dismissed. In fact, Judge Miles T. Granger, who would be hearing the trial, dismissed everyone who had formed *any* kind of opinion. After a while, this angered Samuel Jones, who thought that many of these would have been fair in listening to the evidence. He took exception to Judge Granger's approach on this, but got nowhere except to anger the judge.[24]

One prospective juror bore the last name of Hotchkiss, and Jones, not wanting to get burned again by a holdout vote, inquired whether he had any relatives in the town of Prospect. George Hotchkiss assured him he had not. And the *New York Times* reporter covering the trial took special pains to inform his readers that *this* Hotchkiss "has an intelligent appearance and is not the Mr. Hotchkiss . . . who stood alone for conviction" in the Hayden trial.[25]

By chance, the twelve jurors selected were all blond and the newspapers thought that was amusing. A reporter asked Jones if it was done intentionally. Jones gave a cryptic smile and said, "Blonds are preferred in some quarters, you know."[26]

Because of Judge Granger's decision to eliminate everyone who had an opinion on the case, jury selection had taken a week. However, once the trial started, Granger proved himself to be a no-nonsense judge: he moved everything right along, allowed no wrangling between attorneys such as had dominated the Hayden trial, and cut short everything that he considered a waste of time. Moreover, Granger tended to let *all* evidence come in, reserving his decision as to its admissibility until a later time. Legal observers said he was afraid of being reversed by a higher court, so he tended to be overly cautious in this regard. But in spite of Judge Granger's speed, the Malleys' Superior Court trial would last as long as Hayden's had.[27]

Sheriff Byxbee and his deputies had learned something from their experiences during the Hayden trial. Instead of opening the doors and allowing a rush for seats, they let in only one spectator at a time. When the allotted seats were filled, the doors were closed.[28]

There were two special boxes for women to use, and if these were filled, women could sit in the men's section. Men, however, could not sit in the women's section even if all the seats were not being used there. The reporters took great delight in filling in their readers with the numbers and kinds of women who had attended court that day: whether young or old, rich or poor, ugly or beautiful, all were described in unsparing detail.[29]

There was an insinuation that women who attended murder trials were less than proper ladies. The *Boston Pilot* said that the women's section was filled at the Cramer trial during some of the most disgusting parts (probably the testimony regarding rape), even though the judge had forewarned them that the testimony was about to take a "delicate" turn. The *Pilot* thought the judge might have done as a famous Irish judge once did during a particularly racy segment of a trial when he made that same announcement and many women still remained. The lawyer who was asking questions hesitated to proceed because there were ladies present. "I think you are mistaken," the judge replied sarcastically. "All of the *ladies* went out a little while ago."[30]

A *New York Times* editorial emphasized this point. Admonishing a public that treated the Cramer trial as if it were a circus or theater entertainment, it singled out the many women who were "unwilling to lose a word of the medical testimony" and criticized both sexes for imitating the ancient Romans at the gladiatorial fights.[31]

The prosecution's opening statement on April 25, 1882, outlined its theory of what had happened to Jennie Cramer: that Jennie had begged James to marry her and save her honor. James did not want to marry her but was afraid of what her brother might do. Walter and Blanche were at Branford Point on Friday night, the State admitted, but then later all four went to Savin Rock.[32]

As he had twice before, Asa Curtiss testified to the appearance of the body when he found it. Curtiss was extremely animated during his time on the stand and could not sit still during interruptions by the defense. He talked of a bad odor that had come from Jennie's mouth when he turned her over, which S. L. Marsden had also smelled. Curtiss said it wasn't alcohol and it wasn't anything he had ever smelled before. He thought it might be chloroform. Whatever it was, it stayed with him for days. (Bodies with arsenic often have a strong garlic odor, and it was probably this, along with decomposition, that Curtiss had smelled.[33])

Drs. Durell Shepard and Henry Painter said that Jennie's shoes were wet, but not saturated, and it was this, along with other signs, that caused them to think she had not been in the water long. The estimate of when the rape occurred was based on the fact that the torn areas had not yet begun to heal. Their conclusions as to the degree of violence and the time span were corroborated by Dr. Leonard Sanford, who had testified for the defense in the Hayden case.[34]

Another Hayden alumnus was called by the State for the date rape issue: Dr. Moses C. White, who was probably rejoicing that George Watrous had declined to be on the defense team. White said that the kinds of injuries Jennie incurred to her sexual organs were never achieved without brutality. Notwithstanding the absence of Watrous, however, Dr. White was not to escape unscathed: in his cross-examination, Samuel Jones brought up the blood-on-the-stone fiasco that had marred White's credibility in the Hayden case.[35]

During Mrs. Cramer's testimony, Blanche had the good grace to look embarrassed when Jennie's mother recounted how James Malley had assured her that Blanche was "all right." Mrs. Cramer knew she was *not* a lady, though, because of "her countenance," which must have had a hard edge to it.

Still proud of her daughter's popularity in life, Christina Cramer spoke of the many letters she had found among Jennie's things after her death.[36]

Mrs. Klippstein came back again to testify to what she had seen from her observation post across from the Elliott House. Conspicuously missing in action, however, was "Happy Jack" Gilchrist, in spite of the State's considerable efforts to locate him.[37]

Samuel Mattoon, the clerk in the drugstore under the Elliott House, still maintained that Blanche and Jennie had come in to drink soda water on Thursday at 7:00 P.M. John Hubbell, who was standing across the street at the time, verified this. Asked by the defense as to how he happened to notice the two girls, Hubbell responded that it was because of "a contrast in their dresses."[38]

Charles Rawlings, the maître d'hôtel at the Redcliffe Restaurant, could not be shaken in his insistence that Walter, Blanche, and the lady in white who had had breakfast that morning with Blanche came in for a supper of lamb chops at 10:00 P.M. Thursday.

John Lovejoy, the constable who had seen both Jennie and Jimmy on the Green at the noon hour on Friday, fixed the time by the city hall bell, the noon factory whistle, and the rush of people into Maine's dining room.[39]

George Audley had gone to school with James Malley and had known him for about ten years. He was standing eight feet from him at 3:00 P.M. on Friday when he saw him with a young lady who wore two rings on each hand. Audley also said a Malley detective had approached him about his testimony and told him that he (the detective) would approach Edward Malley about getting enough money "to buy the crowd" so they wouldn't testify.[40]

According to Charles Whedon, a former attorney for Edward Malley, one of the Malley detectives had come to his office to tell him that Edward had "put up a job" to entrap Charles Rawlings from Redcliffe's. However, the trap didn't work and it was never explained what exactly it was.[41]

Henry Allen, the barber-chair witness, repeated his story and was subjected to some humorous, if caustic, cross-examination by William Case regarding Allen's bursting into tears over his identification of James Malley:

Allen: I knew these young men were confined there in jail in more or less trouble and I felt for them.

Case: You saw other prisoners in the jail, did you not? Did you slop over them?

Allen: I did not weep, but felt full of emotion on account of them.

Case: That capped the climax, I suppose?

Allen: Yes, sir, I felt sorry for all of them but more so for James.

. . .

Case: Suppose you had seen the young man you afterward met on Church street and thought was [James], would you have wept over him?

Allen: I guess not.

Case: Why not—you want to be impartial in your weeps, don't you?

Allen: I don't know what you mean.

Case: You are in possession of all your faculties, I suppose?[42]

This particular exchange illustrates the problem the State had in encouraging witnesses to come forward. Many were reluctant to testify because of the humiliating treatment of well-meaning witnesses on the part of the defense.

There were hints dropped to the reporters that Blanche Douglass had told one of the State's detectives of the purchase of arsenic by one of the Malleys around the time of Jennie Cramer's death. But no purchase could ever be found in any of the drugstores in New Haven or its adjoining areas, and the most that could be turned up was Walter's purchase of four ounces of white powder arsenic in September 1880. Because it was far removed in time from Jennie's death, and because the Malley store had rats, it was decided not to present this evidence. Even so, this would have proved that the Malleys at least had it on hand and didn't have to purchase any.

Nor had the prosecution told the jury of Blanche's account of the events in the Malley mansion that Wednesday night. Of course, it had been in the newspapers, but that could not be considered evidence. The only way to get this testimony in, as well as that of the alleged arsenic purchase, was to put Blanche on the stand, and the State did not want to do that. Any possible benefit to be gained would have been offset by the damage of Blanche's ever-shifting testimony and her occupation, and would have been quickly eroded by competent cross-examination.

How could Blanche Douglass have been put on the stand by the State if she were a *defendant* in this trial? It was because Blanche had always been promised immunity from prosecution if she would testify against the Malleys, and at any time she could be made the State's witness. The attorneys she had, Dow and Stoddard, were both selected, hired and paid for by the State. Stoddard had been the law partner of the prosecutor, Doolittle. But because Blanche had never given the State any information that would shed light on Jennie Cramer's death, the State did not feel it had to honor that promise if it didn't want to, a situation Blanche felt very bitter about.

The State tried to get around its Blanche-as-witness problem by putting Sheriff Peck on the stand to testify to her midnight confession. But eventually the judge denied its admission into evidence because Blanche had been offered inducements of money (the two rewards) and protection in exchange for her confession. This was a violation of her rights, and the statements were therefore "poisoned at the fountain." Moreover, Blanche had not been represented by counsel at that time.[43]

As the State prepared to conclude its case, many observers wondered, "Is that all there is?" Unless there was a surprise waiting in the wings to be produced at the last moment, there was nothing to connect the Malleys with arsenical poisoning. The two were scoundrels, there was no doubt about that, but the State hadn't proved they were murderers.

A constant problem arose during the Malley trial that either was not evident at Hayden's trial or not focused on: the failure of many witnesses to speak loudly enough to be heard by jurors and reporters. For example, Mrs. Malloy, the milliner, spoke in such a low tone of voice that a nearly deaf juror couldn't hear her at all and another one fell asleep. Reporters were at their wits' ends trying to write down inaudible testimony, especially since the configurations of the courtroom forced them to write with their backs to the witnesses.[44]

Finally, Joe Howard of the *New York Herald* came up with a suggestion, which he posed to Judge Granger: since the reporters were there on business and not pleasure, and since they represented millions of readers, why not let the reporters have some of the good seats currently occupied by curiosity-seekers? Or, why not turn the reporters' table the other way? Judge Granger said he always left these things to the sheriff, so Howard was sent to talk to Byxbee.

Unfortunately, Howard had already come to the negative attention of Byxbee. On the first day of trial, Howard, who was bald, wore a skullcap to protect his head from drafts. He fought with the sheriff, who insisted he remove his headgear inside the courtroom. To add insult to injury, an anonymous donor (probably a rival newspaperman) sent Joe a black wig to wear on cool days.

Another time, Howard took Edward Malley's vacant seat in order to hear "a zero-voiced" witness. The sheriff had to kick him out of the seat, and Howard did not go quietly. And the day before he wanted to ask the favor of Byxbee, Howard had written in his daily *Herald* article that the New Haven deputies were "a set of bumpkins whose leading characteristics were boorish incivility and a superior degree of ability in expectoration of tobacco juice."

When Howard approached him with the auditory problem, Byxbee said the table idea had been tried during the Hayden case and didn't work. Howard kept at him, though, and finally Byxbee said, "Mr. Howard, you have been growling ever since you came here. None of the other reporters have any trouble. You have set out to ridicule this court and its officers."

Undaunted, Howard retorted, "Now if you have got through with your impertinence, let's return to common sense and business." An exchange followed wherein Byxbee threatened to bar the *Herald* from the proceedings and Howard taunted him that he had no power to do that. Byxbee said he had his duties to perform, and Howard said part of those duties seemed to be "sitting up in a high chair and sleeping three or four hours a day." Blanche Douglass was able to overhear the whole exchange and was heartily amused by it. But the problem of hearing the witnesses remained unsolved.[45]

In the middle of the defense's case, one of the jurors came down with erysipelas (St. Anthony's fire), an acute strep infection that is today practically nonexistent because of antibiotics. However, in the nineteenth century it was life-threatening, and it was feared the juror might die. The death of a juror would cause a mistrial, and the whole thing would have to be done over again if the State chose to refile its case.[46]

The court adjourned until it could be determined what would happen with Juror Lovejoy. Back in his jail cell, Walter told a reporter that the State would never retry the case and had only done so in the first place because of public opinion. However, he said he would much rather have another trial than have it end as the Hayden case did: without a clear acquittal.

Walter vowed to search for the truth to the end of his days: "I am not through with the case when the trial is over, for I shall never be satisfied and will not rest until the affair is cleared up. I shall keep at it until all is explained." There is no indication that he ever did so.[47]

But the seventy-four-year-old juror recovered and the trial, in the words of Lewis and Clark, "proceeded on." The Malley sisters came forward again with their detailed itinerary of the happenings in the Malley household on that Friday night in August 1881. Minnie Quinn was put on to repeat her prodigious feat of memory. Maggie Kane and her flying horses contingent were on hand once more.

As before, the defense chose to go with only one expert witness: Dr. Pliny Jewett. He repeated his opinion from the preceding year that Jennie's death could have been caused by drowning and that the lack of inflammation of the stomach probably meant that Jennie was an arsenic eater. Dr. Jewett also disagreed with the State's experts as to the violence done to the genitals. This, he claimed, was inconclusive.[48]

The State's rebuttal case consisted of still more witnesses to say that, no, it wasn't Maggie Kane and her party at the merry-go-round that night, it was Jennie Cramer.

In his closing argument, Samuel Jones used two tactics he had used in the Hayden trial: criticizing the victim's family and addressing the jurors by name. Jones blasted the Cramers for their negligence in raising Jennie and placed the blame for her death (by suicide) squarely on their shoulders.[49]

If Judge Park's charge to the jury at the end of the Hayden trial was pro-State, Judge Granger's was heavily pro-defense, sounding more like closing arguments than jury instructions. Even Samuel Jones commented on this.[50]

And Jones had worried needlessly about a hung jury: after only one ballot, the jury came back in under an hour with its verdict: Not Guilty.[51]

The Malleys were congratulated by many in the courtroom, although only her attorneys congratulated Blanche. Justice Steven Booth, who had presided at the trial the previous year, went into another room and wept at the verdict.

Immediately after the trial, the Malleys had a party at the Tontine Hotel, which had been prepared for just such a result. Their attorneys, friends, and family members were treated to a lavish repast that included wine, and from there they all went to the Malley mansion to continue the festivities.

But there were no parties for Blanche Douglass, who had to be taken back to jail as she had nowhere else to go.

In an interview the following day, Jimmy declared his intentions to go to Saratoga for a vacation, and Walter said he would be staying home for a while.

If the tide of newspaper opinion had gone toward the Malleys during the trial, it now turned against them and also against the State for botching yet another case. The *New York World* commented, "Following so closely on the acquittal of Hayden for the killing of Mary Stannard, this verdict will be set to make the country think that serial polygamy really is exerting in Connecticut [a] disastrous moral influence." And why was there only one charge? Why not one for accidental death during debauchery, or for inducing Jennie to commit suicide because of their outrageous treatment of her?[52]

Other newspapers stated that, jury decision or no, the Malleys would always be considered guilty of some heinous offense in the minds of the public: "This ought to be a burden to sober and sadden them for the rest of their days."[53]

Perhaps the strongest indictment of the Malleys came from their own hometown newspaper, the *Register*. What were they doing giving themselves parties, it asked? Instead of a "general jollification" and planning resort vacations, they should instead hide their faces from the public. They were lucky to have gotten off, and unfortunately there had only been one charge. This ought to sober them up. Their behavior was "beyond the confines of decency" in contrast to that of their cohort: "To Blanche Douglass, a strumpet, belongs the credit of having behaved in a decorous and becoming way, both before and during the trial."[54]

But there were yet more horrors of indecent behavior in store for New Haven residents. The jurors, who had enjoyed their time together so much that they had a group portrait taken, decided to have a sort of reunion picnic . . . at Savin Rock! Moreover, they chose the date of August 9, only a few days after the first anniversary of Jennie's death there. They had a dinner of seafood and vegetables (tastefully refraining from having steak, mushrooms, and huckleberries), made humorous comments about Blanche Douglass, then visited the sites made famous by the Cramer trial. The picnic was so successful that they thought of making it a yearly occurrence.[55]

Public reaction was swift. The *New York Commercial* thought that "somebody should go up to New Haven and form a nucleus for celebrating the death of those insensate idiots." Have they no decency? cried the *Register*. The *Detroit Free Press* thought the jurors were "as peculiar as the boys themselves," and *The New York Evening Post* had a suggestion for them: the following year they could invite the Malley boys to join them, as "the spot must be full of charm for them."[56]

When all was said and done, however, there was simply not enough evidence to convict the Malleys beyond a reasonable doubt. How could modern forensics have helped? Probably not very much. Since Jennie had been wearing the same clothes as when she was, by their own admission, with the Malleys, fiber evidence would not be probative of their connection with her death.

If semen had been found, a DNA analysis would reveal whether the last man to have intercourse with her was James Malley or someone else, possibly Walter or a stranger from the shore. A lie detector test, while not admissible in court, would have been helpful with respect to all three defendants.

Cause of death could more accurately be gauged by an examination of the eyes for ocular petechiae (pinpoint hemorrhages indicating strangulation or asphyxiation), and perhaps a more sophisticated analysis of the stomach contents would yield more clues as to contents and the time they were ingested.[57]

But, ultimately, Jennie Cramer's death, and the part of the Malleys in it, remains a mystery.

Chapter 18

WHAT HAPPENED TO JENNIE CRAMER?

Only a happy, innocent girl,
With face so sweet and fair,
With long, dark lashes, and dainty curl
In the beautiful, nut-brown hair.

Only a weak and defenceless thing
Caught in the tempter's snare,
Dreaming not of the terrible sting
In pleasures all so fair.

Only a corpse tossed up by a wave
Onto the shining sands,
Alas! too late to help or to save
With strong but gentle hands.

Only a grave without any name,
Only a lonely hearth,
A father bowed down with grief and shame,
A mother crushed to earth.

Only a soul shut out from heaven!
Ah, who shall dare to say?
Pardon divine there must be given
To one so led astray.

—Frank M. Wade, M.D., "Jennie Cramer" (1881)

The two main obstacles to solving the mystery of Jennie Cramer's death are the arsenic and Jennie herself: arsenic makes it difficult to posit an accident, and Jennie's reportedly normal, happy behavior on Thursday and Friday belies suicide.

Even a verdict of "death by misadventure"—perhaps too much laudanum in her drink or too much chloroform to sedate her—is cancelled out by the presence of arsenic, plus the fact that no laudanum or opium derivative was found in her body. And if she were accidentally chloroformed to death, why then use arsenic? How would it get into her bloodstream?[1]

There are the problems of *when* and *where* the death occurred, as well as the one of *how* it happened. That she was alive after Thursday noon is almost certain, and most likely on Friday as well. The witnesses who saw Jennie, Jimmy, Blanche, and Walter together in various combinations on Thursday and Friday could be mistaken as to identity or date, or possibly lying for their own purposes. But not all of them could be wrong. Some of them must have been accurate. The problem is . . . which ones?

There is one small clue that validates the sighting by Minnie Klippstein of Jennie and Blanche at the Elliott House on Thursday afternoon, despite Blanche's repeated denials of having seen Jennie after noon on that day. At the preliminary examination conducted by Drs. Shepard and Painter on the day the body was found, there was evidence of recent and violent sexual intercourse. Yet, the underpants Jennie was wearing were not torn or stained.[2] Therefore, she must have changed her underwear, and she did not do so at home because of the confrontation with her mother.

When the detectives were hunting down Blanche Douglass in New York City, they were acting on the name "Lizzie Bundy" written in some underwear. As it turned out, Blanche and Lizzie had gotten their underwear mixed up, thereby enabling Blanche to be traced to the house of prostitution.[3] But why would the detectives have *Blanche's* underwear? It was much more likely that what they had were the underpants taken from Jennie's body but bearing Lizzie's name. Their hunch was that Blanche had given Jennie a clean pair and maybe threw out the stained pair or took them back to New York. They wanted the stained, torn underwear, which they *did* find with Blanche's things in New York, as proof of the rape.

But what no one seems to have realized is that this fact also provided proof of Jennie's being in the Elliott House after she left her parents' house on Thursday afternoon. Blanche wouldn't have taken an extra pair of underpants to the Malley home on Wednesday evening because she would be going back to the Elliott the next day. And Jennie wouldn't have changed into Blanche's underwear at the Elliott on Thursday morning, since she planned on changing her clothes at home.

Of course, there is the slight chance that Jennie changed *before* going home so that her mother would not see her torn, stained underwear and ask questions about it if Jennie felt she could not dispose of the item without calling attention to it. But it would seem that an item with the name "Lizzie Bundy" written in it would be cause for even more questions than a missing pair of underpants.

What, then, could have happened to Jennie Cramer?

Except for a few melodramatic reporters, no one thought that Jennie Cramer would ever commit suicide, including the young man who was accused of killing her. Those who knew Jennie all said she was too happy and cheerful to take her own life. Viewed from a less sympathetic angle, she was also too vain, shallow, and silly.

Supposedly, Jennie was to have committed suicide over her ruination. But she doesn't seem to have been overly stressed by this. She may have waved jauntily to Walter and Jimmy as she and Blanche were leaving on Thursday morning, and it is not disputed that she had an incredibly hearty breakfast. She wasn't in any special hurry to get home to tell her parents about it, either, not arriving there until 11:00.

Once Jennie got home, she found her mother and told her . . . that her new shoes were bothering her![4] She had come home, she said, to change her clothes and then stay there. It is only when her mother lost her temper that Jennie left the house, and without using the one defense that could have changed her mother's mind: "Mama, they forced me to stay and then James Malley had his way with me against my will."

Those who claim to have seen Jennie at Savin Rock (and surely at least one of them must be telling the truth) said that she seemed to be having a good time.

Jennie wanted to leave home anyway (something her mother never knew she was planning) and perhaps she saw this as her opportunity to get married or move to New York City.

And then there is another problem with suicide: where did she get the Fowler's Solution? Even if it is claimed that she was an arsenic eater (and there was no proof of that), she obviously didn't carry the Fowler's around with her. If she had, at least one of the other three would have noticed it and brought it up as proof of her habit, and the bottle would have been found near her body. No matter where her death occurred—at the Malley mansion, at the Malley beach house at Savin Rock, or in the Foote Building—she had to have access to arsenic in order to kill herself or accidentally overdose.

Perhaps Jennie was drunk and fell off the pier. But she would not have been drinking alone. It is true that, had this happened, the others might have panicked and fled, but there is still that pesky arsenic to account for.

The theory that Jennie was sedated to keep her quiet while Jimmy had sex with her doesn't work because she had already lost her virginity on Wednesday. She would either have been angry at him for this and never want to see him again, or she would have demanded marriage, or she would have consented to be with him on Thursday. A second forceful encounter doesn't seem likely.

Death by misadventure through an experimentation with drugs on the part of the quartet has been raised by at least one analyst as an answer to the mystery.[5] But this would have to have taken place at a time when Jennie could be expected to be all out of sorts: thrown out of her house in shame and rage by the parents she had always seemed to adore, and with an uncertain future ahead of her. What could have induced her to indulge in a carefree, daring undertaking like drug experimentation at a time like that? And if she did so, were not the other three involved in it as well? How convenient, then, that the only one to perish was the very one who could have caused the other three so much legal and social difficulty had she lived!

Could Jennie have had a heart attack or some kind of seizure during all the stress and excitement? It's possible that a heart ailment was part of her medical problem and that Walter might have used Fowler's Solution to revive her. He had been to Yale's Scientific School and would have known that was one of its uses. He may have used too much or she may have died from the heart problem after the Fowler's failed to work.

But the autopsy did not reveal any abnormalities of the heart. And even if there was a defect that did not show up at the post-mortem examination, there was the difficulty of what to do with the body. For if Jennie's death was an *accident* it could only have happened in a place where Fowler's Solution was naturally on hand and not brought there for a darker purpose. This would limit the location to the Malley mansion, where Fowler's Solution was probably right in the medicine chest for heart problems, neuralgia, malaria, heartburn, and any other of its legitimate uses.

How would Jim, Walter, and Blanche get Jennie's body out of the mansion, into a carriage, and down to Savin Rock without anyone seeing them? It would be more of a problem getting a body out of the Foote Building right in the middle of town, and past any hotel employees (and her death in the Foote Building would rule out accident, since Fowler's Solution would not be found there as a matter of course). None of this is impossible, but it makes it more likely that Jennie's death occurred at Savin Rock and not in New Haven.

Murder does seem most probable, simply because Jennie's death so conveniently occurred before she could tell anyone about what had happened to her. But there are difficulties here, too: for example, the carelessness of the other three in being seen around town and at Savin Rock with Jennie on Thursday and Friday—if, in fact, the witnesses are correct. If it was murder, then, it was without much advance planning. And there was also Blanche, a weak link who could not have been trusted to keep her mouth shut if it came down to saving her own skin.

The arsenic has to be seen as the cause of death, since it was obviously administered with that in mind: Whether done by Jennie herself or by the Malleys, and even if Jennie actually died through suffocation, it was the arsenic that was intended to kill her.

Professor Chittenden and the other expert witnesses felt that the arsenic was almost certainly taken in its liquid, soluble form (Fowler's Solution) because of the quickness with which it reached the brain. And, since the prosecution was never able to show a recent purchase of *any* kind of arsenic by either Walter or James, it had to be on hand.

Who had Fowler's on hand? Edward Malley might have, as it was used as a tonic for heartburn, among other things, and could probably have been found in the Malley medicine chest. Jimmy almost *certainly* had some in his home, as he was being treated for neuralgia and malaria while he was in jail. Fowler's is a remedy for both of these, and the Malley family could have easily gotten it from Dr. Andrew O'Malley, Jimmy's brother, who had come from Wilkes-Barre for the trial and attended Jim in jail when he was sick. Therefore, both of the Malleys had the means.

Motive is a little more problematic. Most analysts have looked at the fact that James Malley had a motive because he had ruined Jennie and maybe didn't want to marry her. And this *is*, of course, a problem for him. But is it a big enough one to commit murder? At that time, rape was punishable by a sentence in the state prison, but Jennie's behavior afterward would have given Jimmy much ammunition for a defense of consent. If Jennie's brother or father tried to force a marriage, Jim could simply leave town, as he did after the trial.

Although Mrs. Cramer had indicated that Jennie was welcome back home, Jennie may have said she didn't want to go back because of her shame, or because of the stifling atmosphere there. Jim was not rich like Walter, and so he could not have afforded to buy Jennie off with an apartment in New York. But Walter could have done this for him, and probably would have because of his own involvement in the affair.

So Jimmy's motives for something as drastic as murder were weak, and this has always been the problem with this case.

But there *was* someone with very strong motives to keep Jennie Cramer quiet, and that was Walter Malley. Although Jimmy was not at all ambitious, Walter was. A prosecution for seduction and rape, or accessory to it, was to be avoided at all costs. Even more than that, Walter did not want Edward Malley to find out about it and then to find out about Blanche (he had threatened Rudolph Neumann to keep quiet about his bringing girls up to the Foote Building overnight). And Edward was due home from Saratoga that Saturday.

Edward Malley would not have cared one whit that Walter was going to a house of prostitution in New York (boys will be boys, after all) but it would not have been acceptable for his only son and heir to be seriously involved with such a woman and trying to pass her off as a respectable member of the upper class. Walter's desire to keep this from his father gave him a very strong motive.

Walter and his father were not on the best of terms to start with, and the young man must have felt that this would cause a complete break: perhaps he would lose his home, his job, his inheritance, his position in the community. All of these Walter valued, much more than Jimmy did, and subsequent events (see Aftermath) bear this out.

It was *Walter*, not James, who frantically jumped on a train to New York to keep Jennie from telling Eddie Cramer about the date rape. Eddie would have caused a lot of trouble about it, and Walter must have known that. Moreover, Mrs. Cramer had just let Jimmy know that she suspected that Blanche was not the lady they claimed she was.

Jennie Cramer's fate was sealed when her mother went to Malley's store to confront Jimmy and revealed her suspicion that Blanche was "not a lady."

Who is the idea man in this group? Not Jimmy, but Walter: Walter is the mastermind behind the seduction scheme; Walter is the one Jimmy goes to in a panic after the visit from Mrs. Cramer; Walter is the one writing the notes from Blanche to Jennie and her mother; and Walter is the inventor of the story that Blanche tells the inquest jury.

Jimmy is impulsive, a seeker after pleasure. Tomorrow means nothing to him. Walter, on the other hand, is a thinker, a planner, an organizer. If Jimmy can't be talked into marrying Jennie, or if Jennie cannot be cajoled into going home and keeping her mouth shut, then Jennie will have to die.

Here's how it might have happened: Jennie had either not gone to Savin Rock at all, or came back to the Elliott House after taking a bath down at the shore. She got a change of underwear from Blanche, and maybe even took a bath at the hotel if she didn't go to Savin Rock for one (Blanche testified to having a bath drawn for herself that afternoon).[6] That night, Jennie, Blanche, and Walter had dinner at Redcliffe's. Jimmy was not with them because he was persona non grata with Jennie, and this meshes with the testimony of Charles Rawlings and John Henry.

Walter talked to Jennie about the fact that Jimmy had no plans to marry her, and that she should just go home and not make a fuss. Her mother had forgiven her and was expecting her to come back. But Jennie insisted that she *couldn't* go home and act as if nothing had happened. Besides, this was her big chance to get the money she needed to move to New York, and this was what she wanted: marriage or New York.

The money was not a problem, of course, although Walter was never exactly lavish with it. But if Jennie went to New York, he knew that the Cramers would cause a fuss, a fuss that would come right back to his door.

Walter pretended to assent to the New York plan and said he would make arrangements for it. After the supper at Redcliffe's, he and Blanche drove Jennie down to the Malley beach house on the West Haven shore, where she would be staying out of sight. Perhaps Blanche was assigned to stay there with her.

The next day, Friday, Walter told Jimmy to get himself an unassailable alibi for that night. He may or may not have told Jimmy why, but he could have trusted his cousin's silence because it was Jim, not Wall, who had the obvious motive to kill Jennie.

Jimmy first tried to get Joe Brunt to go with him to Buell's after work, even begging him to change the plans he already had. But when Joe wouldn't go with him, Jimmy made himself conspicuous at home with all that singing and shaving and scolding the girls and yelling at the dogs and demanding mosquito nets. It's no wonder the Friday night alibi sounded so trumped up to the prosecution: it's because it was! Only, the Malley household didn't know it.

It makes more sense to assume that Jimmy *was* at home that night than that all those people made up a story out of wholecloth to protect him. And he still could have sneaked out after he was last seen at 11:00 and come back in by 2:00 or 3:00. Maybe the barking dog he yelled at was barking at him upon his return from Savin Rock!

It is also possible that there *was* no barking dog. The only ones who testified to this were Jimmy and his father. Interestingly, James Malley, Sr., never testified again after the inquest. Had he perjured himself there about the barking dog? If so, he would be reluctant to place himself in a position to be cross-examined, and he probably felt that his son had enough at-home witnesses for that night. The elimination of the barking dog gives Jimmy a window of opportunity from midnight until 6:00 A.M. And if he helped Walter carry Jennie's body down to the water, that would explain the presence of his tie pin in her hat.

Meanwhile, Walter went back to the Malley beach house to see Blanche and Jennie, possibly as early as the afternoon. There, they had something to eat and drank wine. Jennie's wine was doctored with Fowler's Solution, which Walter had brought from home along with the food. He would have known from his Sheffield classes how much would be needed and how long it would take to work. And it is quite possible that he never told Blanche about this.

Later that evening, Walter and Blanche established their own alibi at Branford Point Hotel. Walter even made a fuss about the bill to call attention to himself.[7] Then they headed back to New Haven where they checked the carriage in at 11:00 P.M.

But Blanche never went back to her hotel that night, which she later admitted when confronted with the evidence. And there were horses and carriages to be had near Malley's store that did not require the knowledge of the Malley coachman. So, after Walter got his milk from the housekeeper to establish his presence there, and the household had settled down for the night, Walter and Blanche stole out and got one of those carriages to go to Savin Rock. An alternative is that the coachman (who had originally told a quite different story) and the housekeeper were bribed or threatened to say they had seen Walter at 11:00 when, in fact, he had not come in until much later.

Walter could have chosen to let Jennie die at Savin Rock and have someone find her body. But he couldn't take the chance that she would be found in the Malley beach house. That's why he had to go back to the shore, and he probably had no idea whether she would be alive or dead at that time.

It is possible that he told Jennie to stay in the beach house and not be seen. Or he might have told her to meet them at a particular place at the amusement park. If she died in the house, he and Blanche—or he and Jimmy—would have carried her to the water. If she died at the park, someone would find her and there would be no connection with the Malleys. They would then simply go and clear out any traces of her from the beach house.

It may be that Jennie wandered around to the different Savin Rock locations by herself, or tagged along with others (she was friendly, and not at all shy about hanging out with people she didn't know), and this is why she was seen at the Grove. She may have even felt sick and walked along the water for some fresh air, then collapsed where she was found when the arsenic took effect.

But, if Jennie intruded herself into groups of people she didn't know, why did none of those come forward afterward? Were they afraid of getting involved? It is much more likely that, after two days and nights of drinking and partying, to say nothing of little sleep and the trauma from the violation of her person and the eviction from her home, Jennie simply stayed in the beach house and slept it off. And there would be the gradual effects of the arsenic at work, too. All things considered, she can't have been feeling at all well on Friday, certainly not well enough to be fooling around on the flying horses at the Grove.

Jennie's body was found at 5:30 A.M., and it was later adjudged to have been in the water no more than three to six hours, which means she was put there between 11:30 P.M. and 2:30 A.M. Sheriff Peck had made his last rounds at midnight, but may not have been to that area or may not have seen an object anyway, as the night was overcast and rainy.

At 5:30 A.M. it was nearly high tide, but not completely, so Jennie's body could have been on the beach the previous night before the tide began covering her with water. This would have allowed for a longer time span than three to six hours for the body to have been placed there. But the decomposition factor doesn't fit a longer time frame.

Another problem is Jennie's last meal, taken within eight hours of death: lean and fat meat, mushrooms, and huckleberries. Where did she eat? Did Blanche or Walter bring something down to the shore or cook something for her at the beach house? Did they go to a shore restaurant? Would Walter have risked their being seen with her if he were planning murder?

Huckleberries were in season (the little prodigy Minnie Quinn remembered having them for several meals at the James Malley home), but what about the meat and mushrooms?

It is possible that Jennie died Thursday night at the beach house, eight hours after her Redcliffe breakfast of steak and mushrooms, and was then put into the water on Friday night when the other three had their alibis in place. But, then, how to reconcile all the Jennie Cramer sightings at the shore? She was a distinctive young woman, not to be missed, and her outfit and unusual rings stood out from the crowd. How to reconcile Dr. Painter's statement that decomposition was not yet noticeable when her body was discovered?

On the other hand, there were an estimated 1,500–2,000 people at the shore that day and evening, mingling and moving around. It would have been easy for some—in hindsight, after reading about it in the paper—to imagine that they had seen that same girl at the shore, or to be motivated by a desire for publicity to *say* that they had. Many of the witnesses at Savin Rock did not know Jennie Cramer personally, and so their testimony is to be trusted least.

And then there are those three grains of arsenic, the bare minimum for fatal effect. If Herbert Hayden went overboard with his ninety grains for Mary Stannard, the murderer of Jennie Cramer cut it awfully close. Why not give her enough to make absolutely sure?

There are so many factors about this case that are hard to reconcile in order to come up with a clear, unavoidable theory as to what caused this young girl's death. And her own behavior is the most mysterious of all.

If Jennie had been raped on Wednesday night, why did she act so chipper and nonchalant the next day? And even if she had *consented*, she surely would have had to be in a great deal of pain with a torn fourchette. Yet she didn't act that way at all.

Assuming for a moment that the rape or seduction didn't take place until the next night, Thursday, how to account for Jennie's consenting to put herself back in the control of the very people who had tried to ruin her the previous night and who had caused her to be evicted from her own home? Was she that callous that she could, in effect, spit in her parents' faces by sleeping again with James Malley on Thursday as if it were no big deal? Would it really not have bothered her, even if she thought she was getting married?

There are things about Jennie Cramer that we will never know, because she seems to have been different things to different people. Her mother claimed she was totally open with her in all things and resented Jimmy Malley's sexual pressure. Yet, Jennie continued to see him in spite of this, and we know there were other things that she kept from her mother.

To her family, Jennie seemed virtuous and lively. To the outside world, she appeared loose, frivolous, a flapper ahead of her time. She flirted with young men and teased them, allowing them to give her gifts, or hold her hand, or (at least in the case of Jim Malley) hold her in their arms. She sat on Jimmy's lap and drank too much wine. She continually put herself in compromising and dangerous circumstances.

Yet, Jennie drew the line at sexual intercourse. Was she withholding it as a punishment? (Surely, her flirtatious teasing must have made Jimmy think she would be willing in spite of her protests on the bed that night, that her "No" did not really mean "No.") Was she dangling it as a reward for gifts or marriage? Or did she really want to hold on to this last bastion of her virtue?

And there was yet another of the many puzzles about Jennie Cramer: did she even care for Jimmy Malley? Reading her mother's testimony and the accounts of her behavior around him, it would seem that she really did not. She avoided him often, made excuses for turning down his invitations, and at the time of her death was cheerfully making plans to visit friends in New Britain for a week—hardly the actions of a smitten young lady.[8] Maybe she was just out for a good time, as was Jimmy himself, or maybe she was looking for a high-class marriage, mistakenly thinking Jim was as rich as Walter.

Sometimes Jennie seems so simple as to be almost brainless, and then other times she seems artful and calculating. What were her plans, her motives? Or did she just live from day to day, like Jimmy, for the pleasure of the moment and not think about tomorrow? One newspaper called her "an insipid Gwendolyn"; yet, she doesn't come across as romantic.[9] For all the young men she attracted, there is no evidence that she returned their feelings. Instead, there is at times a hard, purposeful edge to her actions. Was she up to anything other than looking good, shopping, and partying?

What happened to Jennie Cramer? Walter, Jimmy, and Blanche all knew something, which none of them ever revealed. But at the *heart* of the enigma is Jennie herself. She holds the key to her own mystery, and she has not relinquished it yet.

AFTERMATH

The Victims' Families:
The Stannards, Hawleys, and Cramers

Have any of you, passers-by,
Had an old tooth that was an unceasing discomfort?
Or a pain in the side that never quite left you?
Or a malignant growth that grew with time?
So that even in profoundest slumber
There was shadowy consciousness or the phantom of thought
Of the tooth, the side, the growth?

— Edgar Lee Masters, "Eugenia Todd,"
Spoon River Anthology

Those driven to kill often think that the murder will put an end to the difficulty that caused their desperation in the first place. Instead, it is the beginning of a nightmarish journey for everyone: the killers, their families, and the friends and families of the victims. For the Stannards, Hawleys, and Cramers, the deaths of their loved ones continued to affect their lives. They, too, were victimized by the actions of those who killed Mary Stannard and Jennie Cramer.

When the trial was over, Charlie Stannard and Susan Hawley moved in with Ben Stevens, Susan as hired help and Charlie as a laborer. "Old Ben" died in 1881 of gastroenteritis at the age of sixty-four. Charlie died at the same age of heart disease in 1888.[1]

William Victor (Willie) Stannard lived in Guilford and eventually in Durham, where he married in 1901. He and his wife, Ida, had only one child and both wife and daughter died relatively young: Ida in 1936 at age 57 and Edna in 1952 at age 50. As a man, Willie was said to have retained the hot temper he had as a child. He died in Durham on September 4, 1957, a day after the seventy-ninth anniversary of his mother's murder, and is buried in the little Rockland cemetery. He was 81.[2]

Susan Fowler Hawley never married. She took care of her father and Ben Stevens, and after they died she worked in other people's homes. She died of heart problems in a hospital in Middletown on July 21, 1917, at the age of 65.[3] Susan took care of Mary, took care of Willie, took care of Charlie Stannard and Ben Stevens, and took care of the people she worked for. But no one ever took care of Susan.

A lot has changed in the Rockland area since the Haydens and the Stannards lived there, and yet some remnants of the old days remain. There has been much residential development, but the woods where Mary went to meet Herbert Hayden that day in 1878 are still deep, dark, and tangled with underbrush. It is easy to understand Mary's reluctance to penetrate them alone.

The Stannard home is gone, of course, but the foundation is still visible. It is hard to imagine how so many people could have lived in such a small house. The old Durham road that ran past the Stannard place is intact, but is now private property. Up past the Stannards' the spacious remains of the home of Francis and Eliza Mills can be seen.

The house where the Haydens lived has been moved back from the edge of the Durham Highway (Route 79), but the "Rockland Watchtower" across the way (the Luzerne Stevens home) keeps its vigil still.

Reading the gravestones in the cemeteries at Rockland and Madison is like reading a cast list for the Hayden trial: Benjamin Stevens, Francis Mills, Rachel and Abner Stevens, Henrietta Young, Loren and Cornelia Stevens, J. Sherman Buell, Sereno Scranton, Andrew Hazlett, Sylvester Hawley, Henry B. Wilcox.

In spite of the fact that Rockland residents intended to collect money to put up a stone at Mary's grave, her final resting place has no marker.[4] Her plot, along with those of others who could not afford headstones, lies somewhere toward the back of the cemetery, marked only by the sinking of the soil.

As for Jennie Cramer's family, the tragedy that began with her murder did not end with the trial. Since Jennie's death in August 1881, the Cramers' cigar store had fallen into neglect, and with Jacob's suicide that December, the business stopped altogether. After the trial was over in July 1882, Eddie tried to convince his mother and sister to live with him in Brooklyn. He felt they needed watching over, and New Haven held too many bad memories for them to remain there. But Christina and Minnie wanted to stay a little longer in the family home at 179 Grand Street, and Eddie went back to his job as telegraph operator in New York.[5]

Eddie's position at the telegraph office had enabled him to read the dispatches that came through on the Hayden trial, and his feeling was that the

State in the Malley case had made a crucial error in charging them with only one indictment (arsenic) instead of including one for drowning. And he also thought the Malleys should have been charged with rape or seduction, since there was plenty of proof for that.

Often throughout the proceedings and after the trial Eddie had thought of killing James Malley and possibly Walter as well. But the only thing that could have come of that, he realized, would have been a prison sentence and more heartache for his mother.

By 1883, the Cramers had fallen on such hard times that Christina was forced to go to the city and ask for an exemption from her taxes. And she was showing increasing signs of mental disturbance, becoming convinced that the dead girl found at Savin Rock was not Jennie, and that her daughter would soon be coming back home.[6]

In 1884, Eddie married Mary Dwyer, an Irish girl from Pennsylvania, and at that point Mrs. Cramer and Minnie moved down to Brooklyn. A year later, in August, that month of awful memories for the Cramers, Mary gave birth to a son, Charles.[7]

But, in spite of their happiness over the new little life, the Cramers continued to experience more tragedy. In January 1886, young Minnie, who had been the reason Jennie was evicted from her home, died of consumption, the same disease that had afflicted her father for so many years. She was just eighteen.[8]

Christina Cramer had now suffered the loss of her husband and four of her five children, and her instability was increasing. Around 1890, Eddie's mother-in-law, Kate Dwyer, came to live with them also, and this caused some conflict with Christina. The two mothers had their own ways of doing things and did not get along. In July 1891, Christina, in desperation, decided to move back to New Haven.[9]

Eddie did not approve of his mother's decision, as she had been giving indications of irrationality, but Christina could be stubborn and so he gave in against his better judgment. Somewhat unwisely, Mrs. Cramer found an apartment on the same street where the family had lived before. She was just a few blocks away from the home where the Cramer family had once been so happy.

In New Haven Mrs. Cramer was lonely and depressed. After she settled in, she visited another German woman in her building and told her the story of her daughter, Jennie. The woman had not been living in New Haven at the time, and so had known nothing about it. When Christina finished her sad tale, she went back down to her own apartment and sat in the doorway for several hours, just staring. The next day she told her new friend that she hadn't been able to sleep that night.[10]

Ultimately, the memories and the lack of companionship unsettled Christina Cramer so much that she decided to go back to her son's home in Brooklyn, despite the difficulties there. She began packing her things and waited for Eddie to respond with a telegram. But a telegram never came.

At supper time on Thursday, July 16, a resident in Mrs. Cramer's building was going by her apartment when his attention was drawn to a piece of white paper fluttering under the doorway. He picked it up and read: "Send for my son Edward. Address No. 185 Broadway, New York, care of Postal Telegraph Company. Mrs. C. Cramer." The resident thought it disburbing and gave it to Leslie Daggett, a nearby grocer. Daggett read it, then passed it on to a police officer going by.

Officer Lanigan got no response when he knocked on Mrs. Cramer's door. He went back to the precinct, got another officer, Reilly, and the two went back to the apartment. Lanigan crawled through a window on a ladder, then opened the door for Reilly and the two officers proceeded through the rooms. In the kitchen they found Christina Cramer hanging from a clothesline rope.

The method of suicide showed that it was no impulse but had been well thought out. Mrs. Cramer had opened two cupboard doors so that they were facing each other. On the inside of one door was a large screw to which she attached the clothesline, then drew the rope over the top and closed the door. Next, she draped it over the second door, made a loop and put a box on a chair beneath it. Before standing on the box, she arranged several layers of towels around her neck so that it would not be disfigured by the rope. Then she stood on the box and kicked it out from underneath her.

In the meantime, Eddie had sent his mother a telegram from New York on Wednesday, the day before she was found, but got no answer. When he sent another one on Thursday morning, the response came back saying "Boy cannot get in." Alarmed, Eddie took the train to New Haven and arrived at his mother's home just as the police officers had finished cutting her down. "My God!" he shouted. "That's my mother!"[11]

That night, as the news spread about the suicide of Jennie Cramer's mother, curious onlookers gathered outside the apartment building to stare and gossip. Among them was Walter Malley.[12]

Christina Cramer, age fifty-three, was buried in Evergreen Cemetery with her husband, her youngest son, and her two daughters, completing the wake of destruction caused by the Malleys. Her death report was filed by the city's Medical Examiner: Dr. Moses C. White, who had been an expert witness at both the Hayden and the Malley trials.[13]

Like Mary Stannard and Susan Hawley, the Cramers have no headstones marking their graves.

Today, of course, Mrs. Cramer's problem would be recognized as post-traumatic stress disorder. But was her grief exacerbated by the haunting memory of her last words to her daughter ("When your sister comes home, we will have to find another place for you to live")? Was it compounded by the realization of her own contribution to Jennie's death with her indulgent leniency, or by the fact that blame had been laid at her door by the press and by the defense attorneys?

Those cannot have been easy thoughts to live with: "If only . . . "

The Defendants' Families: The Haydens and Malleys

Yes, here I lie close to a stunted rose bush
In a forgotten place near the fence . . .
You have succeeded, I have failed
In the eyes of the world.
You are alive, I am dead.
Yet I know that I vanquished your spirit;
And I know that lying here far from you,
Unheard of among your great friends
In the brilliant world where you move,
I am really the unconquerable power over your life
That robs it of complete triumph.

—Edgar Lee Masters, "Amelia Garrick,"
Spoon River Anthology

After the trial ended in January 1880, the Haydens moved to New Haven permanently. It is hard to imagine why they did this, unless they were told not to leave the county. In that case, they must have felt that its largest city would provide their best chance for relative anonymity.

Herbert Hayden briefly went on the lecture circuit. His topic: "The Evils of Circumstantial Evidence." His speaking style was described as repetitious and boring. An interesting side note is the presence of another famous defendant at Hayden's New York City lecture in March 1880: Jesse Billings of Ballston Spa, New York, whose several murder trials for the shooting death of his wife in 1878 had also ended in a hung jury. After the lecture, the crowd swarmed around both Hayden and Billings as if they were war heroes.[14]

His lecture tour unsuccessful, Hayden went back to New Haven and took up a series of laboring jobs: carriage maker, carpenter, and grocery clerk. (However, in the 1880 census, he somewhat pompously gives his occupation as "Lecturer and Retired Minister" and in the City Directory as "Retired Lecturer.") Because of the possibility that he could be re-arrested should the State find more evidence, he was never invited to preach again.[15]

In his autobiography, which he began in jail and completed in 1880, Hayden conveniently forgot his and his wife's testimony at both trials and claimed that they hired Mary Stannard as soon as she had recovered from giving birth to her illegitimate child. As a result of the good example of the Haydens, other Rocklanders followed suit to forgive her fall from grace and give her work as well.[16]

The truth was that the Haydens did not hire Mary until April 1877, a full year after Willie was born, and then only because Rosa had become ill. Their neighbors highly recommended Mary Stannard as a caretaker for both Mrs. Hayden and the children. Because of her immense popularity with Rockland residents, Mary had never had trouble finding work.

Hayden's autobiography is a pompous document that puts a self-serving spin on the whole sordid mess of the Mary Stannard murder and his part in it.

As she had done in Rockland, Rosa Hayden continued to supplement her family's income by opening a day school in their home.[17] Perhaps she also home-schooled her own children, thereby saving them some of the notoriety they would suffer in attending a public school.

In October 1896, seventeen years after The Great Case began in New Haven, the State of Connecticut filed a nolle prosequi, which meant that it would never try the matter again.[18] The legal cloud was finally removed from over Hayden's head, although, thanks to David Hotchkiss, he could never claim that he had been found "not guilty."[19]

Rosa Hayden died in 1906 at age fifty-seven and her husband Herbert followed her a year later, dying of cancer of the liver at the age of fifty-seven.[20]

After the trial for the murder of Jennie Cramer, the entire James Malley family moved out of New Haven, thereby giving proof to the rumors of a split between the elder Malleys. James, Sr., moved to Easthampton, Massachusetts, where he died before 1900.[21]

Lizzie Malley Wolfe died in Wilkes-Barre, Pennsylvania, only a few years after the trial.[22] She had moved there with her husband, the drugstore owner Nathaniel Wolfe, after their marriage in November 1881.

Dr. Andrew P. O'Malley continued his successful practice in Wilkes-Barre. But in late August 1882, right after the trial was over, another doctor there made an insulting remark about Jimmy and Walter. Andrew punched him and knocked him down, then was arrested and fined for assault.[23]

Jimmy Malley went to Wilkes-Barre when the trial was over and worked for a while as a salesman in his brother-in-law Nat Wolfe's drugstore.[24] But he soon got restless and moved to New York City, running into Blanche Douglass on occasion.[25] In New York he conceived a "get-rich-quick" plan that will be familiar to modern readers: he decided to sue the newspapers for the negative things they had said about him before and during the trial.[26]

For his targets, Jimmy selected the New Haven *Register* and the New York *Staats-Zeitung*, a German newspaper that could be expected to have been sympathetic to the victim and her family. He filed his suits in August 1883, asking for $50,000 from each newspaper, but nothing seems to have come of them.

When Jimmy visited New Haven in order to prepare and file his papers, he tried to stay with Edward and Walter in their mansion on Derby Avenue, but they refused to have anything to do with him. He was forced to stay in what one paper called "a second-rate hotel" instead.

When Walter was interviewed by the *New York Times* at the time of Christina Cramer's suicide in 1891, he said that Jim was in the West Indies—which may or may not have been true, as Walter might have been trying to throw reporters off the scent in case they tried to look up Jimmy.[27] Whatever the case, there is no official record of James Malley, Jr., in Pennsylvania, Massachusetts, New York, or Connecticut after August 1883. He simply vanished without leaving a paper trail.

Edward Malley remarried in January 1884. His new wife was twenty-year-old Mary A. ("Mamie") Carey of New York. Although Edward was nearly sixty, he listed his age as forty. They got married in New York City, and not a moment too soon, as their son, Arthur W. Malley, was born two months later.[28]

Three years after that they had a daughter who was usually known as Jane. However, her official name was Jennie, a fact which reveals Edward's insensitivity or perhaps his indifference.[29]

Edward's new wife died in 1891, the same year of Christina Cramer's suicide, at the age of twenty-eight. But she did not die in New Haven, and she is not buried with her husband in St. Bernard's Cemetery.[30]

Edward continued his suits against the insurance companies to recover money he had lost in the 1882 fire, and the insurers remained steadfast in their adherence to the letter of the law in his taking on of a partner. He was ultimately unsuccessful.[31]

In his old age, Edward became blind. After that, his health began to break down completely until he died on July 26, 1909, just before his eighty-third birthday. (Ironically, Edward Malley had been born on August 6, the date that Jennie Cramer's body was found.)[32]

In a move Edward would not have approved, the Malley store was closed on the day of his funeral. Mourning wreaths were put on all the doors with sprays of carnations on each, as these were his favorite flowers and the ones he most often wore in his lapel. There was standing room only at his funeral, a solemn high requiem Mass in St. Mary's Roman Catholic Church.[33]

Edward is buried in St. Bernard's Cemetery next to his first wife, Mary Ward, the woman he may have poisoned. The obelisk over the plot is so tall that a visitor gets a crick in the neck trying to look to the top. It is a monument depicting both wealth and admiration. Was it put up by Walter?

Edward Malley was said to have been worth several million dollars when he died, which would have been a great deal of money in 1909. He left it to his two children by his second wife, Arthur and Jane, and to his grandson. He left nothing to his son Walter.[34]

Perhaps Edward felt that Walter had established himself on his own and had no need of the money. At the time of Edward's death, Walter was vice-president of his father's company and assumed the presidency after that. And he was still living in the Malley mansion, so the rift, if rift there was, was not complete. But was Edward still punishing Walter for the Jennie Cramer–Blanche Douglass affair by purposely omitting him from the will?

Walter's post-trial story is the strangest of all. While he was in jail, he had composed a waltz, entitled "Under the Elms," which he published after the acquittal and dedicated to the people who had remained faithful to him at that time.[35]

But he had also composed a march while at Seton Hall, aptly entitled "Setonia," and somehow (probably through his notoriety) he convinced New Haven's American Band to play it at one of their summer evening concerts. It was played the evening of August 9, 1882, just a few days after the first anniversary of the death of Jennie Cramer.[36]

The next day an irate citizen wrote to the newspaper that "we have had enough of the name ringing in our ears for the last year" and that it was poor taste to play anything by someone many people considered guilty of "the outrage and death of one of [our] beautiful young girls." Walter should not be treated like a hero.[37]

Another opinion stated that the American Band should mind its own business and not remind New Havenites of "this unpleasant tragedy" and called the "Setonia" march "a wierd [sic] fleshly thing."[38]

Walter did not give up his association with Blanche Douglass. He followed her to New York and spent many nights with her immediately after the trial, even though he told the New Haven *Register* in early August that he had no idea where she was.[39] Throughout that summer, he wrote to her several times a week and visited her when he could.

Edward Malley refused to give Walter any money apart from his salary, leaving him to rely on the inheritance from his mother (which may have been in the form of a trust).[40] Perhaps Edward knew the use to which his own money would be put if he were to give any to his son.

Walter continued his project of trying to make Blanche into a lady.[41] He made her promise not to return to her old life and not to associate with those people any more. He sent her money for food, clothes, and rent, and constantly sent books for her to read and notebooks for her to practice her writing in. His letters were filled with advice and exhortation: read every day, practice your writing, move out of New York City, don't go out so much. (He seems to have wanted her to become a recluse like himself.) At one time he scolded her because he thought she was trying to get back in touch with Sadie Monroe, her old roommate at Lizzie Bundy's.

Walter worried that his inability to be in New York as much as he wanted, coupled with his relative lack of finances, was hurting his chances with Blanche. He knew she could have more fun with other people, he told her, but hoped she would be patient with him.

In the entire annals of this case, there is nowhere a word or an indication of Walter Malley's being considered anything but stiff, humorless, friendless, supercilious, and arrogant. Yet his courtship of this poor, uneducated Irish prostitute shows a vulnerable side that redeems him. He becomes human for once, and his letters to her reveal a weakness that is not manifest in any other part of his life:

I enclose you a slip of paper with all the letters on, large and small, and how they are to be written, above, on, or below the line. . . . There is no need of telling you how pleasantly the time went to me. I only hope you enjoyed it. . . .

> Yours as ever,
>
> Wall

New Haven, July 30, 1882
My Dearest Nellie—[Walter had designated the names Walter and Nellie Maxwell for their correspondence.]
Your long and expected letter received this morning, and the only fault I have with it, is the shortness. Can't you manage to write more at a time, or do you think I should be satisfied with only so much?

New Haven, Aug. 20, 1882
My Dear Nellie—
I expected a letter from you yesterday, but to this (twelve o'clock) have not received one. Now, is that quite fair? . . . Be sure and take the train stated and I will meet you at the depot, wishing and waiting for the train to go by hurriedly. Yours, with bushels of **** [omitted in newspaper as "unfit to print"]

> Wallace

New Haven, Aug. 24, 1882
My Dear Nellie—
. . . You promised me faithfully to keep away from all such who may call themselves your friends. I have done what I was able for your comfort and happiness. I would like

to be able to do more, but getting no help from father I can only ask you not to blame me but be contented with what I am able to do myself for you until better times. I ask you once more, will you avoid that class of people? I think if you should be led back to that horrible old life it would kill me. . . . Knowing my feeling toward you you cannot blame me. . . .

Wall

And what of Blanche all this time? Quite possibly, she reciprocated at least some of his feelings for her, as this excerpt from a letter shows:

Sunday, Aug. 13, 1882
My Dear Wall—
Your very kind and loving letter received, and glad to hear from you always, and when I get your letters I read them over six times a day. It is a month since you were down, and it looks like six months to me. . . .

Yours very truly,
Nellie

But, it appears as if Blanche was still hanging out with the wrong crowd. In October, Walter received a letter from a man in New York who said his name was James Baldwin and claimed to have over two dozen of the letters Walter had written to Blanche, both before and after the trial. He wanted $500 for them or he would have them published.

Walter wasted no time in contacting his former attorney, Levi Blydenburgh, about the problem. Blydenburgh hired some detectives in New York, and then he and Walter went down to meet the blackmailer, supposedly to complete the trade. At the agreed-upon meeting place, three young men showed up to confront Walter. Unbeknownst to them, however, Blydenburgh and the two detectives were watching them from hiding places.

As soon as the money and a letter changed hands, the detectives came forward and arrested Edward (Ned) Hanley, William Pratt, and John Gourivan, all in their early twenties. The story, gleaned from Hanley and also from Annie Snyder, Blanche's landlady, was that Hanley, who had been introduced to Snyder as Blanche's brother-in-law, got a key from the landlady to enter Blanche's apartment when she wasn't there. He broke open the trunk and stole the letters, which the newspapers claimed were mostly "unfit to print."

Hanley claimed to be Blanche's boyfriend and that they had been living together at one time. This is how he knew of the letters in the trunk. He also claimed Blanche was in on the blackmail and was to share in the proceeds. (However, another witness said that Blanche had gone to the Bleecker Street bar where Hanley worked and asked for the letters back, so this is probably not true.)

Walter and Blanche pressed charges against the three and filed complaints, which Blanche laboriously signed as "Annie Zimmerm," apparently not as far along in her copying practice as Walter had hoped.

At a court hearing, Blanche had to take the stand to show that the letters had been stolen, her hat feather quivering nervously the whole time. The defense attorney afterward kept her for two hours asking her embarrassing (and probably inadmissible) questions. Some of her answers revealed that she had slept with many men, both before and since the trial, and that she spent a great deal of time in the saloons of Houston and Bleecker Streets.

Walter cannot have been terribly pleased, but he remained attentive and solicitous throughout the proceedings. The newspapers, however, were merciless, saying that Blanche had grown heavy since the trial but wasn't any better looking. They described her attire in great detail, and stated that it was perfectly obvious by looking at her "to what class she belongs." Quite possibly, Walter's money wasn't being spent to the best advantage.

And yet, amazingly, it is quite possible that Walter married Blanche Douglass. Although there is no definitive proof, no one fact that links them conclusively, the conincidences are too many and too close to ignore.

Walter's wife and Blanche Douglass had the same first name (Anna), year and place of birth (1860, New York City), and both their fathers were named Frank.[42] Anna Malley's maiden name is given as Madden on her death certificate. This was not a name that was ever brought out in connection with Blanche, but these two were very adept at making up pseudonyms and would have avoided one that could be traced to her.

On her death certificate, Anna Malley's birthday is listed as March 22. There is no available birth certificate for Blanche Douglass, and she may not even have known her actual birthday. However, March 22 is the day of her mother's death, and exactly the kind of memorable date she would have chosen when creating her new life as Anna Malley. (It will be recalled that at the inquest Blanche had such trouble remembering the fake address they gave her that Walter had to write it on her handkerchief.)

And, even more telling, there is no record of any Anna Madden born in New York City from 1858 to 1864. In that same time span, there is *no* Madden child, male or female, with a father named Frank or Francis, or born on March 22.

Walter and Anna were not married in New Haven, New York State, or New Jersey, at least not under their own names. Was it a secret marriage? Were they trying to avoid publicity?

The son of Walter and Anna Malley, Wallace Ward Malley, was born in East Orange, New Jersey, in 1886, but did not go to New Haven until he was a boy.[43] Yet, the 1900 census lists Walter as living with Edward, still single, and there is *no* listing for Anna or Wallace in Connecticut, New Jersey, or New York under either Madden or Malley. Why were Walter's wife and son not living with him?

The person who gave the information to the New Haven census taker either did not know that Walter was married (if, indeed, he was) or lied to cover it up. But if Anna Madden were someone *other* than Anna Kearns/Blanche Douglass, then why keep her under wraps, especially when she had a child?

The child's name, Wallace Ward Malley, is also revealing. "Wallace" was one of the names Walter used in writing to "Nellie Maxwell" after the trial. "Ward" is *his* mother's maiden name, when the usual practice would be to use the *child's* mother's maiden name.

Wallace Malley graduated from Yale's Sheffield Scientific School in 1909, the year Edward Malley died. Yet, Edward was aware of his existence, for he left him a legacy in his will.[44] Perhaps Edward's omission of Walter was because of his having married the prostitute after all and then trying to hide it from him. On the other hand, maybe it was never hidden from Edward but only from the outside world so that those who might have remembered what Blanche Douglass looked like had forgotten or passed away. It would be entirely like Edward to be concerned with the *appearances* of a thing rather than the thing itself.

In his *Times* interview outside Mrs. Cramer's apartment house in 1891, Walter said that Blanche Douglass had died in a hospital outside Chicago a few years prior to that.[45] If this was true, it means that Walter, even though married and with a child, was still keeping tabs on Blanche Douglass. If *not* true, then he must have been blowing smoke at the reporter for a reason, possibly so he wouldn't try to track her down.

Whoever she was, Anna Malley kept a quiet profile throughout her life. She devoted herself to charitable works, especially to those involving children, whom she dearly loved. She and her husband took trips to Europe, Lake Placid, and elsewhere, and were married for about fifty-eight years. Anna lived until the age of eighty-three, dying in February 1944.[46]

It would be nice to think that Blanche Douglass had managed to achieve some peace and comfort in her life after all its early turmoil. Although she must have known or suspected what had happened to Jennie Cramer back in 1881, her role was undoubtedly a small one—a sordid one, granted, but small nonetheless.[47]

Walter Malley lived a long life as well. He was active in many clubs and organizations, and he gave much money to charity. He and his family moved to a large residence at 305 St. Ronan Street, today the home of the Bethesda Lutheran Ministry.

Ever the Pygmalion, Walter spent a great deal of his money in getting people to sing and enjoy fine music. He paid for music and singing lessons, and formed a chorus at the Malley Company. He donated heavily to the New Haven Symphony Orchestra and to a youth orchestra. Yet, the only pieces he ever composed himself were the "Setonia" march and "Under the Elms."

Like his father, Walter became blind in old age. He had turned over the operation of the business to his son, Wallace, and also gradually divested himself of the other obligations he had amassed: board of directors of the library, Chamber of Commerce, Knights of Columbus, and the like. Then, on February 23, 1948, four years after Anna, he died at his home a few months before he would have turned 92.[48]

A story, probably apocryphal, was told to Professor Robin Winks of Yale. A woman who had been a former employee at the Malley Company said that when Theodore Dreiser's sensational novel, *An American Tragedy*, came out in 1925, Walter Malley told her to remove all the copies from the store's shelves.[49]

The novel, which is based on a real incident that occurred in 1906, bears a strong resemblance to the Jennie Cramer case. However, one has to wonder how the books got on the shelves at the Malley Company in the first place if Walter objected to them. Also, in 1925, Walter would have been nearly seventy years old and possibly not as active in the affairs of the store. And removing the books would have called more attention to them than leaving them there. The novel was a best-seller, and the Malley Company's banning it would not prevent it from being acquired elsewhere.

But the fact that the story is told at all is indicative, as with all folklore, of the feelings of the people about the Jennie Cramer incident. Perhaps, in reading the novel, someone thought, "Hmmm . . . wonder if that Walter Malley is squirming in his chair right now. Well, he ought to be!"

That Walter was ambitious can be seen in his decision to stay in New Haven despite the negative publicity that followed. He was criticized in the newspaper for acting superior, for having a weak mouth that he was trying to hide with a puny mustache, and for a general lack of masculinity in his appearance.[50] And there was a story about a woman from Boston who "felt sick, weak, and oppressed with fear" every time a strange gentleman shared her table in the hotel restaurant. She was later told by a waiter that her companion had been Walter Malley.[51]

Walter stuck it out, as James did not, and soon all references to Jennie Cramer disappeared from the newspapers.

That Walter also tried his whole life to be accepted by his father is poignantly evident in his gravestone. In St. Lawrence's Cemetery in West Haven, across from Yale Field, the Malley graves are topped by an immense Celtic cross. Underneath, they are neatly lined up in a row: Walter, Anna, their son and his wife, and their grandson. Anna and their son's wife are "Beloved Wife of . . . ," while Wallace and his son Ward are "Beloved Husband of . . . " Walter's stone, on the other hand, reads, "Walter E. Malley, 1856–1948, Son of Edward Malley." It says volumes about how he thought about himself, how he defined himself. Was it so important to him that he committed murder for it?

The huge monuments of the Malleys and the substantial Hayden gravestone stand in stark, ironic contrast to the emptiness and anonymity of the final resting places of their victims: Mary Stannard's grave cannot be located with accuracy, nor can Susan Hawley's; and Evergreen Cemetery no longer has a record of the Cramers.

It is not supposed to end this way, that the killers prosper and the victims continue to be victimized. Yet, real life is not Hollywood, and the bad guys do not always get their due in the final frame. Whether they were able to achieve inner peace, of course, is a different issue, and we would like to think that their actions in 1878 and 1881 haunted their dreams and their memories for the rest of their lives. We will never know this, and it is very probable that they managed to convince themselves it never happened or that they never had a hand in it.

But there is one thing we *do* know: the decisions that Herbert Hayden and the Malleys made back then were not forgotten by the families of Mary and Jennie. There was no peace for them while they lived, and no great monuments for them when they died.

NOTES

The following abbreviations have been used for newspaper citations:

HDT   The *Hartford Daily Times*
NHER   The *New Haven Evening Register*
NHJC   The *New Haven Morning Journal and Courier*
NYT   The *New York Times*

CHAPTER 1: MARY

1. "The Rev. Mr. Hayden Free," *NYT*, 30 October 1896.
2. "The Hayden Case," *NHER*, 13 October 1879.
3. "The Hayden Case," *NHER*, 11 October 1879.
4. "The Hayden Case," *NHJC*, 14 October 1879.
5. "Mr. Hayden's Defense," *NHER*, 6 December 1879; "Mrs. Hayden's Testimony," *NYT*, 21 September 1878.
6. Willie was reportedly ill-behaved, and the Studleys had put that stipulation in the agreement. See "Mrs. Hayden's Testimony," *NYT*, 21 September 1878, and "Hayden's Wife's Story," *NYT*, 11 December 1879.
7. *Poor Mary Stannard: A Full and Thrilling Story of the Circumstances Connected with Her Murder* (New Haven: Stafford Printing Co., 1879), 28. This volume was put together by reporters of the *New Haven Union* after the inquest trial.
8. "Hayden's Wife's Story," *NYT*, 11 December 1879.
9. *Poor Mary Stannard*, 6.
10. "The Rev. Mr. Hayden Free," *NYT*, 30 October 1896.
11. "The Madison Mystery," *NHJC*, 23 September 1878.
12. "A Celebrated Case," *NHER*, 13 September 1878.
13. "State's Suppressed Evidence," *NYT*, 4 October 1878.
14. "The Hayden Case," *NHJC*, 8 January 1880.
15. "Rev. Mr. Hayden's Trial," *NHER*, 2 January 1880.
16. "State's Suppressed Evidence," *NYT*, 4 October 1878.
17. "The Rockland Tragedy," *NHER*, 6 September 1878; "The Hayden Case," *NHER*, 11 October 1879.

18. "Susan Hawley's Story," *NHER*, 2 December 1879. This is the only newspaper that reproduced what most likely was Mary's original spelling, and even this may have been cleaned up somewhat. The spelling and handwriting were so bad as to be nearly illegible. The misspelling of Stannard is discussed in the defense's closing argument, so it must have been spelled that way.

19. "The Hayden Case," *NHJC*, 6 December 1879 ("damnedest ugliest boy"); "The Hayden Case," *NHER*, 11 December 1879 (Mary's plan and Studley's objection to it).

20. "The Hayden Case," *NHER*, 11 December 1879.

21. "The Hayden Case," *NHJC*, 6 December 1879.

22. "The Long Murder Trial," *NYT*, 21 November 1879. See also "The Hayden Trial," *NHJC*, 10 December 1879.

23. Madison Birth Records, 1878.

24. "The Madison Tragedy," *NHJC*, 11 September 1878. Tansy tea was used as an abortifacient because it stimulated the menstrual flow. See B. Frank Scholl, M.D., *Library of Health* (Philadelphia: Historical Pub. Co., 1927), 1408.

25. "Susan Hawley's Story," *NHER*, 2 December 1879.

26. "The Great Hayden Case," *NHER*, 13 December 1879.

27. "Susan Hawley's Story," *NHER*, 2 December 1879.

28. Marc McCutcheon, *The Writer's Guide to Everyday Life in the 1800s* (Cincinnati: Writer's Digest, 1993), 165.

29. "State's Suppressed Evidence," *NYT*, 4 October 1878.

30. Madison Birth Records, 1856.

31. "The Madison Tragedy," *NHER*, 10 September 1878.

32. "The Hayden Trial," *NHJC*, 12 December 1879.

33. "The Madison Murder," *NHER*, 9 September 1878.

34. Ibid.; Madison Death Records, 1874.

35. *Poor Mary Stannard*, 16.

36. "The Hayden Trial," *NHJC*, 3 January 1880.

37. "The Madison Murder," *NHER*, 9 September 1878.

38. "Mrs. Hayden's Story," *NHER*, 10 December 1879.

39. "The Hayden Case," *NHJC*, 21 November 1879.

40. "Susan Hawley's Story," *NHER*, 2 December 1879. The stomach contents consisted only of pieces of egg white, and blackberry seeds and pulp ("Searching for Arsenic," *NYT*, 18 October 1879). Mary probably ate blackberries while waiting for Hayden to show up.

41. "The Hayden Trial," *NHJC*, 3 January 1880.

42. "The Hayden Case," *NHJC*, 22 November 1879.

CHAPTER 2: THE REVEREND HERBERT H. HAYDEN

1. Information about Hayden's background comes from his trial testimony and his autobiography: Herbert H. Hayden, *An Autobiography* (Hartford: Press of the

Plimpton Mfg. Co., 1880). See also "The Great Hayden Case," *NHER*, 30 December 1879.

2. *Wesleyan University, Catalogue*, 1873–1875 (Hartford: Case, Lockwood & Brainard, 1875), 21–22.

3. "Reverend Mr. Hayden's Accusers," *NYT*, 21 October 1878.

4. "Mrs. Hayden's Testimony," *NYT*, 21 September 1878.

5. "Mary Stannard's Murder," *NYT*, 7 September 1878.

6. Records of the Rockland Methodist Episcopal Church, Madison, CT, 1833–1906.

7. This is speculation based on hints brought out at the trial. See, for example, "Denying His Story," *NYT*, 1 January 1880.

8. "Mrs. Hayden's Testimony."

9. "Mary Stannard's Murder," *NYT*, 7 October 1879.

10. Information from the testimony of both Haydens.

11. "The Madison Mystery," *NHJC*, 23 September 1878.

12. "The Madison Tragedy," *NHJC*, 11 September 1878.

13. "Properties of Arsenic," *NYT*, 29 October 1879.

14. Rosa Hayden testified that it was she who sent her husband home that night, for the purpose of putting the children to bed. However, since the hour was late and they had hired Mary to babysit, this doesn't make sense. The children were used to Mary and minded her well, so there would be no need for Hayden to put the children to bed. It is more likely that he told her he was leaving and she gave him the injunction to check on things at home.

15. This sentiment is outlined in J. H. Kellogg, M.D., *Man, the Masterpiece* (Battle Creek, MI: Modern Medicine Pub. Co., 1885, 1894), 417–423; see also McCutcheon, 205–206.

16. "The Great Hayden Case," *NHER*, 8 January 1880.

17. "The State's Suppressed Evidence," *NYT*, 4 October 1878.

18. "The Hayden Case," *NHER*, 13 October 1879; "The Great Hayden Case," *NHER*, 9 January 1880; *Poor Mary Stannard*, 7.

19. The conversation between Hayden and Mary in the barn is based on "The State's Suppressed Evidence." Although the Haydens denied that he and Mary were ever in the barn alone, they were seen by the neighbors across the road, and Mary told Susan Hawley she had talked with him there. (See "The Hayden Murder," *NYT*, 26 November 1879).

20. "Hayden's Story Finished," *NYT*, 24 December 1879.

21. "Mr. Hayden Testifying," *NYT*, 19 December 1879.

22. "Mary Stannard's Murder," *NYT*, 19 September 1878; *Poor Mary Stannard*, 20.

23. "Hayden's Story Finished," *NYT*, 24 December 1879. Although it is never directly stated, there is an undercurrent of irritation about the tools. Hayden had fulfilled his part of the bargain, yet the tools were never ready for him.

24. Ibid.

25. "The Hayden Trial," *NHJC*, 19 December 1879.

26. "The Trial of Mr. Hayden," *NYT*, 31 October 1879.

27. Hayden's questions of Dr. Bailey suggest the possibility that he went to Middletown specifically to obtain an abortifacient, ostensibly for his wife. See "Reverend Mr. Hayden's Accusers," *NYT*, 21 October 1878 and "Mary Stannard's Murder," *NYT*, 7 October 1879.

28. "The Hayden Trial," *NHJC*, 10 December 1879.

29. The conversation between Mary and Hayden is a hypothetical one, based on what most likely would have transpired between them and on what Mary later told Susan.

30. No one besides his wife saw Hayden leave for the woodlot, and they both claimed it was around 2:15. The prosecution tried to show that he left earlier than that, around 1:00, but in reality he had enough time to commit the murder with a 2:15 departure. Hayden is supposed to have told Mary to meet him at 1:00, or "after dinner." Susan said she left around 1:15; Charlie Stannard and Ben Stevens said she left between 1:00 and 2:00. Why did she leave so early? And why did Hayden tell her to meet him then when he made no effort to get away before 2:00? The answer may lie in something established at the trial: "after dinner" in Rockland meant 1:00. Thus, Hayden could have said "an hour after dinner" and Mary could have left closer to 2:00. It is also possible that she left earlier to do what she said: pick blackberries. No blackberries were found in her pail, which could either mean she was too agitated to pick them, or that Hayden tossed them out of the pail to put the water in for her to swallow the "quick medicine."

31. The spice tin story told at the trial (see Chapter 8) may not have been made up of wholecloth. Hayden's account of disposing of the wrappers and string is in "Hayden's Story Finished," *NYT*, 24 December 1879.

32. "Denying Hayden's Story," *NYT*, 1 January 1880.

33. This was the prosecution's theory of the route taken, although they also tried to show that Hayden had gone to the woodlot first. Hayden most likely did *not* go to the woodlot until early the next morning.

34. *Poor Mary Stannard*, 4.

35. "Rev. Mr. Hayden's Trial," *NHER*, 30 December 1879; "Hayden's Trial Resumed," *NYT*, 30 December 1879.

36. "Defending Mr. Hayden," *NYT*, 12 December 1879.

37. The time frame followed in this reconstruction coincides with a departure time a little after 2:00 and puts Hayden in the road where Mrs. Ward sees the man (see Chapter 10). It also fits the time of the scream heard by Mrs. Mills (see Chapter 4).

38. Hayden wouldn't have brought a weapon with him, assuming the arsenic would do the trick. He would have grabbed something close at hand, and there was plenty of wood lying around. Moreover, it was determined that a blunt instrument caused the wound on Mary's head.

39. The contusion on the back of Mary's hand was thought to be a defense wound (see "Mary Stannard's Murder," *NYT*, 7 September 1878), but a defensive

posture would more likely have caused injury to either the palm of the hand or the forearm.

40. "Hayden Testifies for Himself," *NYT*, 25 September 1878.

41. "The Stannard Murder," *NHER*, 25 September 1878.

42. "Madison's Tragedy," *NHER*, 25 September 1878; *Poor Mary Stannard*, 31.

CHAPTER 3: THE STANNARD-HAWLEY CLAN

1. "Mary Stannard's Murder," *NYT*, 7 September 1878.

2. "The Hayden Trial," *NHJC*, 10 December 1879.

3. "The Long Murder Trial," *NYT*, 21 November 1879 (Charlie moving in); U.S. Census, 1850, 1860 (for children).

4. "Rev. Mr. Hayden's Fate," *NHER*, 10 October 1879.

5. "The Hayden Case," *NHJC*, 21 November 1879.

6. "The Long Murder Trial," *NYT*, 21 November 1879.

7. Madison Birth and Death Records.

8. "Mary Stannard's Death," *NHER*, 19 September 1878.

9. "Mary Stannard's Death," *NYT*, 20 September 1878.

10. *Poor Mary Stannard*, 8.

11. "James Hawley's Death," *NHER*, 19 December 1879; "Dayton Hawley's Death," *NHER*, 7 January 1880.

12. "The Great Hayden Case," *NHER*, 3 December 1879.

13. The U.S. Census records for 1860, 1870, and 1880 show Hawley as a laborer in various households.

14. "Mr. Hayden's Story," *NHER*, 19 December 1879.

15. "The Hayden Case," *NHJC*, 15 January 1880.

16. "The Madison Mystery," *NHJC*, 10 September 1878. Although Charlie denied he had said this, it had probably been reported by someone. It is believable that he would say it, but judging from their family relationship it is doubtful he would have followed through with it.

17. "The Hayden Trial," *NHJC*, 2 January 1880; "Hayden's Story Attacked," *NYT*, 2 January 1880. Charles Hawley did not say what he meant by this, but did admit he was angry at Mary. It is my supposition as to the reason.

18. "The Hayden Trial," *NHJC*, 3 January 1880.

19. Charlie's movements on September 3 are taken from his testimony: "The Hayden Case," *NHJC*, 21 November 1879; "The Long Murder Trial," *NYT*, 21 November 1879; "Trial of Mr. Hayden," *NHER*, 20 November 1879.

CHAPTER 4: DISCOVERY: THE ROCKLAND
COMMUNITY TAKES OVER

1. "The Madison Case," *NHJC*, 14 September 1878; U.S. Census, 1880 (age information).

2. This is my interpretation based on the melodramatic style of her testimony.

3. *Poor Mary Stannard*, 17.

4. Information on the Wallingford tornado is from the *New York Times* of 10–13, 15, and 30 August 1878.

5. Eliza Mills' testimony can be found in *Poor Mary Stannard*, 17–18; "The Madison Case," *NHJC*, 14 September 1878; "The Madison Tragedy," *NHJC*, 16 September 1878 (Freddie Mills).

6. *Poor Mary Stannard*, 4.

7. "The Nails on the Heel," *NHER*, 7 November 1879.

8. "The Hayden Case," *NHJC*, 6 October 1879.

9. "The Madison Tragedy," *NHJC*, 16 September 1878.

10. "Rev. Mr. Hayden's Defense," *NYT*, 15 September 1878.

11. "The Hayden Case," *NHJC*, 15 January 1880.

12. Ibid. See also "The Hayden Murder Case," *NYT*, 26 November 1879.

13. "The Hayden Case," *NHJC*, 26 November 1879.

14. Ibid.

15. "The Hayden Case," *NHJC*, 16 January 1880.

16. In Connecticut at this time, inquest juries were formed as quickly as possible by engaging anyone who happened to be available. More often than not, this meant witnesses and bystanders at the scene. Once sworn in as an inquest juror, a member had the right and the duty to investigate the crime in the same way police do today.

17. "The Madison Murder," *NHJC*, 20 September 1879.

18. "Mary Stannard's Death," *NHER*, 19 September 1878.

19. "The Madison Murder," *NHER*, 9 September 1878.

20. "A Young Woman's Ruin and Death," *NYT*, 6 September 1878; *Poor Mary Stannard*, 17.

21. "The Hayden Trial," *NHER*, 23 December 1879.

22. "The Madison Murder," *NHJC*, 20 September 1878.

23. This is my interpretation of his activities at the woodlot.

24. "The Madison Tragedy," *NHJC*, 16 September 1878.

25. "A Sick Man's Testimony," *NYT*, 3 January 1880.

26. "The Madison Murder," *NHJC*, 25 September 1878.

27. "The Hayden Case," *NHJC*, 13 December 1879. This was a denial by Mrs. Davis that Mrs. Hayden had said this, but it seems like a perfectly natural thing for a wife to say. Mrs. Davis was probably reluctant to have the jury think there was even the slightest discord between the Haydens.

28. This is my conjecture as to his motive. However, FBI profiler John Douglas says that it is also common for certain killers — those who have lost control of a situation and felt forced to kill their victims, much like Hayden — to revisit the crime scene out of remorse (*Journey Into Darkness*, New York: Scribner, 1997, 67–68).

29. "Rev. Mr. Hayden's Defense," *NYT*, 15 September 1878.

30. "Hayden's Defense Closed," *NYT*, 31 December 1879. Mrs. Hayden testified that she had never said anything to her husband about Mary's menstrual periods

("The Great Hayden Case," *NHER*, 7 January 1880). Therefore, he must have heard it from Mary herself.

31. "The Madison Murder," *NHJC*, 20 September 1878.
32. "Hayden's Defense Closed," *NYT*, 31 December 1879.
33. "The Great Hayden Case," *NHER*, 7 January 1880.
34. "The Great Hayden Case," *NHER*, 8 January 1880.
35. "The Hayden Trial," *NHJC*, 12 December 1879.
36. "The Hayden Case," *NHJC*, 16 October 1879.
37. "Mary Stannard's Murder," *NYT*, 7 September 1878.
38. "Still Waiting for the Verdict," *NHJC*, 19 January 1880.
39. "The Hayden Case," *NHER*, 13 October 1879.
40. *Poor Mary Stannard*, 27.
41. This is my conjecture as to what Hayden might have told his wife to get her to protect him.
42. Pumpkin cells were found on Lennie's knife by Dr. Treadwell ("Tracing Stains of Blood," *NYT*, 13 November 1879).
43. "The Madison Mystery," *NHJC*, 23 September 1878.
44. "Rev. Mr. Hayden's Trial," *NHER*, 20 October 1879.
45. "Spiritual Practice at Law," *NYT*, 22 September 1878.
46. "The Madison Mystery," *NHJC*, 26 September 1878.
47. "The Great Hayden Case," *NHER*, 8 January 1880.
48. "Trial of Mr. Hayden," *NHER*, 11 December 1879.
49. "Testifying for Hayden," *NYT*, 13 December 1879.
50. "The Great Hayden Case," *NHER*, 8 January 1880.
51. "Last of the Evidence," *NHER*, 10 January 1880.
52. "The Great Hayden Case," *NHER*, 9 January 1880.
53. "Sympathy for Rev. Mr. Hayden," *NYT*, 2 October 1878.

CHAPTER 5: JUSTICE COURT TRIAL: PRELUDE TO "THE GREAT CASE"

1. "Looking for a Murderer," *NYT*, 10 September 1878.
2. Madison Death Records.
3. *Poor Mary Stannard*, 4.
4. "Mary Stannard's Murder," *NYT*, 7 September 1878.
5. Ibid.
6. FBI profiler John Douglas, in his 1997 book *Journey Into Darkness*, analyzes O. J. Simpson's post-crime behavior, and says it was not consistent with appropriate, expected behavior from an innocent person: "You would expect an innocent person accused of such a crime to respond with outrage, to deny it with every fiber of his being" (354).
7. These facts were gleaned from the various reports of the trial, as covered by the *New York Times*, the *New Haven Evening Register*, and the *New Haven Morning Journal and Courier*.

8. "Looking for a Murderer," *NYT*, 10 September 1878.

9. The hiring of Samuel Jones by the Methodists is covered in *Poor Mary Stannard*, 5. Facts concerning the Methodist Church were found in Madison Methodist Church Records, vol. 1, 1870–1923.

10. "Rev. Mr. Hayden's Defence [*sic*]," *NHER*, 21 September 1878.

11. "The Madison Case," *NHJC*, 14 September 1878.

12. "The Hayden Case," *NHJC*, 17 October 1879.

13. "The Feeling in Durham," *NHER*, 13 September 1878.

14. Brian Marriner, *On Death's Bloody Trail: Murder and the Art of Forensic Science* (New York: St. Martin's Press, 1991), 80.

15. Forensic uses of guaiacum gleaned from trial testimony.

16. "The Madison Case," *NHJC*, 14 September 1878.

17. "Madison's Tragedy," *NHER*, 13 September 1878.

18. "The Madison Tragedy," *NHJC*, 16 September 1878.

19. "Mary Stannard's Death," *NYT*, 20 September 1878.

20. Marriner, 92–94.

21. "The Stannard Murder," *NHER*, 25 September 1878. An interesting footnote regarding the knife is recounted by Joel Helander in *Noose and Collar*: in 1910 a descendant of Ben Stevens, then living in Hayden's former house in Rockland, found a large knife behind a wall in the kitchen. The implication is that Hayden hid it there, but the connection is too remote to be definitive. Also, the finder only told one other person, and the knife was never brought forward until 1978 (78).

22. "The Madison Tragedy," *NHJC*, 16 September 1878.

23. "Rev. Mr. Hayden's Accusers," *NYT*, 21 October 1878.

24. This problem was mentioned constantly throughout the Cramer case. See, for example, "The Murder Case," *NHER*, 2 June 1882.

25. Prof. Wayne N. Renke, "Evidence Course Modules: Module 12," http://www.law.ualberta.ca/courses/575/575.lp12.html.

26. "Is Hayden Guilty?" *NHER*, 20 September 1878.

27. "Mary Stannard's Murder," *NYT*, 4 October 1878.

28. "Looking for a Murderer," *NYT*, 10 September 1878.

29. "The Murder of Mary Stannard," *NYT*, 13 September 1878; "Mary Stannard's Death," *NYT*, 20 September 1878. Although a definitive answer to the Solon Shingle reference could not be found, the context in which it was used indicated a fictional bumpkin lawyer who took on silly cases. In addition, the *Register* often featured small snippets of the doings of obviously made-up characters called Jimmy Tuffboy and Charlie Smallface. Their antics were humorous, and sometimes acted as commentary on current events or fads. I am assuming that Solon Shingle is a character in this vein.

30. "Mary Stannard's Death," *NYT*, 20 September 1878.

31. "The Madison Murder," *NHJC*, 20 September 1878.

32. *Poor Mary Stannard*, 23.

33. "Mrs. Hayden's Testimony," *NYT*, 21 September 1878. The rest of her testimony is taken from this account, as well as those in the *New Haven Register* and the *New Haven Morning Journal and Courier*.

34. *Poor Mary Stannard*, 27.

35. Shakespeare, *Macbeth*, act I, sc. vii, line 60.

36. "Hayden Testifies for Himself," *NYT*, 25 September 1878.

37. For an account of the dismissal, see "The Preacher Acquitted," *NYT*, 26 September 1878, and "The Madison Mystery," *NHJC*, 26 September 1878.

CHAPTER 6: INTERIM: PREPARING FOR "THE GREAT CASE"

1. In his book *Noose and Collar*, Joel Helander relates a story told by the son of one of the witnesses at the trial: unhappy with the results, some of Hayden's neighbors went to his home one night and took him to the railroad station, telling the conductor to "take him to hell" (85). Although it is not stated which trial was meant, it must have been the Justice Court trial, as Hayden had been out of jail over a week after it. Besides, his family had moved to New Haven during the Superior Court trial. I interpret the train incident as a message to Hayden to get out or be lynched.

2. "Hayden in His Pulpit," *NYT*, 30 September 1878.

3. *Poor Mary Stannard*, 38.

4. Psalm 27:3–4 (Douay Version).

5. Matthew 5:10–11 (Confraternity Edition).

6. "Hayden in His Pulpit."

7. "The Madison Murder," *NHJC*, 7 October 1878.

8. "Sympathy for Rev. Mr. Hayden," *NYT*, 2 October 1878.

9. "Mr. Hayden and His Brother Clergymen," *NYT*, 7 October 1878.

10. "Sympathy for Rev. Mr. Hayden," *NYT*, 2 October 1878.

11. "The Hayden Case," *NHJC*, 10 January 1880.

12. "Rev. Mr. Hayden Rearrested," *NYT*, 9 October 1878.

13. "The Madison Tragedy," *NHJC*, 10 October 1878. Don W. Weber and Charles Bosworth, Jr., in *Silent Witness* (New York: Onyx, 1993), speak of what they call "guilty-man syndrome": "An innocent man stunned by his false arrest and humiliated by booking would be damned angry by now, and he would be letting his captors know it" (239). The guilty man, on the other hand, is calm and accepting of his fate (190).

14. "The Madison Tragedy."

15. Ibid.

16. "The Madison Murder," *NHER*, 10 October 1878; "Searching for Arsenic," *NYT*, 18 October 1878.

17. "Hayden's Indictment," *NHER*, 16 October 1878.

18. "The Re-Arrest of Rev. Mr. Hayden," *NYT*, 10 October 1878.

19. "Mary Stannard's Murderer," *NYT*, 19 October 1878. Although it was reported to be Ben Stevens's daughter-in-law involved in this incident, it was more

likely the wife of his next-door neighbor, Edgar Stevens. Edgar Stevens was not related to Ben, but was the brother of Luzerne Stevens, Hayden's neighbor.

20. "Ben Stevens Gets Mad," *NHER*, 21 October 1878.

21. "Another Way to Look at Hayden Case," *NHER*, 22 October 1878.

22. "The Stannard Murder Mystery," *NYT*, 20 October 1878.

23. "Mary E. Stannard's Murderer," *NYT*, 23 November 1878.

24. "The Madison Excitement," *NHJC*, 21 October 1878.

25. Ibid.

26. "Does It Amount to Anything?" *NHER*, 23 November 1878.

27. "The Stannard Murder," *NHER*, 26 November 1878.

28. "Before the Grand Jury," *NHER*, 14 October 1878.

29. "Searching for Arsenic," *NYT*, 18 October 1879.

30. "Tracing Stains of Blood," *NYT*, 13 November 1879.

31. "The Rockland Mystery," *NHER*, 22 October 1878.

32. Ibid.

33. *Poor Mary Stannard*, 41.

34. "Important Testimony," *NHER*, 26 August 1881.

35. "A Woman's Misfortune," *NYT*, 29 December 1878.

36. "Released on Bonds," NHJC, 27 January 1880.

37. "The Hayden Trial," *NHER*, 28 October 1879; Madison Death Records.

CHAPTER 7: THE GREAT CASE

1. Mark S. Hoffman, ed., *The World Almanac Book of Facts* (New York: Pharos Books, 1988), 157.

2. Ibid., 158–159.

3. Advertising in *NHER* and *NHJC*, 1878–1882.

4. See, for example, "The Hayden Trial," *NHJC*, 10 December 1879, where the jurors tried to get the attorneys to sing *Pinafore* songs on their trip to Rockland.

5. "A Closer Look at George Caldwell," *Moscow (Idaho)–Pullman (Washington) Daily News*, 16 July 1998, 1.

6. "Quotations—Pedestrianism," http://fox.nstn.ca/~dblaikie/uw-aquah.html. See also "Entertainment," *NHJC*, 3 November 1879, and "Arrival of Charles Rowell," *NHJC*, 4 September 1882.

7. "More Craziness," *NHER*, 15 December 1879.

8. See, for example, "Courtney-Hanlan," *NHER*, 16 October 1879, and "An Immense Fraud," *NHER*, 8 October 1879.

9. "Tickets for Hayden's Trial," *NHER*, 6 October 1879; "The Hayden Murder Trial," *NHJC*, 7 October 1879.

10. "The Hayden Trial," *NHJC*, 18 October 1879.

11. "Before the Grand Jury," *NHER*, 14 October 1878; "Rev. Mr. Hayden's Fate," *NHER*, 10 October 1879. Throughout both trials, Hayden's extreme indifference and frequent light-heartedness was commented on by all newspapers. FBI profiler John Douglas analyzes similar behavior by O. J. Simpson after his wife's

murder: "And remember that, in addition to being a world-famous football player, he's also naturally very charming and experienced as an actor. He knows how he has to behave to throw suspicion off him, like conversing amiably with people and signing autographs like he always does. In his mind, he's obviously justified the crime. 'She forced me into it.' So he's already got a certain amount of peace with it" (*Journey Into Darkness*, 352). Hayden's experience as a preacher and teacher would have given him that same smoothness in public.

12. "The Murder in Madison," *NYT*, 8 October 1879.

13. "The Hayden Case," *NHJC*, 9 October 1879.

14. "Rev. Mr. Hayden's Fate," *NHER*, 10 October 1879; "The Stannard Tragedy," *NHJC*, 8 October 1879.

15. "The Hayden Case," *NHER*, 13 October 1879.

16. "Free for Five Minutes," *NYT*, 9 October 1879.

17. "Mary Stannard's Murder," *NYT*, 7 October 1879. Waller was elected governor of Connecticut two years after the Hayden trial.

18. Events of the first day can be found in "The Stannard Tragedy," *NHJC*, 8 October 1879.

19. "The Hayden Case," *NHJC*, 9 October 1879.

20. "The Hayden Case," *NHER*, 11 October 1879.

21. Ibid.

22. "The Hayden Case," *NHER*, 13 October 1879.

23. "A True Bill Found," *NHER*, 14 October 1879.

24. Jury selection can be found in *NYT* for 8, 15, and 16 October 1879; *NHJC* for 15–16 October 1879; and in *NHER* for 14 October 1879.

25. This juror was exactly the kind the O. J. Simpson defense team was advised to get by its high-priced jury selection experts, Decision Quest. See Mark Miller, "How the Jury Saw It," *Newsweek*, 16 October 1995, 39.

26. Dr. White's testimony can be found in "The Hayden Case," *NHJC*, 16 October 1879; "Rev. Mr. Hayden's Trial," *NHER*, 16 October 1879; "The Hayden Case," *NHJC*, 17 October 1879; and "Evidence from the Grave," *NYT*, 17 October 1879.

27. "Mary Stannard's Plea," *NHER*, 28 October 1879.

28. "The Hayden Trial," *NHER*, 28 October 1879. Information that she was collecting witness fees comes from Helander, 80.

29. "Mrs. Studley's Funeral," *NHER*, 5 November 1879; "Funeral of Mrs. Daniel Studley," *NHJC*, 6 November 1879.

30. "The Hayden Case," *NHJC*, 25 November 1879.

31. "Preaching About the Hayden Case," *NHJC*, 18 November 1879.

CHAPTER 8: ARSENIC AT CENTER STAGE

1. This would be changed, at least in Connecticut, after the Hayden trial. See Chapter 16.

2. "The Trial of Mr. Hayden," *NYT*, 31 October 1879.

3. Hayden was so ignorant about arsenic he didn't know that it was the same thing as ratsbane ("Mr. Hayden's Story," *NHER*, 19 December 1879). To give an idea of the popularity of ratsbane, an estimated 3,000 boxes of Rough on Rats were sold in New Haven in a three-month period in 1881 ("Jennie Cramer Poisoned!" *HDT*, 3 September 1881).

4. Scholl, *Library of Health*, 1376.

5. This would become an issue in the Cramer case.

6. "The Murder in Rockland," *NYT*, 1 November 1879.

7. "Rev. Mr. Hayden Rearrested," *NYT*, 9 October 1878 (his story as to what he did with the arsenic); "The Hayden Case," *NHJC*, 31 October 1879 (sheriff's story about seeing shelves and closets in the house). It must have occurred to someone to look in the almost-empty barrel Hayden claimed to have thrown the paper and string into. If they were really there, it seems the defense would have displayed them prominently. If they *weren't* there, how did he explain it? The fact that this never came up is further proof that Hayden made up the arsenic story or his attorneys made it up for him.

8. "The Rearrest of Mr. Hayden," *NYT*, 10 October 1878.

9. Ibid.

10. Professor Johnson's testimony can be found in "Searching for Arsenic," *NYT*, 18 October 1879; "The Crystals of Arsenic," *NYT*, 23 October 1879; and "Ninety Grains of Arsenic," *NYT*, 19 October 1879.

11. "A Lecture About Arsenic," *NYT*, 24 October 1879.

12. "Dr. E. S. Dana Dies; Famed Geologist," *NYT*, 18 June 1935.

13. Ibid.

14. Professor Dana's testimony can be found in *NYT*, 22–25, 29, 30 October 1879; *NHJC*, 22–25, 29, 30 October 1879; and *NHER*, 23–25, 27–29 October 1879.

15. "Under the Microscope," *NYT*, 30 October 1879.

16. "The Crystals of Arsenic," *NYT*, 8 November 1879.

17. The stomach experiment can be found in "Under the Microscope," *NYT*, 30 October 1879.

18. "The Trial in New Haven," *NYT*, 6 November 1879 (McKee); "The Murder in Rockland," *NYT*, 1 November 1879 (David Tyler); "The Trial of Mr. Hayden," *NYT*, 31 October 1879 (George Tyler).

19. "Mr. Hayden's Re-Arrest," *NHER*, 9 October 1878.

20. "The Hayden Case," *NHJC*, 31 October 1879.

21. "The Hayden Case," *NHJC*, 16 January 1880.

22. In his cross-examination of McKee, Jones asked if he had ever bought any drugs in Hartford. McKee said he had never bought arsenic there, but he had purchased some non-drug items from Talcott Brothers. It is possible that, after the experts pointed out Talcott Brothers' arsenic sample as identical in form to the "barn arsenic," Jones felt he needed to come up with an explanation. See "The Trial in New Haven," *NYT*, 6 November 1879.

CHAPTER 9: EXPERTS ON PARADE

1. "The Great Hayden Case," *NHER*, 3 December 1879.

2. "Hayden's Persecution," *NHER*, 24 November 1879. The Parkman-Webster case is an important one for the use of circumstantial evidence. See Robert Sullivan, *The Disappearance of Dr. Parkman* (Boston: Little, Brown, 1971).

3. "Abate the Nuisance," *NHER*, 24 November 1879.

4. "Summing Up of Hayden Case," *NHER*, 24 November 1879.

5. "Tracing Stains of Blood," *NYT*, 13 November 1879.

6. Marriner, 80.

7. Ibid., 83.

8. Dr. Treadwell's testimony can be found in *NYT*, 13 and 14 November 1879; *NHJC*, 12–14 November 1879; and *NHER*, 12 and 13 November 1879.

9. "The Hayden Case," *NHJC*, 12 and 13 November 1879.

10. Marriner, 215–216.

11. "The Trial of Mr. Hayden," *NYT*, 15 November 1879.

12. "Rev. Mr. Hayden's Trial," *NHER*, 18 November 1879.

13. "The Great Trial," *NHER*, 5 November 1879.

14. "The Murder in Rockland," *NYT*, 19 November 1879.

15. Testimony on the ovarian tumor can be found in "The Trial of Mr. Hayden," *NYT*, 15 November 1879.

16. Boot heel testimony can be found in "The Nails in the Heel," *NHER*, 8 November 1879; "The Hayden Trial," *NHER*, 11 November 1879; and "Heel Marks on a Cheek," *NYT*, 27 November 1879.

17. The defense's expert testimony can be found in "The Hayden Case," *NHJC*, 13 December 1879, and "The Hayden Trial," *NHJC*, 18 December 1879.

CHAPTER 10: LAY TESTIMONY

1. "The Hayden Case," *NHJC*, 3 December 1879.

2. "The Murder in Rockland," *NYT*, 19 November 1879.

3. "The Hayden Trial," *NHJC*, 17 January 1880.

4. "The Great Hayden Case," *NHER*, 26 November 1879.

5. Ibid.

6. "The Hayden Case," *NHJC*, 21 November 1879.

7. Ibid.

8. "The Hayden Case," *NHJC*, 7 November 1879.

9. "The Great Hayden Case," *NHER*, 6 January 1880.

10. "The Hayden Case," *NHJC*, 7 November 1879.

11. "The Hayden Case," *NHJC*, 5 January 1880.

12. "The Hayden Case," *NHJC*, 21 November 1879.

13. Mrs. Ward's testimony can be found in "Adverse to Mr. Hayden," *NHER*, 25 November 1879; "The Hayden Murder Case," *NYT*, 26 November 1879; and "The Hayden Case," *NHJC*, 26 November 1879.

14. The testimony of Rachel Stevens and Henrietta Young can be found in "The Hayden Case," *NHJC*, 26 November 1879; "The Hayden Murder Case," *NYT*, 26 November 1879; and "The Great Hayden Case," *NHER*, 26 November 1879.

15. "The Hayden Case," *NHJC*, 10 December 1879.

16. "The Hayden Case," *NHJC*, 22 November 1879.

17. Charles Hawley's testimony can be found in "The HaydenTrial," *NHJC*, 2 January 1880. See also "Rev. Mr. Hayden's Trial," *NHER*, 2 January 1880:

Watrous (pointing to his head): You know this is where people keep their memory?

Charles: I don't know whether I keep mine there or not.

Watrous: Well, it's somewhere between your head and your feet, isn't it?

Charles: I s'pose so.

18. "The Hayden Case," *NHJC*, 21 November 1879.

19. "Trial of Mr. Hayden," *NHER*, 20 November 1879.

20. "The Great Hayden Case," *NHER*, 21 November 1879. This was in marked contrast to the openly derisive attitude of the defendants in the Cramer case.

21. "The Hayden Case," *NHJC*, 21 November 1879.

22. "Susan Hawley's Story," *NHER*, 2 December 1879.

23. Included in Hayden, 8. Much of Hayden's book is devoted to puffing himself up and trashing Mary Stannard and her family.

24. Susan Hawley's testimony can be found in "The Hayden Case," *NHJC*, 2 December 1879; "The Hayden Trial," *NHJC*, 5 December 1879; "The Great Hayden Case," *NHER*, 3 December 1879; "The Hayden Case," *NHJC*, 16 January 1880; "Susan Hawley's Story," *NHER*, 4 December 1879.

25. "The Hayden Case," *NHJC*, 30 December 1879; Hayden, 90.

26. "Mr. Waller questioned exceedingly kindly and gently in all" ("The Hayden Case," *NHJC*, 11 December 1879).

27. "Mary Stannard's Death," *NHER*, 19 September 1878.

28. "Madison's Tragedy," *NHER*, 24 September 1878.

29. "The Hayden Case," *NHJC*, 8 December 1879.

30. Ben Stevens' testimony can be found in "The Hayden Trial," *NHJC*, 3 January 1880.

31. "The Madison Tragedy," *NHER*, 12 September 1878.

32. "The Hayden Case," *NHJC*, 11 December 1879.

33. "Mrs. Hayden's Story," *NHER*, 10 December 1879.

34. Mrs. Hayden's testimony is taken from "The Hayden Case," *NHJC*, 11 December 1879.

35. "Susan Hawley's Story," *NHER*, 4 December 1879.

36. "The Hayden Case," *NHJC*, 16 December 1879.

37. "Trial of Mr. Hayden," *NHER*, 11 December 1879. In fact, Mrs. Hayden cried or almost cried throughout both trials whenever a reference was made to her husband's fidelity. See *Poor Mary Stannard*, 23.

38. Hayden's cross-examination is contained in his autobiography at 78 et seq., indicating that he was pleased with his performance. See also *NHER*, 19 and 22–24

December; *NYT*, 19, 23, 24, and 30 December 1879; and *NHJC*, 19, 24, and 30 December 1879.

39. "The Hayden Trial," *NHJC*, 24 December 1879.

40. "The Hayden Trial," *NHER*, 23 December 1879.

41. "Andrew Hazlett, Charles Stannard and myself went down where Burr had been burning coal" ("Madison's Tragedy," *NHER*, 25 September 1878); his denial that he used the name Hazlett is in "The Hayden Trial," *NHER*, 24 December 1879.

42. "The Hayden Trial," *NHJC*, 24 December 1879. His testimony is peppered with "I don't remember," "I don't recollect," "I cannot tell," "I cannot say," "I don't think so," "I don't know."

CHAPTER 11: VERDICT

1. Closing arguments and the judge's charge to the jury can be found in "The Hayden Case," *NHJC*, 15 and 16 January 1880, and "The Hayden Trial," *NHJC*, 17 January 1880.

2. Jury deliberations and the verdict can be found in "Still Waiting for the Verdict," *NHJC*, 19 January 1880; "Waiting for the Verdict," *NHJC*, 17 January 1880; "At Last!" *NHJC*, 20 January 1880; and "Hayden Not Convicted," *NYT*, 20 January 1880.

3. "The Hayden Case," *NHJC*, 5 January 1880.

4. Helander, 67.

5. Ibid., 70.

6. "The Great Hayden Case," *NHER*, 9 January 1880.

7. *Poor Mary Stannard*, 8.

CHAPTER 12: "DRIFTING WITH THE TIDE"

1. "Following Many Clues," *NYT*, 26 August 1881. Of all the articles that mentioned Dr. Creed, only this one indicated that he was "a colored man." In this era, newspapers routinely mentioned a person's ethnic background and this was always true of African Americans. Even more surprising is the respectful tone used in talking about Dr. Creed and his background.

2. For a description of President Garfield's wound, see "The President's Wound," *HDT*, 21 September 1881, and "General Garfield's Wound," *HDT*, 30 September 1881.

3. Whitney Medical Library Archives, Yale University.

4. *Obituary Records of Graduates of Yale University, 1901–1910*, pp. 91–92; "Death of C.V.R. Creed," *NHER*, 8 August 1900.

5. "Jennie Cramer's Death," *NHER*, 6 August 1881.

6. Ibid.

7. "A Beautiful Girl's Fate," *HDT*, 8 August 1881. In this era, stockings were made of cotton lisle. Why Jennie would have worn two pairs in the summer heat was not mentioned. Perhaps it was a requirement of Victorian modesty to make sure no

flesh would show through. At the same time, the plunging neckline of her bodice would seem to go against that modesty.

8. "Jennie Cramer's Death," *NHER*, 6 August 1881.

9. "Local News," *NHJC*, 20 October 1879.

10. "Jennie Cramer's Death," *NHER*, 6 August 1881; "A Beautiful Girl's Fate," *HDT*, 8 August 1881. However, Peck would later change his story and say he had *not* seen either Jennie or Jimmy that night.

11. "Jennie Cramer's Death," *NHER*, 6 August 1881.

12. Ibid.

13. Information about Jacob Cramer's early life comes from his obituary, "Died of Consumption," *NHER*, 21 December 1881; the children's ages and Minnie's name come from the U.S. Census for 1860–1880.

14. "Jennie Cramer's Death," *NHER*, 6 August 1881.

15. This segment is a composite taken from "Jennie Cramer's Death" and from the various trial testimonies of Mr. and Mrs. Cramer.

16. James Malley's statement about the shore was ambiguous. Mrs. Cramer assumed it meant that he was going to Savin Rock with Jennie; however, he never said it was Jennie he was going to be seeing, or that "the shore" meant Savin Rock, and under the circumstances it is doubtful he would have meant either.

17. "Jennie Cramer's Death," *NYT*, 13 August 1881.

18. "Jennie Cramer's Death," *NHER*, 6 August 1881.

19. Ibid.

20. "Two Doctors Testify," *NHER*, 7 September 1881.

CHAPTER 13: JENNIE, JIMMY, WALL, AND BLANCHE

1. "The New Haven Mystery," *NYT*, 15 August 1881; "Pretty Jennie Cramer," *NYT*, 16 August 1881.

2. "New Haven's Astute Jury," *NYT*, 18 August 1881.

3. This is an assumption based on Mrs. Cramer's actions and statements concerning her daughter, including her disapproval of one of Jennie's suitors because of his lowly occupation (barber).

4. "The Malley Trial," *NHER*, 5 May 1882.

5. "Mr. Cramer's Body," *NHER*, 9 May 1882; "The New Haven Mystery," *NYT*, 15 August 1881.

6. *The Beautiful Victim of the Elm City* (New York: M. J. Ivers & Co., 1881), 3.

7. Ibid., 46; "The West Haven Tragedy," *NYT*, 29 August 1881.

8. "The Cramer Mystery," *NHER*, 3 September 1881.

9. "The Malley Trial," *NHER*, 5 May 1882; "Jennie Cramer's Character," *NHER*, 13 May 1882.

10. *The Beautiful Victim*, 3.

11. "The Cramer Mystery," *NHER*, 22 August 1881.

12. "Jennie Cramer's Death," *NHER*, 8 August 1881.

13. U.S. Census, 1870, 1880; "Pretty Jennie Cramer," *NYT*, 16 August 1881.

14. The sources only mention a "slight speech impediment." My interpretation comes from Judge Blydenburgh's statement to the inquest jury that if they didn't try to hurry him they'd do better ("Last Evening's Testimony," NHER, 10 August 1881), and from the description in "Plea Not Guilty," *NHER*, 5 April 1882.

15. "Testimony for an Alibi," *HDT*, 29 August 1881.

16. "The Difference Between the Malleys," *HDT*, 17 August 1881.

17. Apart from James Malley, Sr.'s, position in his brother's store, there is also the fact that their house was not big enough for each of the girls to have her own room, and the statement of the personnel at Branford Point Restaurant that, while they were very familiar with Walter and Edward Malley, they knew none of the James Malley, Sr., family. See "The Malley Trial," *NHER*, 25 May 1882.

18. This interpretation of Walter Malley's relationship with his father is based on characteristics of both men, especially the interview with Edward Malley, "Talks With the Malleys," *NYT*, 20 August 1881.

19. Ibid.

20. "Gossip About the Trial," *NHER*, 30 May 1882.

21. Seton Hall University Archives.

22. "Local News," *NHER*, 22 October 1879.

23. Yale University Archives.

24. "Defending the Malleys," *NYT*, 23 August 1881.

25. "Talks with the Malleys," *NYT*, 20 August 1881 (for money amount); New Haven Death Records (for date of death). Mrs. Malley's reason for leaving her money to her son is based on the hypothesis of Walter's relationship with his father, which is strengthened by the fact that the money actually belonged to Edward (see Chapter 14).

26. There were many versions of Blanche's past, told by her, by Lizzie Bundy, by her stepfather Matthew Hines, by James Reilly, and by her ex-husband John Zimmermann. This is a composite of what is actually known as well as what is most likely. For example, the story she told in her midnight confession regarding seduction by her stepfather's employer and a subsequent child by him was probably fabricated to gain sympathy. No one else mentions this story, and the time line is not likely: she was married to John Zimmermann in December 1877, when she was fifteen or sixteen.

27. New York City Marriage Certificate No. 6700, December 16, 1877; New York City Death Certificates No. 260556 (1877) and No. 356437 (1880).

28. "Poor Jennie Cramer," *HDT*, 12 August 1881.

29. Ibid. See also "Trial of the Malleys," *NHER*, 20 May 1882.

30. "Poor Jennie Cramer," *HDT*, 12 August 1881.

31. "Jennie Cramer's Death," *NYT*, 20 May 1882.

32. "Poor Jennie Cramer."

33. "Last Evening's Testimony," *NHER*, 10 August 1881.

34. "The Cramer Tragedy," *NHER*, 8 August 1881.

35. "Mrs. Cramer's Story," *NHER*, 5 May 1882.

36. "The Cramer Tragedy," *NHER*, 8 August 1881.

37. *The Beautiful Victim*, 53. This is substantiated by the comment by one of the jailers that Jimmy was the sharpest prisoner he had ever seen and was better at cross-examining than most lawyers: "If you talk with him on any subject, he will find out all you know and when you get through you'll find out he hasn't told you anything" ("A Sharp Prisoner," *NHER*, 30 August 1881).

38. Information for the remainder of this chapter comes from "The Cramer Tragedy," *NHER*, 8 August 1881.

CHAPTER 14: BOYS WILL BE BOYS

1. "Ghastly Riddles," *NHER*, 31 August 1881; "Citizen Train," *NHER*, 15 August 1881; "Murder Mysteries," *HDT*, 6 October 1881.

2. "The Cramer Tragedy," *NHER*, 8 August 1881.

3. "Trial of the Malleys," *NHER*, 4 May 1882.

4. "The Cramer Tragedy," *NHER*, 8 August 1881.

5. Ibid.

6. Ibid.

7. "Jennie Cramer's Death," *HDT*, 9 August 1881.

8. "Talks with the Malleys," *NYT*, 20 August 1881; "End Comes to Edward Malley," *NHER*, 26 July 1909.

9. "Various Matters," *NHER*, 13 October 1879; "Local News," *NHJC*, 18 October 1879; "Personal," *NHJC*, 19 January 1880.

10. "Pretty Jennie Cramer," *NYT*, 16 August 1881.

11. "The Malley Boys," *HDT*, 20 August 1881. This is my own interpretation of why she gave Walter the money.

12. "Mrs. Edward Malley," *NHER*, 10 May 1880; New Haven Death Records, 1880.

13. "Trial of the Malleys," *NHER*, 16 May 1882.

14. "Talks with the Malleys," *NYT*, 20 August 1881.

15. Ibid. See also *The Beautiful Victim*, 46.

16. "The Cramer Tragedy," *NHER*, 8 August 1881.

17. Ibid.

18. "Jennie Cramer's Death," *NHER*, 18 August 1881; "The Malley Boys," *HDT*, 20 August 1881.

19. Ibid.

20. "Jennie Cramer's Death," *HDT*, 9 August 1881. However, Blanche *had* lived on Spring Street: she was born there, possibly at that same address (New York City Marriage Certificate No. 6700, December 16, 1877).

21. "Jennie Cramer's Death," *NHER*, 8 August 1881.

22. "Miss Douglass' Story," *NHER*, 9 August 1881.

23. "Jennie Cramer's Death," *HDT*, 9 August 1881.

24. "Dr. Prudden's Evidence," *NHER*, 6 September 1881.

25. "The Suffocation Theory," *NHER*, 20 August 1881.

26. "Birmingham Affairs," *NHER*, 20 August 1881.

27. "Jennie Cramer's Death," *NHER*, 8 August 1881. Even at this early stage there were many snide remarks by the reporters regarding "the fair Miss Blanche" and "just like a proper lady." Her looks and/or dress must have given her away, as they obviously did with Mrs. Cramer.

28. Blanche's testimony is taken from "Miss Douglass' Story," *NHER*, 9 August 1881, and "Who Killed Jennie Cramer?" *HDT*, 10 August 1881.

29. "Poor Jennie Cramer," *HDT*, 12 August 1881.

30. "Miss Douglass' Story."

31. Ibid.

32. James Malley's testimony is taken from "Last Evening's Testimony," *NHER*, 10 August 1881, and "Who Killed Jennie Cramer?" *HDT*, 10 August 1881.

33. Although all the other newspapers merely summarize this testimony, there is one intriguing report in the *Hartford Daily Times* as to what was really said by Carroll to James Malley. According to William Mountain, whose counter was across from Jimmy's, Patsy Carroll approached Jim at about 11:00 that morning and said, "A lady friend of yours has drowned" ("James Malley, Jr.'s, Alibi," *HDT*, 1 October 1881). Instead of asking who it was, which would seem to be a normal response, Jimmy said, "Oh, no, you're kidding!" However, the newspaper could have left out the intervening question and response. But if there *was* no question, it means that Jimmy already knew Jennie was dead. And right after Patsy Carroll told him this, Jimmy ran up to see Walter. Perhaps they did not expect the body to be found so fast.

34. Walter Malley's testimony is taken from "Last Evening's Testimony," *NHER*, 10 August 1881, and "Who Killed Jennie Cramer?" *HDT*, 10 August 1881.

35. "Poor Jennie Cramer," *HDT*, 12 August 1881.

36. "The Malleys in Jail," *NHER*, 15 August 1881.

37. "Trial of the Malleys," *NHER*, 20 May 1882.

38. "Jennie Cramer's Death," *HDT*, 16 August 1881, and "The Cramer Tragedy," *NHER*, 16 August 1881.

39. Ibid. See also "The Malley Boys," *HDT*, 13 September 1881.

40. Ibid. See also "Trial of the Malleys," *NHER*, 10 May 1882 ("this man tried to impress upon my mind . . . " and "they tried to have me think . . .").

41. This was a filler piece (no title), in *HDT*, 20 August 1881.

42. "Following Many Clues," *NYT*, 26 August 1881.

43. "Light on the Mystery," *NHER*, 17 August 1881.

44. Ibid.

45. "Jennie Cramer's Death," *HDT*, 15 August 1881.

46. "The West Haven Tragedy," *NYT*, 29 August 1881.

47. "The Cramer Mystery," *HDT*, 20 September 1881.

48. "The Case Against the Malleys," *HDT*, 18 August 1881.

49. "The Cramer Mystery," *HDT*, 20 September 1881.

50. "The Case Against the Malleys."

51. "Jennie Cramer's Death," *NHER*, 18 August 1881.

52. "The Cramer Murder Case," *NHER*, 26 May 1882.

53. "The Cramer Mystery," *NHER*, 12 August 1881.

54. "The Suffocation Theory," *NHER*, 20 August 1881.

55. "The Cramer Murder," *HDT*, 19 August 1881; "Jennie Cramer's Fate," *HDT*, 29 August 1881.

56. "Jennie Cramer's Fate."

57. Ibid.

58. "The Malleys in Jail," *NHER*, 15 August 1881.

59. Edward Bulwer-Lytton is famous today for a style that is so awful there is a "bad writing" contest in his name, wherein contestants try to outdo each other in creating an introductory paragraph of the most horrendous purple prose in the Bulwer-Lytton manner. For background on Bulwer-Lytton (author of the phrase "It was a dark and stormy night"), as well as the history and rules of the contest, see "The Bulwer-Lytton Fiction Contest Home Page" at www.bulwer-lytton.com. Penguin Books has issued a series of collections of the entries, entitled (appropriately) *It Was a Dark and Stormy Night*.

An interesting side note to this is that one of Bulwer-Lytton's most popular novels, *Eugene Aram*, was a romanticization of an eighteenth-century murderer and thief who was also a teacher and scholar. Did Walter see himself in Aram? Did he find him worthy of admiration? For more on the Aram mystique, see Nancy J. Tyson, *Eugene Aram: Literary History and Typology of the Scholar-Criminal* (Hamden, CT: Archon, 1983).

60. "The Malleys," *HDT*, 16 August 1881; "Testimony for an Alibi," *HDT*, 23 August 1881.

61. "Jennie Cramer," *HDT*, 22 August 1881.

62. "Light on the Mystery," *NHER*, 17 August 1881.

63. "Tried on Five Counts," *NHER*, 5 September 1881.

64. "The Malley Boys," *HDT*, 20 August 1881.

65. "The Cause Ascertained," *NHER*, 19 August 1881; "Sent to Jail at Last," *NYT*, 30 August 1881.

66. "Sent to Jail at Last," *NYT*, 30 August 1881.

67. "Selecting the Jurors," *NHER*, 18 April 1882.

CHAPTER 15: AN END AND A BEGINNING: INQUEST VERDICT

1. "The Cramer Tragedy" and "Blanche Douglass," *NHER*, 16 August 1881. For the photo ads, see issues of the *New Haven Evening Register* from 27 August 1881 into September.

2. "Beginning the Trial," *NHER*, 25 April 1882.

3. See, for example, "Not Quite So Well," *HDT*, 30 August 1881, and "His Condition Very Serious," *HDT*, 5 September 1881.

4. "The New Haven Tragedy—A Horrible Development," *HDT*, 17 August 1881.

5. "The Elder Malley Arrested," *HDT*, 15 August 1881. Either the charge was dropped for lack of evidence or because Edward Malley paid what she was asking, as there is no further word of this in the newspapers.

6. "The Cramer Tragedy," *NHER*, 8 August 1881; "Duty of the Authorities," *NHER*, 12 August 1881; "The West Haven Shore," *NHER*, 26 August 1881.

7. "The Case Against the Malleys," *HDT*, 18 August 1881 (Blanche's heart attack); "The Cramer Mystery," *NHER*, 20 August 1881 (Blanche escaped); *The Beautiful Victim*, 38 (Jimmy shot himself); "The New Haven Mystery," *NYT*, 6 September 1881 (Jennie in Philadelphia); "The Cramer Mystery," *NHER*, 22 August 1881 (Spanish fly).

8. "Poisoned by Cantharides," *NHER*, 22 August 1881. See also Robert H. Dreisbach and William O. Robertson, *Handbook of Poisoning* (Norwalk, CT: Appleton & Lange, 1987), 429.

9. B. Frank Scholl, M.D., *Library of Health* (Philadelphia: Historical Pub. Co., 1927), 1243.

10. "Several Love Letters," *NHER*, 23 October 1882.

11. "The Cramer Murder," *HDT*, 18 August 1881.

12. "The Cramer Mystery," *NHER*, 22 August 1881.

13. "Blanche Douglass in Jail," *HDT*, 30 August 1881.

14. "Fishing for Clues," *NHER*, 27 August 1881.

15. "The Malleys in Jail," *NHER*, 15 August 1881.

16. "Blanche Douglass in Jail," *HDT*, 30 August 1881; "Sent to Jail at Last," *NYT*, 30 August 1881.

17. "Jennie Cramer's Death," *NYT*, 24 August 1881.

18. "Jennie Cramer's Death," *HDT*, 19 August 1881.

19. Ibid.

20. "The Cause Ascertained," *NHER*, 19 August 1881; "Talks with the Malleys," *NYT*, 20 August 1881.

21. "Important Testimony," *NHER*, 26 August 1881; *The Beautiful Victim*, 56.

22. "The Boat Theory," *NHER*, 24 August 1881.

23. "Jennie Cramer's Death," *NYT*, 31 August 1881.

24. "The West Haven Trial," *NHER*, 15 September 1881; "Jennie Cramer's Fate," *HDT*, 15 September 1881.

25. "Inquest on Jennie Cramer," *HDT*, 26 August 1881; "Important Testimony," *NHER*, 26 August 1881; *The Beautiful Victim*, 55–56.

26. "Fishing for Clues," *NHER*, 27 August 1881; "The Cramer Mystery," *NHER*, 29 August 1881.

27. "Testimony for an Alibi," *HDT*, 23 August 1881.

28. Ibid. See also "Defending the Malleys," *NYT*, 23 August 1881; "Making Slow Progress," *NHER*, 3 October 1881; "Clara Louise Malley," *NHER*, 5 October 1881; "Was It Jennie Cramer?" *NHER*, 6 October 1881.

29. "Jennie Cramer's Death," *HDT*, 19 August 1881. The line is from "I Am the Monarch of the Sea." See Deems Taylor, ed., *A Treasury of Gilbert and Sullivan* (New York: Simon and Schuster, 1941), 63–65.

30. "Jennie Cramer's Fate," *HDT*, 24 August 1881. After this news broke, Timothy Fox rushed to the jail and had a half-hour private conference with Jimmy ("The Cramer Case," *HDT*, 25 August 1881). Dr. Shepard was disappointed at Mrs. Cramer's indiscretion, as he felt it allowed Jimmy to prepare himself ("Fishing for Clues," *NHER*, 27 August 1881). And the *New York Times* questioned whether a young man of Jimmy's fancy tastes in dress would have only one pin, and a cheap one at that ("The New Haven Mystery," *NYT*, 25 August 1881).

31. "Following Many Clues," *NYT*, 26 August 1881.

32. A possible reason is that Minnie may have been African American. Only one newspaper mentions this, however (see "Jennie Cramer Tragedy," *HDT*, 1 September 1881), and in all her various testimonies, it never comes up again. John Henry, on the other hand, is described as "the colored waiter" each time his name is brought up.

33. Ibid. See also "The Cramer Mystery," *NHER*, 3 September 1881, and *The Beautiful Victim*, 60–61.

34. "The Jennie Cramer Tragedy," *HDT*, 1 September 1881.

35. "Blanche Douglass in Jail," *NHER*, 30 August 1881; *The Beautiful Victim*, 57–58.

36. "Jennie Cramer Poisoned!" *HDT*, 3 September 1881; "The Cramer Mystery," *NHER*, 3 September 1881; "Jennie Cramer Poisoned," *NYT*, 4 September 1881.

37. Information on the verdict comes from *The Beautiful Victim*, 64.

CHAPTER 16: JUSTICE COURT TRIAL IN WEST HAVEN

1. "The Fate of Miss Cramer," *HDT*, 13 August 1881.

2. "The Late Jennie Cramer," *NHER*, 1 August 1882.

3. "How Blanche Douglasses Are Made," *NHER*, 3 August 1882.

4. "Pretty Jennie Cramer," from the *Philadelphia Record*, in *NHER*, 16 August 1881.

5. For a history of the suit, see "The Malley Store Attachment," *HDT*, 26 September 1881; "The Malley Attachment," *NHER*, 27 September 1881; "Local News," *NHER*, 27 September 1881; "A Writ of Habeas Corpus," *HDT*, 30 September 1881; "The Carroll Habeas Corpus," *NHER*, "The Malley-Carroll Case," *NHER*, 31 October 1881.

6. "The Accused Malleys," *HDT*, 20 October 1881.

7. For a good "you-are-there" account of the particulars and how the country reacted, see the black-bordered issue of *NHER* for 20 September 1881, which includes the melodramatic title, "He Goes Out with the Ebbing Tide."

8. "Blanche Douglass," *HDT*, 26 October 1881.

9. "The Cramer Mystery," *NHER*, 3 September 1881.

10. "New Haven's Astute Jury," *NYT*, 18 August 1881.

11. "Trial of the Malleys," *NHER*, 4 May 1882.

12. "Tried on Five Counts," *NHER*, 5 September 1881.

13. Later, as agriculture waned in America and there was an increase of workers on assembly lines, the hallmark of leisure would be the tan, signifying someone who did not have to work in a factory. And with our current awareness of the dangers of skin cancer, it may be that the pale complexion will come back into vogue.

14. "The Arsenic Purchase," *NHER*, 18 May 1882.

15. "Blanche Douglass' Husband," *HDT*, 12 September 1881.

16. "Jennie Cramer's Death," *NHER*, 10 August 1881.

17. Ibid. See also *The Merck Manual*, http://www.merck.com and "Primary Amenorrhea," Thriveonline, http://www. thriveonline.com.

18. "The West Haven Tragedy," *NYT*, 29 August 1881.

19. In *Man the Masterpiece* at p. 419, Dr. J. H. Kellogg says that people are like the animals in that women only feel lust, if at all, once a month; before the onset of menstruation and at menopause, therefore, women don't feel passion. This may have been the thinking behind Dr. Lindsley's comment about Jennie.

20. "Dr. Prudden's Evidence," *NHER*, 6 September 1881.

21. Interview with Carl Koenan, M.D., of the Asotin County (Washington) Coroner's Office, February 1998.

22. Keith D. Wilson, M.D., *Cause of Death* (Cincinnati: Writer's Digest Books, 1992), 110.

23. Asa Curtiss: "Beginning the Trial," *NHER*, 25 April 1882; Dr. Case is quoted in Weber and Bosworth, *Silent Witness*, 356.

24. Professor Chittenden's testimony can be found in "The Cramer Murder Trial," *HDT*, 7 September 1881, and "Trial of the Malleys," *NHER*, 6 September 1881.

25. No decomposition: "Two Doctors Testify," *NHER*, 7 September 1881; slight stiffening: "The Malley Boys' Hearing," *HDT*, 8 September 1881.

26. Flexible: "Two Doctors Testify," *NHER*, 7 September 1881; rigor in mouth and jaw: Michael Kurland, *How to Solve a Murder* (New York: Macmillin, 1995) 48.

27. Ibid. See also Wilson, 67.

28. Post-mortem lividity: Kurland, 49; Wilson, 67; Mr. Cramer's problem of recognition: "A Comparison," *NHER*, 30 August 1881.

29. "Two Doctors Testify," *NHER*, 7 September 1881.

30. "The New Haven Murder," *NYT*, 9 September 1881.

31. "Yesterday's Testimony," *NHER*, 9 September 1881; "Local News," *HDT*, 9 September 1881.

32. "Trial of the Malleys," *NHER*, 12 September 1881; "Blanche Douglass' Husband," *HDT*, 12 September 1881. "What Zimmerman Says," *NHER*, 12 September 1881.

33. "Trial of the Malleys," *NHER*, 12 and 14 September 1881.

34. "A Dramatic Court Scene," *HDT*, 9 September 1881.

35. "The Cramer Murder," *HDT*, 10 September 1881.

36. "The Malley Boys," *HDT*, 13 September 1881.

37. "Jennie Cramer's Fate," *HDT*, 15 September 1881.

38. Ibid. See also "The Jennie Cramer Case," *HDT*, 16 September 1881.

39. "The Foote Building," *NHER*, 7 October 1881, and "The West Haven Trial," *NHER*, 8 October 1881.

40. Ibid. See also "The Cramer Mystery," *HDT*, 20 September 1881.

41. "The Cramer Mystery," *HDT*, 20 September 1881.

42. Ibid. It is also a possibility that Walter could have changed the soiled sheet himself to avoid detection.

43. "The West Haven Trial," *NHER*, 15 September 1881.

44. "The Malley Trial," *NHER*, 15 September 1881; "The West Haven Trial," *NHER*, 16 September 1881.

45. "The Cramer Tragedy," *NHER*, 17 September 1881.

46. "The New Haven Murder," *HDT*, 24 September 1881.

47. "The West Haven Trial," *NHER*, 21 September 1881.

48. "Jennie Cramer Poisoned!" *HDT*, 3 September 1881.

49. "Maggie Kane's Story," *NHER*, 22 September 1881.

50. "The Murder of Jennie Cramer," *HDT*, 23 September 1881.

51. "The Cramer Case," *HDT*, 29 September 1881.

52. "James Malley, Jr.'s, Alibi," *HDT*, 1 October 1881.

53. For Minnie Quinn's testimony, see "James Malley, Jr.'s, Alibi," *HDT*, 1 October 1881; "The Malley Trial," *HDT*, 3 October 1881; "The Malley Boys' Defence," *HDT*, 5 October 1881; "The West Haven Trial," *NHER*, 1 October 1881; "The Malley Alibi," *NHER*, 1 October 1881; "Minnie Quinn's Life," *NHER*, 3 October 1881; "The Malley Defense," *NHER*, 5 October 1881.

54. "The Malley Boys' Defence," *HDT*, 5 October 1881. For an account of the Jennie Cramer–like case, see "One More Unfortunate," *HDT*, 4 October 1881.

55. "Jennie Cramer's Death," *HDT*, 6 October 1881.

56. "The Malley Boys' Defence," *HDT*, 5 October 1881.

57. The U.S. Census for 1880, taken in late June of that year, lists Lizzie in her father's household in New Haven, and in her brother's household in Wilkes-Barre.

58. "The West Haven Trial," *NHER*, 6 October 1881.

59. "On a Junketing Tour," *NHER*, 11 October 1881, and "The Cramer Mystery," *HDT*, 11 October 1881.

60. Ibid.

61. "The Malley Boys' Defence," *HDT*, 12 October 1881.

62. For Dr. Jewett's testimony, see "Jennie Cramer's Fate," *HDT*, 14 October 1881, and "The West Haven Trial," *NHER*, 14 October 1881. There were so many exceptions to the inflammation problem that it cannot be taken as a serious contradiction (see "Trial of the Malleys," *NHER*, 3 May 1882). His statement minimizing the injuries to Jennie's vaginal area is a truly irresponsible one, considering the evidence. And there is his own statement to a reporter in 1882 in response to a question as to whether Dr. Painter would know what he was talking about on this subject: "Yes, he knows pretty well about it" ("Trial of the Malleys," *NHER*, 26 April 1882).

63. "Defending the Malleys," *NYT*, 23 August 1881.

64. "Waiting Up All Night," *NHER*, 18 October 1881.

65. "Testifies in Rebuttal," *NHER*, 18 October 1881.

CHAPTER 17: SUPERIOR COURT TRIAL IN NEW HAVEN

1. New Haven Marriage Records, 1881; "The Trial Tomorrow," *NHER*, 17 April 1882.

2. "The Cramer Tragedy," *NHER*, 24 August 1881.

3. New Haven Death Records, 1881.

4. For accounts of Jacob Cramer's death, see "Died of Consumption," *NHER*, 21 December 1881; "The Jennie Cramer Mystery — Death of Her Father," *HDT*, 21 December 1881; "Jennie Cramer's Father Dead," *NYT*, 21 December 1881.

5. "New Haven's Astute Jury," *NYT*, 18 August 1881.

6. "Malley's Mammoth Fire," *NHER*, 28 February 1882; "Fire Marshal's Inquiry," *NHER*, 1 March 1882; "The Malley Fire," *NHER*, 2 March 1882; "The Malley Insurance," *NHER*, 8 March 1882.

7. "Local News," *NHER*, 1 March 1882.

8. "The Malley Insurance Case," *NYT*, 6 April 1883 (overvaluation and fraud).

9. "The Malley Insurance," *NHER*, 29 December 1883; "The Malley Insurance Cases," *NYT*, 30 December 1883; "Insurance Companies Sued," *NYT*, 17 March 1883; "The Malley Insurance Case," *NYT*, 5 April 1883.

10. "Opinion," *NHER*, 25 August 1881.

11. "The Malley Case," *NHER*, 21 January 1882; "The Cramer Murder Case," *NYT*, 28 January 1882.

12. "The Cramer Murder Case," *NYT*, 22 April 1882.

13. "The Cramer Tragedy," *NHER*, 28 January 1882. The odor of decomposition was so bad that Blydenburgh had to leave after two minutes. Fox, however, stayed throughout the autopsy.

14. "The Trial Tomorrow," *NHER*, 17 April 1882. Walter said Bulwer-Lytton was his favorite author, and that he had never read Hawthorne.

15. "Discipline at the Jail," *NHER*, 1 March 1882.

16. "Walter Malley," *NHER*, 2 March 1882.

17. "Jail Manners," *NHER*, 2 March 1882.

18. Guiteau's lawyer, Charles Read of Chicago, came to the courtroom during jury selection in the Malley trial and talked to Lewis Cassidy ("Not Eager to Serve," *NHER*, 20 April 1882).

19. "Plea Not Guilty," *NHER*, 5 April 1882.

20. "Several Love Letters," *NHER*, 23 October 1882.

21. "Jennie Cramer's Death," *NHER*, 13 October 1881.

22. "Beginning the Trial," *NHER*, 25 April 1882. However, Cassidy had not expected the case to drag on as long as it did. He tried commuting from Philadelphia and attending to his caseload there, but eventually had to give Andrew his resignation. He didn't think Jimmy was in any special danger of being made the scapegoat by Walter's lawyers ("An Expert Testifies," *NHER*, 15 June 1882).

23. "The Cramer Murder Case," *NYT*, 20 April 1882.

24. "Not Eager to Serve," *NHER*, 20 April 1882.

25. Ibid. See also "Jurors in the Malley Trial," *NYT*, 21 April 1882.

26. "The Jury Picked Out," *NHER*, 21 April 1882.

27. "The Arsenic Analyses," *NHER*, 28 April 1882.

28. "Chittenden's Methods," *NHER*, 2 May 1882.

29. See, for example, "Not Eager to Serve," *NHER*, 20 April 1882.

30. "The 'Ladies,'" *NHER*, 12 May 1882.

31. "The Cramer Trial," *NYT*, 19 May 1882.

32. "Beginning the Trial," *NHER*, 25 April 1882.

33. Ibid. For the garlic smell resulting from arsenic ingestion, see "Trial of the Malleys," *NHER*, 3 May 1882, and Wilson, 118.

34. "Beginning the Trial" and "Trial of the Malleys."

35. "The Malley Trial," *NHER*, 4 May 1882.

36. "Mrs. Cramer's Story," *NHER*, 5 May 1882.

37. "Mr. Gilchrist's Letters," *NHER*, 19 May 1882.

38. "Beefsteak and Mushrooms," *NHER*, 10 May 1882.

39. "Trial of the Malleys," *NHER*, 11 May 1882.

40. Ibid.

41. "Two Witnesses Heard," *NHER*, 12 May 1882.

42. Ibid.

43. "Blanche's Admissions," *NHER*, 19 May 1882.

44. "The New Haven Mystery," *NYT*, 1 June 1882 (Mrs. Malloy); "A Reporter's Troubles," *NHER*, 12 May 1882 (configuration of seats).

45. "A Reporter's Troubles." See also "Dragging Slowly," *NHER*, 9 May 1882.

46. "The Malley Case Adjourns," *NYT*, 3 June 1882.

47. Ibid.

48. "An Expert Testifies," *NYT*, 16 June 1882. See Note 62, Chapter 16.

49. "Trial of the Malleys," *NHER*, 29 June 1882.

50. "The Malleys Acquitted," *NYT*, 1 July 1882.

51. For the verdict and post-trial Malley party, see "The Malleys Acquitted" and "The Malleys at Home," *NHER*, 1 July 1882.

52. "Opinions of the Press," *NHER*, 1 July 1882.

53. Ibid.

54. "The Malley Cousins," *NHER*, 3 July 1882.

55. "The Malley Jurors," *NHER*, 9 August 1882.

56. "Persons and Things," *NHER*, 10 August 1882; "As Peculiar as the Boys," *NHER*, 16 August 1882; "The Malley Jurors," *NHER*, 21 August 1882; "Full of Charm for Them," *NHER*, 11 August 1882.

57. Marriner, 157; Kurland, 58.

CHAPTER 18: WHAT HAPPENED TO JENNIE CRAMER?

1. Chloroform leaves burn marks around the mouth and these were not found in Jennie's mouth. See Marriner, 119.

2. "The Cramer Murder," *HDT*, 19 August 1881; "The Cramer Mystery," *NHER*, 20 August 1881.

3. "Poor Jennie Cramer," *HDT*, 12 August 1881; "Clothes and Bail," *NHER*, 20 August 1881 (Jennie's underwear found in New York).

4. Richard Waite noticed a cut across her new shoes, as if she had done it to ease discomfort ("The Cramer Tragedy," *NHER*, 8 August 1881) and when Jennie first went downstairs to see her mother Thursday morning, she "said something about her shoes" ("A Beautiful Girl's Fate," *HDT*, 8 August 1881).

5. "The Murder of Jennie Cramer," lecture given by Professor Robin Winks of Yale at the Whitney Library on 15 October 1997.

6. "Miss Douglass' Story," *NHER*, 9 August 1881; "Trial of the Malleys," *NHER*, 22 September 1882.

7. "Proving the Alibi," *NHER*, 26 May 1882.

8. "Mrs. Cramer's Story" and "The Malley Trial," *NHER*, 5 May 1882.

9. "Somebody's Idea of It," *NHER*, 7 September 1881.

AFTERMATH

1. U.S. Census, 1880; Madison Death Records.

2. Information about Willie is from Helander, 84; dates of death are from the gravestones.

3. U.S. Census, 1880, 1900; City Directories for Guilford, Wallingford, and Middletown; Middletown Death Records.

4. *Poor Mary Stannard*, 42.

5. "Edward Cramer and His Mother," *NYT*, 4 July 1882.

6. "The Malley Trial Recalled," *NYT*, 28 August 1883.

7. U.S. Census, 1900.

8. New Haven Death Records, 1886. (Although Minnie died in Brooklyn, she was brought to New Haven for burial. New Haven Vital Statistics noted the date, place, and cause of death for such people even though they died outside the jurisdiction.)

9. "The Death of Mrs. Cramer," *NHER*, 17 July 1891. The neighbor interviewed said Mrs. Cramer was upset with her son's new wife, but this does not correspond with the facts, as Eddie had been married quite some time. However, as the 1900 Census shows Mrs. Dwyer living with her daughter and Eddie, it is more likely that the mother-in-law was the precipitating cause of Mrs. Cramer's distress.

10. "Jennie Cramer's Mother," *NHER*, 17 July 1891.

11. Ibid.; New Haven Medical Examiner's Report, July 16, 1891.

12. "A Murder Case Recalled," *NYT*, 17 July 1891.

13. New Haven Medical Examiner's Report.

14. "Hayden on the Platform," *NYT*, 12 March 1880. For an example of Hayden's speaking style, see "The Rev. Mr. Hayden's Lecture," *NYT*, 19 February 1880, which quotes extensively from his talk on circumstantial evidence.

15. Madison Methodist Church Records, vol. 1, 1870–1923.

16. Hayden, 30–31.

17. New Haven City Directories.

18. "The Rev. Mr. Hayden Free," *NYT*, 30 October 1896.

19. Joel Helander, author of *Noose and Collar*, tells of contacting one of Lennie's sons for an interview for his book in 1979. In spite of being confronted with genealogical proof, he politely but firmly denied that he was Herbert Hayden's grandson. (Personal interview, June 1998.)

20. New Haven Death Records; "A Buried Mystery," *NHER*, 14 May 1907.

21. The New Haven City Directory for 1883 reported the move to East Hampton, MA. However, he does not appear in the 1900 U.S. Census for Massachusetts, Connecticut, Pennsylvania, or New York.

22. Wilkes-Barre City Directories show Nat Wolfe moving to a hotel in 1889. The 1900 Census shows him boarding with a nonrelative in Philadelphia. Lizzie Malley Wolfe does not appear in the 1900 U.S. Census in Pennsylvania, and Luzerne County records prior to 1893 have been destroyed by fire.

23. "Knocked Him Down," *NHER*, 24 August 1882.

24. "The Malley Trial Recalled," *NYT*, 28 August 1883. A New Haven newspaper reported Jimmy as a "practicing physician in Pennsylvania," but this is unlikely as he had no post-secondary education ("Mrs. Cramer Kills Herself," unknown newspaper source, files of the New Haven Colony Historical Society, July 1891). Shortly after the trial, Walter said Jim was in Wilkes-Barre ("Personal," *NHER*, 7 August 1882).

25. "Several Love Letters," *NHER*, 23 October 1882.

26. "The Malley Trial Recalled."

27. "A Murder Case Recalled," *NYT*, 17 July 1891.

28. New York City Marriage Records; U.S. Census, 1900, 1910.

29. She is listed as Jennie B. Malley on her birth certificate and in one census report. Another census report and the obituaries of Edward and Walter list her as Jane.

30. Edward Malley's obituary gives the year of death ("End Comes to Edward Malley," *NHER*, 26 July 1909), but she is not listed in the New Haven Death Index, 1881–1895, and is not in Edward's cemetery plot.

31. "The Malley Insurance Case," *NYT*, 6 April 1883.

32. "End Comes to Edward Malley."

33. "Multitude at Malley Funeral," *NHER*, 28 July 1909.

34. Edward's estate was estimated at three million dollars ("Multitude at Malley Funeral"). The New Haven Probate Index lists only his children Arthur and Jane, and his grandson Wallace Ward Malley, as legatees.

35. Cover sheet of "Under the Elms." See also "Personal," *NHER*, 7 August 1882.

36. "The Band Concert," *NHER*, 9 August 1882.

37. "Walter Malley's March," *NHER*, 10 August 1882.

38. "Opinion," *NHER*, 21 August 1882; "Persons and Things," *NHER*, 28 August 1882.

39. "Personal," *NHER*, 7 August 1882.

40. Walter tells Blanche that his father won't help him ("Several Love Letters").

41. Ibid. The letters printed in this article give evidence of this. For a full account of the blackmailing incident, see also "Blanche Douglass' Secrets," *NHER*, 24 October 1882; "This Time Witnesses," *NHER*, 26 October 1882; "Walter Malley's Letters," *NYT*, 26 October 1882; "Blackmailing Walter Malley," *NYT*, 27 October 1882.

42. In 1881 Blanche variously gave her age as nineteen, which would make her year of birth 1861/1862, or as "about 20" (see *NHER*, 20 May 1882), which would make it 1860/1861. But she also said she got married in 1877 at age seventeen, which would make her year of birth 1859/1860 (see "Who Is Miss Douglass?" *NHER*, 19 August 1881), and her husband, John Zimmermann, corroborates this.

It may be that Blanche was not exactly sure of her age, as seems to be the case with so many poor people back then. On her application for a marriage certificate in December 1877, she reports her "age at next birthday" as sixteen and her place of birth as New York City. She gives her father's name as Frank and her mother's name as Ellen Kerrigan.

Anna Madden Malley's gravestone gives her year of birth as 1860, but her death certificate (filled out by Walter) says 1859. Her place of birth on the death certificate is listed as New York City and in the U.S. Census as New York. Walter gave her father's first name as Frank and indicated that he did not know her mother's name.

There is another discrepancy on the death certificate, in that Walter states his wife's "length of time in this community" as sixty years, which would make it 1883 or 1884. However, Anna Malley was not brought to New Haven until some time between 1900 and 1910.

43. "W. W. Malley Dies at 72 in New Haven," *NHER*, 11 January 1959. The birth certificate for Wallace that is filed in New Jersey was not filled out until 1937, when he was fifty and Walter (who filled it out) was eighty. He must have needed it for something (possibly Social Security, which had only recently been established) and there was nothing on file for him. This means that there was nothing filed back in 1886, or that it was filed under another name.

44. New Haven Probate Index.

45. "A Murder Case Recalled," *NYT*, 17 July 1891.

46. "Mrs. Walter E. Malley Dies; Funeral Tomorrow," *NHER*, 11 February 1944; "Many Present at Services for Mrs. Malley," *NHER*, 13 February 1944.

47. Walter and Anna's only child, Wallace Ward Malley, was also the subject of criminal action. In 1914, at the age of twenty-six, he was speeding down New York City's Madison Avenue and struck a pedestrian, hurling the victim several feet. Young Malley kept on going despite being chased by police who tooted their horns and fired shots to get his attention. When he was finally pulled over, he claimed not to have been aware of either striking anyone or of being chased. The case seems to have been dropped eventually. The victim was not hurt badly and Walter probably paid a fine to keep his son out of jail. See "Police Fired Shots at Malley Thinking He Was Trying to Flee," *NHER*, 7 February 1914; "Policemen and Watchman Shoot to Stop Malley, Who Struck a Man," *NYT*, 8 February 1914;" Malley's Bail Increased," *NYT*, 10 February 1914.

48. "W. E. Malley Funeral Due on Thursday," *NHER*, 24 February 1948.

49. Letter to author, 15 October 1997.

50. "The Malley Trial Recalled," *NYT*, 28 August 1883.

51. "A Psychological Oddity," *NHER*, 24 October 1882.

SELECTED BIBLIOGRAPHY

The Beautiful Victim of the Elm City. New York: M. J. Ivers & Co., 1881.

Botanical.com. "Poisons and Antidotes: Arsenic." In *Stedman's Shorter Medical Dictionary.* Online at http://www.botanical.com/botanical/steapois/ars08.html. Accessed February 1998.

Census Records of the Federal Government for Connecticut, New York, Pennsylvania, Massachusetts, New Jersey.

Douglas, John, and Mark Olshaker. *Journey Into Darkness.* New York: Scribner, 1997.

Dreisbach, Robert H., and William O. Robertson. *Handbook of Poisoning: Prevention, Diagnosis, and Treatment,* 12th ed. Norwalk, CT: Appleton & Lange, 1987.

Gray, Henry, FRS. *Anatomy, Descriptive and Surgical* (Gray's *Anatomy*), 1st Am. ed. New York: Bounty Books, 1901.

Guilford, CT. Births, Marriages, Deaths, 1875–1904.

Hayden, Herbert H. *An Autobiography.* Hartford: Press of the Plimpton Mfg. Co., 1880.

Helander, Joel. *Noose and Collar.* No publisher, 1980.

Kellogg, J. H., M.D. *Man the Masterpiece, or: Plain Truths Plainly Told about Boyhood, Youth, and Manhood.* Battle Creek, MI: Modern Medicine Pub. Co., 1885, 1894.

Kurland, Michael. *How to Solve a Murder: The Forensic Handbook.* New York: Macmillan, 1995.

Madison, CT. Births, Marriages, Deaths, 1850–1960.

Madison Methodist Church Records, vol. 1, 1870–1923.

Manhattan Death Index, 1875–1881.

Manhattan Marriage Index, 1875–1877; 1879–1887.

Marriner, Brian. *On Death's Bloody Trail: Murder and the Art of Forensic Science.* New York: St. Martin's Press, 1991.

Masters, Edgar Lee. *Spoon River Anthology.* New York: Collier Books, 1914, 1962.

McCutcheon, Marc. *The Writer's Guide to Everyday Life in the 1800s.* Cincinnati: Writer's Digest Books, 1993.

Middletown, CT. Death Records 1915–1920

Middletown City Directories, 1900–1930.

Miller, Mark. "How the Jury Saw It." *Newsweek*, 16 October 1995: 37–39.

Miller, Sigmund S., ed. *Symptoms: The Complete Home Medical Encyclopedia*. New York: Avon Books, 1978.

New Haven, CT. Deaths, 1879–1888; Marriages, 1877–1896.

New Haven, CT. Probate Index.

New Haven City Directories, 1883–1920.

New Haven Coroner's Records, 1885–1891; 1906–1909.

New York City Birth Index, 1859–1864.

New York City Death Certificates, 1867, 1877, 1880.

New York City Marriage Certificates, 1877; 1884–1885.

Poor Mary Stannard: A Full and Thrilling Story of the Circumstances Connected with Her Murder. New Haven: Stafford Printing Co., 1879.

"Quotations—Pedestrianism." Online at http://fix.nstn.ca/~dblaikie/uw-aquah.html. Accessed February 1998.

Records of the Rockland Methodist Episcopal Church, Madison, CT, 1833–1906.

Renke, Prof. Wayne N. Evidence Course Modules, Module 12: Particular Exceptions to the Hearsay Rule, 2d ed., 1995. Online at http://www.law.ualberta.ca/courses/575/575.lp12.html. Accessed November 1997.

Scholl, B. Frank, Ph.G., M.D. *Library of Health: Complete Guide to Prevention and Cure of Disease*. Philadelphia: Historical Pub. Co., 1927.

Seton Hall University Archives, 1870–1881.

Stevens, Serita D., R.N., B.S.N., with Anne Klarner. *Deadly Doses: A Writer's Guide to Poisons*. Cincinnati: Writer's Digest Books, 1990.

Taylor, Deems, ed. *A Treasury of Gilbert and Sullivan*. New York: Simon and Schuster, 1941.

Wallingford, CT. City Directories, 1889–1894.

Weber, Don W., and Charles Bosworth, Jr. *Silent Witness: The Karla Brown Murder Case*. New York: Onyx, 1993.

Wellman, Francis L. *The Art of Cross-Examination*, 4th ed. New York: Collier Books, 1903, 1936.

Wilkes-Barre, PA. City Directories, 1882–1910.

Wilson, Keith D., M.D. *Cause of Death: A Writer's Guide to Death, Murder, and Forensic Medicine*. Cincinnati: Writer's Digest Books, 1992.

Yale University Archives, 1857–1901.

Index

About the Author

VIRGINIA A. McCONNELL teaches English, literature, and speech at Walla Walla Community College's Clarkston Center in Clarkston, Washington. A native of Syracuse, New York, she has degrees from the College of St. Rose, Purdue University, and Golden Gate University School of Law. She has taught high school in upstate New York and in Sacramento, California, and has practiced law in San Francisco. She lives on thirty acres of land in Idaho. Having researched historical true crimes for many years, she aspires to become the "Ann Rule of Victorian true crime."